HENRY MILLER

~~~~~~

The Major Writings

Leon Lewis

SCHOCKEN BOOKS • NEW YORK

First published by Schocken Books 1986
10 9 8 7 6 5 4 3 2 1   86 87 88 89
Copyright © 1986 by Leon Lewis

Library of Congress Cataloging in Publication Data
Lewis, Leon.
  Henry Miller : the major writings.
  Bibliography: p.
  Includes index.
  1. Miller, Henry, 1891–   —Criticism and interpre-
tation. I. Title.
PS3525.I5454Z7148   1986   818'.5209   84–16059

Design by Nancy Dale Muldoon
Manufactured in the United States of America
ISBN 0–8052–3952–9

PERMISSIONS ACKNOWLEDGMENTS

We gratefully acknowledge permission to use excerpts from the following:

Always Merry and Bright by Jay Martin. Copyright © 1978 by Jay Martin. Reprint-
ed by permission of Capra Press, Inc., Santa Barbara, Calif.
Genius and Lust: A Journey through the Major Writing of Henry Miller by Norman
Mailer. Copyright © 1976 by Norman Mailer. Reprinted by permission of
Grove Press, Inc.
Henry Miller Letters to Anaïs Nin, edited by Gunther Stuhlmann. Copyright ©
1965 by Anaïs Nin; Introduction copyright © 1966 by Gunther Stuhlmann.
Reprinted by permission of Putnam Publishing Group.
The Rebel by Albert Camus, translated by Anthony Bower. Copyright © 1956 by
Alfred Knopf, Inc. Reprinted by permission of Alfred A. Knopf, Inc.
Sexual Politics by Kate Millett. Copyright © 1969, 1970 by Kate Millett. Reprinted
by permission of Doubleday & Company, Inc.

New Directions has given permission to use excerpts from the following works
by Henry Miller:

The Air-Conditioned Nightmare. Copyright © 1945 by New Directions Publishing
Corporation.
Big Sur and the Oranges of Hieronymus Bosch. Copyright © 1957 by New Directions
Publishing Corporation.
The Colossus of Maroussi. Copyright © 1941 by Henry Miller.
Henry Miller on Writing. Copyright © 1964 by Henry Miller.
Remember to Remember. Copyright © 1947 by New Directions Publishing Cor-
poration.
Stand Still like the Hummingbird. Copyright © 1962 by Henry Miller.

For Florence and Jesse,
and Dixie

Contents

'Tis dangerous when the baser nature comes
Between the pass and fell incensed points
Of Mighty Opposites.

Shakespeare, Hamlet

Introduction: "Acolytes and Adversaries"

LIKE Menelaos in the land of Lakedaimon, like an old warrior after his last battle, Henry Miller spent the final years of his life amidst celebration and recollection in the Los Angeles suburb of Pacific Palisades. In his mid-eighties and nearly bedridden, divorced from his fifth wife and living with two of his children, Miller continued to write about one of his great themes—the possibilities of love. Reluctantly admitting, on the one hand, "I was hopelessly in love with my work," as an explanation of his failure to find lasting marital happiness, Miller also proclaimed about a woman friend, Brenda Venus, "We are mad with love, to put it bluntly." Addressing her with characteristic ardor, Miller declared, "Lead me, O blessed one, wherever." And as he continued to look toward the future, he maintained his contact with his origins, completing three collections of reminiscenses about the comrades of his earlier years for Noel Young's Capra Press.[1]

Miller's life and art remained typically intertwined in his ninth decade as he reached back into the past to recall the warmth of many friendships, and alternately, looked forward to one last romance which would finally satisfy all his expecta-

tions and permit him to transcend the limits and disappoint-
ments of his previous romantic experiences. To the end of his
days, he was still trying to confront the contradictory impulses
of his spirit and his will, and to unite in his life and art the
contrary forces which made his writing so vital, original and
often troubling for his legion of readers and friends.

A vision of transcendence drove Miller throughout his life as
an artist, but its focus was blurred by the ambivalence of psychic forces straining in divergent directions. Here was a man
afflicted with the restlessness of a permanent wanderer who
could celebrate the *spirit of place* of lands he visited more acutely
than most of the inhabitants; who maintained through his long
life a courtly, virtually medieval concept of romantic love while
writing scenes of erotic abandon extraordinary in intensity and
magnitude; who looked to the past for inspiration and the future for salvation, while proclaiming his conviction that the artist must live in Whitman's "eternal here and now"; who saw
himself as a kind of gangster and desperado of art when he
wasn't lecturing his readers on the necessity for social reform;
who sounded like a street-smart superrealist when he wasn't
writing surreal, cinematic fantasies about the landscape of his
mental voyages; who disparaged American culture with great
energy and invention while demonstrating his tremendous affection for the variety and style of life in America; and who,
perhaps most of all, proclaimed the power of an almost mythic
male ego-impulse while struggling without real success to convey the nature of the feminine reality he knew to be its necessary complement. It is a measure of both the ultimate disappointment of Miller's work, as well as a part of its perplexing
fascination, that there is no real rendering of an equivalent
feminine spirit to match the masculine one which Miller
expresses, for this is the one case where the conflict of contrary
impulses has not been balanced by contending forces of similar
gravity. Miller's inability to envision or write about a harmonious blending, or even an equal contest, must be reckoned a
"failure"—particularly in terms of his great ambitions—but the
manner in which he struggled with the question is at the heart
of his achievement as well.

Had Miller worked consistently toward any of his goals, his work might have been more easily accepted and understood. But even a modest version of literary "success" eluded Miller for so long that he felt compelled to shift his strategies throughout his career, and when he was finally successful, that "success" itself altered his perspective on his accomplishments. The crab that moves sideways to advance, one of his emblems for himself, is well chosen. Because of the shifts in his economic and spiritual well-being, his writing career was marked by what appeared to be a refusal to be bound by any familiar rule of consistency, and the commentary he has received has suffered accordingly.[2] Both his acolytes and adversaries have been confounded by an inability to see fully what Miller was trying to do, and have concentrated their support or censure specifically on that aspect of his writing which they favored or disdained. A brief outline of Miller's working life will illustrate the pattern of evolution which runs through his writing.

When he began to write in the 1920s, Miller was convinced that eventually his work would be treated with the serious critical attention reserved for those artists (Dostoevski, D. H. Lawrence, Whitman, and Balzac) he admired and hoped to equal. While he never totally surrendered these expectations, various rebuffs had given him another sense of himself by the time *Tropic of Cancer* was published in Paris in 1934 by Jack Kahane's Obelisk Press, a house that specialized in pornography for British and American tourists. Miller now had recast himself as an artist/rebel eternally at war with a genteel culture and the critics of a literary gentility, appreciated only by fellow members of the underground and other outcasts. Until *Cancer* was published in the United States by Grove Press in 1961, Miller lived and worked in an ethos of fierce partisan support from his friends and nearly constant abuse and vilification from those people who were enraged by his work or what they thought it represented. Then, after numerous court cases, which had a substantial effect upon the public's right to read what it wishes and which were necessary for the book to be published in this country, and a fair amount of money abruptly available after decades of financial stress, Miller found himself cast rather suddenly at the end of his life as a revered seer whose work was beginning to be recognized as a basic part of the American literary tradition.

Because of these radical readjustments in Miller's reception by the public and because of some confusion in Miller's own mind about what he had achieved, there has been an almost overwhelming tendency to see Miller as the agent of an extremist sensibility; a talented farceur forever tumbling into excess. Both his advocates and adversaries have made extravagant, absolutist claims about the man and his writing that have submerged or obscured the work itself. The greatest difficulty has been Miller's use of erotic and obscene material, and in a bizarre and ironic development, just at the point when a relatively objective discussion of erotic writing was becoming possible, the emergence of a long-overdue feminist aesthetic and the beginnings of a revisionist counterattack to the so-called "sexual revolution" added additional elements to a complex situation. As Kate Millett's sometimes devastating critique of Miller suggests, it is still easier for most critics to see Miller as a limited, single-issue author, but this continuing practice has kept the field of Miller criticism rather narrow in scope.[3] To fully understand the problem, one must consider the actual publishing history of Miller's books in the 1930s.

James Laughlin was studying in Rapallo with Ezra Pound in the mid-1930s at Pound's "Ezuversity" when Pound gave Laughlin his Obelisk Press edition of *Tropic of Cancer* to read. Laughlin recalls that he "wrote Henry a fan letter when I was there in Rapallo, and correspondence started which later led to our publishing association when New Directions got started."[4] Unfortunately for Miller, Pound didn't get Laughlin to begin New Directions until Miller had already written the *Tropics;* Miller was interested in editorial guidance during the 1930s and was unable to get the help he wanted. In 1932, he wrote to Anaïs Nin, "That you found the old novel (*Crazy Cock*) good in parts and that you think it could be doctored and made publishable is well. Sure I would be delighted if you would go over it and prune it. . . . Perhaps I could reciprocate some time by doing the same for you. . . . And after you get through with it

I believe I would have sufficient enthusiasm to make further revisions myself."[5] And when he was finished with the manuscript of *Tropic of Cancer*, in 1933, he turned again to his friends:

> It was probably my third year in Paris. Almost from the start I had begun writing the *Tropic of Cancer*. At last it was finished. But before thinking about a publisher, I knew it had to be edited, trimmed down especially. I looked about me in vain for editorial guidance. Anaïs Nin was out of the question. It was not her type of book. One day, perhaps at Fred's own suggestion, I asked him if he would help me.[6]

Alfred Perlès and Nin assisted Miller as much as they could, and Jack Kahane, the head of Obelisk Press, made suggestions too, but he was too concerned with commercial and legal problems to be of much help.

Ultimately, Kahane's method of presentation invited attacks on *Cancer* as soon as it was published, and Miller's friends moved directly to the defense.[7] Perhaps because the attacks were so vehement, they supported Miller the man, suggesting the work was "okay" since he was a fine fellow. Karl Shapiro's claim is typical: "As a writer Miller may be second or third rate or no rating at all; as a spiritual example he stands among the great men of our age. Will this ever be recognized?"[8]

Many of Miller's supporters saw his writing as a new testament to an ideal life, and Alfred Perlès, one of his earliest friends and his roommate in Paris at the famous Villa Seurat, epitomized their opinion in his comment that Miller was an illustration of all that is good in the American character, "the best 'ambassador' the United States could have wished for."[9] This type of praise offers a deceptive picture of Miller—one that reduces him by the conventional nature of its rhetoric—and when praise in this vein is applied to Miller's books, it can lead to some very misleading evaluations. Lawrence Durrell, who was one of Miller's earliest supporters and firmest friends, repeatedly refers to Miller as some kind of saint. Robert Fink picks up Durrell's theme in the *International Henry Miller News Letter* and suggests that "American literature begins and ends with the meaning of what he has done."[10] Durrell himself offers the not unreasonable assertion that Miller might be compared with Whitman and Melville, and then goes on to claim that *Cancer* must be placed next to *Moby Dick* in American letters.[11] This is the overblown language of advertising, and it is designed to "sell" the reading public and the respectable citizen a product that they not only wouldn't buy but were anxious to keep off the shelves. Even the prominent critics who dealt with Miller's work in the 1940s and 1950s, including Philip Rahv, Herbert Read, and Edmund Wilson, addressed themselves primarily to the legend and storm surrounding Miller's life, not to his writing.[12]

When one considers the range and intensity of the attacks on Miller, and the fact that there was no close parallel or precedent for him in American letters—except, possibly for Whitman who was taught only in carefully chosen *selections* even in American universities until recently—all of the earnest attempts at a defense of Miller's work are quite understandable. It may have seemed a little academic to discuss literary distinctions and artistic criteria when Miller's work was banned in Europe and the United States and book stores faced prosecution if they stocked it. The vituperative nature of the attacks on Miller demanded a response that did not concern itself with shades of meaning. Exaggeration was often met with exaggeration, as Miller was reviled by people like the "critic" in the Philadelphia trial of *Cancer* who had this to say about Miller's brilliant paean to Matisse:

> There is simply no beauty or literary value. The book simply has no literary value, either in language or structure or thought. Even the few attempts at something like literary writing are marred, as follows: "At the periphery the light waves bend and the sun bleeds like a broken rectum." There is literature for you, huh? When I was in the Army we called such people swine.[13]

So much for surrealist art in the United States army. But this tone of smug assurance remained consistent through three decades of outrage.[14]

Miller's friends resisted the attacks made on him in the name of "decency" and their strength and courage gave Miller the support he needed to continue the struggle, but the controversy around the publication of his books shifted the ground for those critics who might have been able to give Miller some intensive examination on purely literary issues. Even Rahv felt the need to answer objections about Miller's choice of subject, and to explain why Miller lived the way he did. As Miller's work ranged over great areas of psychic sensibility, he seemed to be describing a man who was both saint and swine, and most of the commentary about Miller written prior to 1960 reflected a response to one of the two polar extremes, assuming that Miller was actually *all* one way or the other in his life and his work. The insistence on reducing the complexity of Miller's "I" narrator into a relatively familiar and moderately manageable creation effectively prohibited most of the commentators from recognizing (much less analyzing) the crucial paradox at the core of the work; namely, that categories can converge and eventually coalesce into something altogether new and different. Even Millett and Mailer, in the sophisticated brilliance of their interpretations, have essentially chosen to see Miller at one or other of the extremes.

The struggle between the two "public" versions of Henry Miller fed a legend which defied a critique. But the widespread success of the *Tropics* in the United States in the 1960s and the concomitant collapse of the outer shell of a puritan public morality have lessened the necessity for partisan strategies. Consequently, it is not surprising that books have begun to appear during the last twenty years, which, taken together, offer a reasonably firm base for studying Miller's work. As one considers these pioneering efforts, one sees a gradually widening angle of vision, as well as a reflection of the main currents of American literary scholarship through the last two decades.

Kingsley Widmer's *Henry Miller* (1963) makes the accurate claim that it is the "first reasonably thorough (study) of Miller's published writings."[15] Widmer points out that he is *not* a friend of Miller, and that he can separate Miller's writing from the myth (or malicious gossip) that threatens to suffocate it:

The truth about Henry Miller is that he is neither the "greatest

living author" and a "unique saint" nor the "foulest writer of
meaningless nonsense" and a "madman." Between cops and cult-
ists it is sometimes difficult to see the who and what. Miller, I
shall argue, is a minor but intriguing writer whose best works are
the rhetorical gestures of a rebel-buffoon.[16]

Widmer's core idea that Miller is a typically American figure
expressing a comic, almost anarchic position ("buffoon" is almost slander, and says more about Widmer's cynicism than
Miller's writing) prevents him from getting below the surface of
Miller's work. He is unable to see much beyond the comedy
and he doesn't understand that very profoundly. The greatest
weakness of his study, though, is that he presents no thesis to
integrate the sometimes perceptive insights he offers. His recognition of Miller's basic subject—"megalopolitan man"—is
unexplored, and his book is most useful for the biographical
information, bibliographical references and cultural checkpoints
it provides, although much of the same material has subse-
quently appeared in more complete form in other books. It is
actually more of a compendium of Milleriana than a critical
study, and Widmer's expertise in scatology is its strongest
point. He has a fifties fondness for the man who laughs and
jests at a horrible society he can't change in order to keep it
from killing him.

What is missing in Widmer's book is some coherent vision of
Miller's work as a literary achievement. Widmer's encyclopedic
arrangement minimizes the differences that are such an important part of Miller's books and suggests, by implication, that
the various pieces are of equal merit. Perhaps Widmer's real
contribution is that he got things started, for it was at about the
time that his book was published that William Gordon began
The Mind and Art of Henry Miller (1967), a much more traditional
piece of literary scholarship, and in the eyes of Lawrence Durrell, the book which finally filled the vacuum which had existed
in that area.[17] Durrell laments in the foreword that Miller has
had "a pitifully small band of supporters" among the critics,
and that this book is "an accurate and penetrating study of the
artist's growth; it cites the works and experiences of the author
in a coherent pattern, and illustrates the gradual evolution of

Miller toward his own self-liberation through art. And it makes the right claims for the books."[18]

Gordon's thesis is that Miller is the "ultimate romantic." He describes Miller's work as a form of autobiography which he calls "progressive self-creation" and maintains that Miller is involved in a process of continuous self-discovery as an artist—a process which leads to his fulfillment as a man. He tells us that Miller's quest is remarkably similar to that undertaken by Whitman (whom Miller admired) and Wordsworth (whom Miller found unreadable), and that Miller's "sexual bravado" is an attempt to reconcile, in the "auto-novel," the instinctual or unconscious aspect of his nature with a desire for maximum growth of the spiritual self. Consequently, he sees Miller's use of obscene and erotic material as a part of a primarily Freudian self-analysis in which all of the repressed material is dredged up, expressed symbolically and eventually exorcised. For Gordon, the entire description of Miller's early life—his "youthful" sexual extravagance especially—can be seen as "imaginative acting out of basic instinctual levels, a bringing into the day what had been restricted to the night."[19] This interpretation depends upon Durrell's interesting contention that:

> . . . he has retained (as every artist must) an abnormally large part of his childhood fantasy life intact—with all its wounds and ardours and fantastically *unreasonable* demands upon the world of men. He has re-enacted it all as an adult, and then written it all out, unwittingly providing a catharsis for the dammed-up fantasy life of the Anglo-Saxon.[20]

Gordon observes, "There can be little doubt that the levels of life which Miller is expressing are highly regressive, associated with infantile demands upon reality."[21]

The orthodox Freudianism of his approach leads Gordon (through Durrell) to a version of the romantic artist as an overgrown child, and tends to rob Miller's work of any specific interest beyond that of the "confession." This approach works reasonably well when Gordon is discussing the *Tropics,* but it is much less successful with the *Rosy Crucifixion.* Just as Durrell was put off by the language in *Sexus* (he calls it "a childish explosion of vulgarity," indicating that his own "dammed-up fantasy life" might not have been as elaborately flamboyant as Miller's), Gordon becomes uneasy when he is discussing some aspect of Miller that does not fit his theories. One of his central points, for instance, is that "Miller used two general levels of technique, the realistic story and the fantasy or dream technique," which, while being a good way to start, ignores Miller's appreciation of André Breton's observation that the fantastic is merely another part of the realistic. Gordon is unable, I feel, to cope with Miller's involvement in what Leslie Fiedler calls "another time," one which is "apocalyptic, anti-rational, blatantly romantic and sentimental; an age dedicated to misology and prophetic irresponsibility; one distrustful of self-protective irony and too-great self-awareness."[22] It is important to see that Miller's mind and art developed during the Proust–Mann–Joyce era which Fiedler uses to represent modernist fiction, as Gordon well knows, but also to see that Miller approaches and anticipates writers like Borges, Pynchon and Barth—people Gordon is totally unprepared to discuss. In many ways, as I will point out, Miller is a genuinely transitional figure, working tentatively in many of those areas that postmodernist writers have made their own. Gordon misses this, and it makes his book incomplete. His material on Miller and the romantic tradition is its strongest part.

Ihab Hassan, on the other hand, approaches Miller from an ultracontemporary viewpoint—a stance that might be labeled "trendy" unless one is aware that Hassan is a critic who has begun, not followed trends. His study of Miller and Samuel Beckett, *The Literature of Silence* (1967), is divided into two separate sections in which each author is considered singly, but the thrust of the book comes from its substantial prologue.[23] Here Hassan attempts to explain his conception of a literature of "silence" in a rapid-transit exposition of nearly every important mode of discourse to become popular in the 1960s. With almost bewildering succession, Hassan touches on and refers to Norman O. Brown, Michel Butor, John Cage, camp, pataphysics, random composition, Wittgenstein's notion of language as game theory and many other features of early postmodernist thinking. The structure of the essay suggests an exercise in the kinetics of montage. The prologue is so full of energy that its ideas occur in blinding but brief flashes of insight without ever properly illuminating the subject. The focus is never sharp enough to give one a precise sense of what Hassan's version of "silence" actually means, and I feel that it was difficult to determine how "literary silence" is actually a part of Miller's theories of composition. The discussion of Miller tends to be somewhat ambiguous and rather amorphous, but it is definitely relevant (if only tangentially) to Miller's work and I believe that it is worth summarizing at this point.

The literature of silence is being written, Hassan claims, as a form of negative transcendence of an absurd universe. It is the expression of a metaphysical revolt against the impossibility of any value system supporting or structuring a coherent vision of the cosmos. The "silence" itself is seen as metaphorical. Its components are outrage, an invocation to apocalypse, the rejection of human identity, revulsion against the self and the desire to alter one's consciousness.

Hassan correctly identifies outrage, obscenity, revulsion and apocalyptic prophecy as important elements in Miller's writing, but he does not work his way through to an adequate explanation of how they operate within it. The difficulty lies in his attempts to show "metaphoric silence" actually emerging from Miller's books. Specifically, Hassan sees metaphoric silence occurring when:

1. The idea of an *absurd creation* causes the artist to depreciate or deny his work;
2. The obscenity which the artist directs outward rebounds and leads him to a deadness or numbness in his language;
3. The artist generates a tone of "radical irony" which carries the negation of any statement within that statement;
4. Chance replaces intentional consciousness in an *art* which refuses to discover or disclose order.

None of these strictures are germane to Miller's writing. The second contention is worth considering in an examination of Miller's use of language, but it will not work as an operative theory to explain Miller's construction of an individual, unusual voice. Perhaps, as Leslie Fiedler suggests, Miller moves not toward *silence* in any of its meanings, but to a "super-garrulousness" related to but diametrically opposite to Hassan's conception.[24] Hassan himself may sense this, because his discussion of the texts largely ignores his original proposition. His most valuable comments are on Miller's short pieces—the travelogue–essays and the philosophical rambles—where he uses his erudition and brilliance to locate Miller with respect to modern culture just as Gordon located him with respect to various established literary traditions. The problem may finally be that Hassan is not very interested in Miller, and like Widmer, he tends to dwell excessively on Miller's more obvious defects while glancing over the works he considers Miller's best. The book is much better on Beckett where Hassan's skill as a critic is combined with a genuine interest in his subject.

Of all the critical writing that has appeared so far, Jane Nelson's *Form and Image in the Fiction of Henry Miller* (1970) is probably the most provocative.[25] In *The Wisdom of the Heart*, Miller makes a statement about his methods that is a typical reflection of his fear that he may be explained or "understood" too easily:

> I haven't the slightest idea what my future books will be like, even the one immediately to follow. My charts and plans are the slenderest sort of guides: I scrap at will, I invent, distort, deform, lie, inflate, exaggerate, confound, confuse as the mood seizes me. I obey only my own instincts and intuitions. I know nothing in advance. Often I put down things which I do not understand myself, secure in the knowledge that later they will become clear and meaningful to me.[26]

Here, Miller is supporting one of his images of himself—the wild, manic, spontaneous, irrepressible literary anarchist. And James Laughlin recalls that "I could never get Henry to rewrite anything."[27] But before Miller delivered his manuscripts, he often revised individual sentences and paragraphs, and in his letters to Durrell, Anaïs Nin and others, as well as several biographical accounts by various friends, there is ample evidence that Miller's "fiction" was a part of an elaborate, preplanned project.[28] In spite of periodic antic denials, Miller worked con-

sciously and subconsciously along the lines of an immense mul-
tibook scheme which he refers to often. Gordon attempts to
explain this plan in Freudian terms, and Nelson brings to Miller's
"fiction" a method designed to reveal a pattern of carefully organized symbology which can be explained with great clarity according to the theories of Carl Jung. Her knowledge of Jung (one
might say her "mastery" of Jung), Eric Neumann and Angus
Fletcher practically turns her book into an explication of Jungian
psychology in terms of Miller's writing, and unless one knows
Jung's thought and principles well, her book is going to seem
very obscure. Miller himself remarked that Nelson, "thinks I'm
a Jungian!" and complained, "I've been looking up the words
she uses—I don't understand what she's talking about."[29] However, even though she sometimes uses Jung as a prayer wheel,
and curiously ignores Miller's own eccentric reading of Jung, her
book is a perceptive critique that tackles a number of the most
crucial aspects of Miller's work.

First, she addresses herself to the problem of the narrator,
the "I" who recounts and presents his exploits and adventures.
According to Nelson, this "I" is describing in his *confession* or
anatomy (the terms follow Northrop Frye's substitutions for
autobiography or *novel*) his struggle to seek independence from
the subconscious forces symbolized by the archetypal feminine.
The "demonic, obsessive quality of the erotic experience" in
Miller is an attempt to dramatize the hero's confrontation with
the archetypal and primordial figures of the terrible mother, the
negative aspect of what Jung called the great mother. The direction of the books is from the fragmentation of the self in *Cancer*
to a kind of integration or maturity which Jung calls "individua-
tion." Second, she locates the settings in which this struggle
takes place as "negative centers" (Paris and New York, specifically, although Miller's experiences in Paris and *Brooklyn* are by
no means entirely negative) which provide a region for the
symbolic descent into the womb, whale's belly, dark night of
the soul or whatever archetype is momentarily appropriate. In
an anagogic sense, destruction of the self must take place before rebirth, and this destruction is delineated in the opening
sections of *Cancer* as Miller's narrator comes in contact with

"visually fragmented female figures" who are "manifestations of devouring, castrating, chthonic Aphrodite, fascinating and deadly aspects of the Terrible Feminine."[30] Because the self is formless and undefined at this point, the hero is vulnerable and uneasy, an "inevitable victim of the vigorous and myriad figures of the sexually aggressive woman (who) functions emblematically in Miller's obscene panorama as potent symbols of the threatening unconscious, as fragments of the Archetypal Feminine."[31]

The relationship of the male narrative consciousness to various forms of female "reality"—psychic and physical—is a part of Miller's work that must be confronted. Nelson's idea that the emerging self of the *Rosy Crucifixion* takes shape as an "androgynous union of opposites . . . negative and positive," is an intriguing suggestion and a more subtle means of trying to understand Miller's complex relationships with women than attacks like that of Kate Millett.[32] Nelson continues her argument by claiming that the "I" narrator finds his final form (his "individuated self") in a process that risks annihilation to find salvation; the goal that is sought is a "positive center"—what Jung referred to as *centroversion,* a state of being akin to Miller's self-description as a "happy rock." In such a condition, Nelson claims, Miller will eventually reject art as an unnecessary sublimation, and she interprets all of Miller's numerous comments on art and the artist as an expression of a basic feeling that "full manifestation of the total personality is more important" than creative work.[33] This, I feel, is a distortion of Miller's life and art: an unfortunate position that Nelson must defend to be consistent with her Jungian analysis. I will discuss it in some detail later.

Even though Nelson carries her thesis beyond its real applicability to Miller's writing, her book is consistently intelligent and often provocative. Her explication of Miller's use of art as therapy is accurate and revealing and her recognition that Miller is not simply attacking or degrading women is an important insight. My primary objection is to her insistence on seeing the books completely as allegory. In restricting herself to a description and identification of the symbol system and the allegorical figures within it, she never makes any critical judgments nor draws any distinctions between the various "novels." Without an evaluation of Miller's efforts, one gets the impression from Nelson that Miller is working at a consistent level of creativity; this is way off the mark. Much of the *Rosy Crucifixion* is quite weak; *Plexus* is practically a disaster and *Nexus* is a revealing disappointment and a strange anticlimax to Miller's quest. While Nelson might know Jung very well, she relies on his terminology without attempting to discuss his thinking, and this tends to reduce the artist's uniqueness to an amorphous mass of archetypes. There is, too often, a sense of some *ur*-artist (in John Simon's words), "spewing up images of carnality, violence, fear and frustration that have a way of being interchangeable with everybody else."[34] Nelson's investigation suggests that Miller is working his way through a Jungian soul analysis in his fiction, and while this is partially true, there are other elements that must be considered in conjunction with this perception. Otherwise, the analysis itself becomes fragmentary except when seen from the confines of its own self-enclosed vision of existence.

What is missing is the more tangible, humane side of Miller's personality that is vital in explaining the spirit of the man. When Nelson talks of negative erotic experience, her description remains clinically distant and unconvincing. The tone of her discussion suggests that her knowledge of the world, especially its darker or "demonic" side, is secondhand. I am certainly not proposing that one must *be* evil to *know* evil, but a certain imaginative activity is probably required to avoid the appearance of a scientist measuring a specimen for various attributes. Nelson cannot have conceived of other than an academic audience for her book, particularly those with an interest in Jungian psychology, and while her book can be useful in studying Miller, its angle of attack is, if not a dead end, what might be called a vortex of ever-narrowing dimensions. The three books on Miller which appeared during the 1970s indicate there there are other possibilities for serious critical appreciation.

The one most like Nelson's is Bertrand Mathieu's *Orpheus In*

Brooklyn: Orphism, Rimbaud and Henry Miller (1976).[35] As the title suggests, it is an attempt to explain the controlling vision of Miller's writing as a conscious retelling and up-dating of the Orpheus myth, and it suggests that the technique that Miller uses is heavily influenced by the work of Rimbaud (the subject of Miller's study *The Time of the Assassins)* and the symboliste movement.[36] Mathieu concentrates only on *The Colossus of Maroussi*, Miller's account of his trip to Greece in 1939, and refers to the auto-novels only incidentally. Even though he devotes more than half of the book to a discussion of Rimbaud, his reading of *Maroussi* is sensitive, thorough and consistent with his readings of Miller's other work. He follows the explication du texte method of classical French criticism and responds to every nuance in the text. There are times when one would almost prefer that he did not try to wring every particle of "meaning" out of each line, and he tends to be a little repetitious, making the same point several ways in different sections of his book, but he has several ideas about Miller that are excellent points of departure for examining the full range of Miller's writing.

Mathieu's familiarity with Rimbaud helps him to identify the poetic qualities in Miller's style, and his discussion of Miller's use of poetic devices in developing a unique voice illuminates one of the major sources of Miller's strength as a writer. In addition, Mathieu's understanding of the symboliste aesthetic enables him to see that the qualities of *music* and *song* which are a part of this voice are central to Miller's appeal to a very wide audience. Mathieu skillfully ties the Orphic tradition's conception of the poet as seer to Emerson's ideas in this area, and shows how Miller's depictions of himself as a prophet of sorts are an outgrowth of this conception. He notes that the Orphic tradition includes the motif of descent or *Katábasis* which parallels both Gordon's and Nelson's insights into the "dark night of the soul" archetype, and he suggests that the third part of *Maroussi* presents a version of paradise which recalls Rimbaud's recollection of a paradise drawn from a notion of childhood innocence. I intend to extend these ideas into areas of Miller's writing beyond *Maroussi* in the course of this study.

Mathieu's book is limited as far as Miller is concerned by his interest in Rimbaud. A small shift in emphasis would make the book a study of *Rimbaud* from the perspective of Miller's use of Rimbaudian elements, and many of the extensive illustrations in the text are from Rimbaud's original French. Also, Mathieu, while trying to keep the life of Miller's work surging through the text, lapses occasionally into jargon almost as hermetic as that of Nelson. The major limitation of the book as far as I am concerned, however, is that it concentrates too intensely on only one of Miller's texts, and makes claims for it that may be hard to accept in spite of Mathieu's comprehensive and often persuasive arguments. As Norman Mailer points out, (about *Maroussi*) "It swims in delight, it tintinnabulates in rhapsody, but sometimes it neglects to describe the very terrain which is furnishing the spiritual equivalent of the old personal hard-on. After awhile, it becomes a trifle suspicious as a book."[37] In other words, for all of Mathieu's claims, is *Maroussi* really at the center of Miller's achievement; is it the best or most essential work of Henry Miller?

An extremely engaging answer to this question is provided in the negative by Mailer in his unusual reader–tribute to Miller, *Genius and Lust: A Journey through the Major Writings of Henry Miller* (1976). Just as Nelson often seems to be too far from Miller's sensibility to really understand it, Mailer frequently seems too close. Miller has the kind of style that encourages affectionate parody, but Mailer enters into the spirit of the occasion so completely that it seems as if he is trying to show that he can equal Miller's verbal sexual gusto, as well as his incredible inventiveness.

His "journey" is the latest in a series of readers (*The Henry Miller Reader*, compiled by Lawrence Durrell [New York, 1959], and *Henry Miller on Writing*, compiled by Thomas H. Moore [New York, 1964]), but it is compiled by an admirer who recognizes the vast unevenness of Miller's writing. Each reader is instructive in terms of what the compiler selects and how he explains and supports his choices. Mailer regards the *Tropics* and the *Rosy Crucifixion* as "the heart of Miller's gargantuan talents *and vices* as a novelist," (my italics) and claims that this talent is a product of the tremendous emotional forces which drove him through his life and work.[38] He believes that Miller's writing must be understood in terms of the patterns those forces directed, and contends, characteristically, that the most powerful of these forces is lust. Mailer maintains that Miller is probably the first writer to really explore the demands of lust, and that Miller's (and his own?) interest in and knowledge of women stems from a recognition of the importance and universality of this force. Mailer takes his contention in this area rather deeply into metaphysical speculation, but he is fully aware of his own predilections, and he demonstrates his ability to measure his own most extreme tendencies in the strongest part of his book, the chapter on narcissism. Here, Mailer writes with psychological insight and aesthetic shrewdness, pointing out that narcissism is characterized by "the fundamental relationship. It is with oneself," and then qualifying this by saying, "it is not love of the self but dread at the world outside the self which is the seed of narcissism," and then recognizing the crucial contradiction, "The narcissist suffers from too much inner dialogue . . . the underlying problem of the narcissist is boredom."[39] The chapter is quite revealing about Miller and Mailer, and it is limited only by Mailer's choice throughout the collection to provide insight and assertion in the place of extended analysis and argument.

Mailer's comments on Miller are of interest to an audience considerably beyond that of academe, and while his position is definitely a partisan one, it is presented in a spirit of enthusiasm and constructed as an excess of appreciation. Mailer's own ideas on the nature of the "feminine" range from the daringly imaginative to the simply preposterous, but his empathetic responses to Miller's attempts to handle the woman/women in his life set off a series of brilliant sparks that illumine what must be regarded as the central feature of Miller's work. While it would be difficult to deny that Mailer's judgment is often warped by his own somewhat eccentric opinions on the feminine psyche, he is not so self-absorbed that he fails to see how another man has become lost in an obsession. At this stage in history, there are many points on which there must be disagreement depending upon one's own sense of the nature of masculine and feminine reality, its divergences and convergences, and both Mailer's and Miller's exploration of this central subject are worth attending to. I will pursue some of Mailer's more specific ideas, including his dispute with Kate Millett, later on.

While Mailer's introductory essays on Miller are described as a "journey" through the "major writing," Jay Martin's *Always Merry and Bright* (1978) is a journey through Miller's life in the form of an "unauthorized" biography. Martin's book offers a sampling of the material gathered in many libraries and is of considerable value in studying the relationship of Miller's life to his art. However, this isn't all that Martin had in mind. Rather, it was his intention to write a book that "is parallel to Miller's life: it exhibits the process of Miller's life."[40]

To accomplish this, Martin has interviewed many of Miller's acquaintances, read all of the critical material he could locate, and read over one hundred thousand pages of material from manuscript collections residing in twenty-three libraries. As he describes it, "Assembling letters, notes, diary and journal entries, marginalia, correspondence from others, contracts, financial records, outlines for books, clippings and jottings, drafts of fiction and essays, wall charts, photographs of different periods, and a varied miscellany of other material, I began to see the shape of Miller's life emerging."[41] For anyone interested in Miller, as a writer and as a human being, Martin's book is a vast source of information. Unfortunately, the manner in which Martin has chosen to present the information may not suit everyone's taste or preference. Aware, no doubt, of biographies like Joseph Blotner's respected work on William Faulkner or Carlos Baker's huge book on Hemingway, Martin has decided that a similar presentation of material from a relatively uninvolved and noninterpretive perspective would clearly defy the spirit of Miller's life and work. His alternative approach has been to put some of the same scenes that Miller made famous into his own shape and form. The contrast between the Martin and the Miller version is a graphic demonstration of the difference between art and descriptive reportage. One can understand Miller's reluctance to see Martin thundering ahead on this project, although in his usual fashion, he showed interest and gave Martin his time and his advice.[42]

Although *Always Merry and Bright* (a mock motto of Miller's) is uneven since Martin has covered certain periods closely and been unable to get much material on others, it is a gathering of Milleriana that far surpasses some of the other "celebrations" compiled by Miller's friends.[43] Martin has spent so much time with Miller's work that he has reached the point where one might fairly consider him an expert. Even if his writing does not always take advantage of his expertise, he offers many momentary, almost offhand comments that are helpful in understanding Miller's intentions. The detailed account of the genesis of *Cancer* is an example of a classic kind of literary scholarship that enriches one's grasp of a work.

Each of the books that I have been discussing offers insights and ideas that enhance one's understanding of Miller's work, and their variety of approaches and styles suggest something of the range and complexity of the artist they are examining. The number of books devoted to Miller is still slight, considering the "industries" in operation on some of Miller's contemporaries, but this modest output may be accounted for by the fact that Miller has not yet been pulled into the mainstream of academic respectability. But a visit to a bookstore almost anywhere in this country, or in an impressive number of countries throughout the world, will demonstrate the enduring appeal of Miller's writing to a very considerable audience—an appeal that cannot be explained solely by Miller's reputation or the erotic content of his writing. Miller's work remains in print and it is widely read. I hope, in my discussion, to illuminate his enduring appeal to so many people.

1 Land, Skin, Space and Time

IN the middle of the nineteenth century, Henry Miller's grandfather arrived in America among many other men from Europe. He settled in the Williamsburg section of Brooklyn, then a rural community with a predominantly German population. The Miller family was living in the Yorkville section of Manhattan when Henry Miller was born, "between 12:30 and 12:45," as his father recalls, on December 26, 1891. A month later, his family moved back across the river to a secure, friendly environment in Williamsburg that was about to die. Manhattan was already recognizable as the tight, crowded slum-ridden island damned and celebrated in the literature of the great immigrant surge of the turn of the century, while Brooklyn retained many of the charming characteristics of a series of small towns. But the German-American community in which the Miller family had lived

comfortably if frugally for several decades was beginning to
vanish. The Brooklyn Bridge was completed in 1883. Many new
settlers from Eastern Europe were arriving in the United States
and they followed the bridge across the East River. When the
Williamsburg Bridge was completed twelve years after Miller
was born, the part of Brooklyn that bordered the river began to
resemble the crowded sections of lower Manhattan that the
new immigrants wished to escape from. Williamsburg was
slowly becoming another metropolitan nightmare, but until
Miller was ten, he lived in a home made strong by his family's
relatively blind faith in the world, and on streets alive with the
promise of love and adventure.

Miller writes about the vital, exhilarating days of his youth in
Black Spring, a book marked by an exuberance and an innocence
absent in almost all of his other work. A part of Miller's appeal
to a broad range of readers is his ability to exhibit an energetic
delight in circumstances which most people would find distressing. Critics have referred to this in terms of what is often
called his "acceptance" of everything, but that is not an accurate way of describing the phenomenon. It is actually not an
acceptance of things as they are, but an expectation that things
will be better, mingled with a delight in diversity. The mock
motto that Martin takes for his biography, "Always Merry and
Bright," has a dark, even bitterly ironic resonance in the context of Miller's work, and it is not so much "acceptance" as
resilience which enables Miller to survive everything he encounters. But in *Black Spring*, Miller is writing about a time before the snake entered the garden, when everything the world
presented could be accepted without an adult's reservation that
there might be something horrible hidden beneath the surface.
If one considers just how much trouble Miller lived through,
his capacity for regenerating a prelapsarian sensibility that temporarily blanks out the full knowledge he has of the adult world
is an indication of the importance of the years he describes in
Black Spring. This brief, golden time in his youth was fixed in
Miller's memory in sharp contrast to the rapid decline in his
fortunes in the next few years, and his recollections of innocence became the foundation for vision of a transcendent existence somewhere in the future.

The intensity with which Miller recalled his childhood was partly a product of how quickly it ended, and how different his life seemed afterward. The neighborhood in which his family lived began to deteriorate, and his family began to collapse both economically and psychologically at the same time.[1] Miller's father's moderately successful tailor shop did less and less business, his mother responded to financial pressures by becoming progressively more rigid and intolerant and his sister Lauretta was discovered in her youth to be the victim of mental retardation, a condition which would keep her helpless throughout her life. Miller spent a few months at City College in 1909 before dropping out with failing grades in everything, and in the next few years, he drifted without any real direction, bored by mundane jobs and involved with several women in protracted, debilitating affairs. His first marriage and the responsibilities it brought concluded a period of early manhood that changed Miller's outlook radically and permanently. The "place" where Miller felt completely at home, alive and aware, was totally wiped out—family, neighborhood and boyhood gone, but growing already in memory and available there for mythologizing into a positive mode of existence to balance a dreary life in the present. Until the publication of *Cancer* in 1934, Miller had no tangible accomplishments to point to, and the vision of his happy childhood grew in imagination and memory, sustaining him by its promise of a way of life that could be reclaimed or restored in his mature years if he should find the right means.

Although Miller, in the early pages of *Black Spring,* could evoke its moods with clarity and describe its scenes with a vividness worthy of comparison to Dickens, he could never quite regain the condition of innocent awareness he describes. He was no longer capable of actually *being* in that world, of completely relocating himself into the mind that existed before childhood's end, but he also recognized the opportunity to use his recollections of that world for his own purposes. Because it could not be recaptured or reentered, Miller was not concerned with producing an objective historical record of its existence. Instead, he felt free to invent it anew, or embellish it according to his inspiration. Eventually, it became both a guide on his quest, and the goal of his search for transcendence. Like Tom Sawyer in Lawrence Ferlinghetti's poem, Miller presents himself in his writing as one who is "perpetually awaiting/a rebirth of wonder."[2]

Of course, the word *awaiting* suggests a passive stance, and one of the primary operating principles of Miller's work is that he is rarely willing to wait for anything.[3] What actually occurs is that Miller works to maintain a condition of mind in which this "rebirth" is not only possible but likely. In order to do this, Miller has sought to recreate or redevelop or rediscover a *place* (psychic or physical, although they cannot really be separated) similar to that one in which he experienced his original *birth* of wonder. This process is informed by three specific objectives:

1. The need to chart a detailed map to replace the lost landscape of his youth in Brooklyn. This part of his quest involved travels in the United States, Europe and Greece, and when none of these led to a completely satisfactory environment, further travels in the landscape of his mind and as a part of this, the landscape of literary history.

2. The need to establish living conditions within a comfortable, familiar terrain similar to those which permitted the full psychic and sensory awareness that he felt in his youth. Not only did Miller need a congenial society to live in, he also had some distinctly individual patterns of behavior which made him a demanding, difficult person to live with, and he needed the support of close friends of both sexes to remain productive and moderately happy. His intricate relationship with the women in his life must be considered here, because he felt in their company a perceptual intensity akin to the child's vital awareness that he treasured in memory.

3. The need to somehow derail or thwart time (he often called it "The Destroyer") which was carrying him further and further away from the moments he remembered as fulfilling and complete. For the first forty years of his life, everything Miller tried failed in one way or another, and even after the publication of *Cancer*, he had to wait almost thirty years to reach modest financial security. Like most artists, throughout his life, he harbored doubts concerning the enduring value of his writing, and

until his death, he remained unsure about joining the company of "immortals"—even after receiving considerable critical acclaim. Therefore, Miller felt inclined to try to arrest or step out of the temporal progression that calibrates history.

Each of these three objectives is crucial in shaping his work. The first objective, the need to explore and map new lands, gave him a sense of setting. As he established a connection to the natural world, nature's realm gradually began to replace his childhood world as a source of inspiration. It is the second objective, the need to describe and understand sensory activity, that helped to give him a sense of style and language. The third objective, the need to escape from time, gave him a sense of structure (loose as it may often be) and a philosophy of composition. All of these *objectives* will be considered as they apply to each of the important books, but because I have been talking in general, almost abstract terms, I would like to develop them further before continuing.

To return to Miller's first objective, the demographic destruction of rural Brooklyn cut Miller loose, and he spent the remainder of his life trying to locate himself within a similarly comfortable environment. His intense contempt for an entire epoch of religious, aesthetic, moral and philosophical dogma might also be seen as a part of a cultural uprooting, and perhaps this too contributed to his desire for a compensatory geographical attachment. Once Miller was able to break away from Brooklyn, he began to seek other lands where he could feel at home. His travels through France, Greece and America were part of what Durrell calls "the search for the spirit of place."[4] When the ethos of each new land turned out to be only temporarily or partially adequate, Miller was driven back to "Brooklyn" and forced to cross and recross the blighted landscape to see if some hidden forces might still be unearthed or exploited. And when these searches turned out to be fruitless, Miller began to chart what was now an elaborate inner landscape. In his later writing, the surrealist excursions into the mind are part of an attempt to create an imaginary landscape which would have to serve as a refuge or sanctuary since there seemed to be no place on earth where Miller could find what he wanted. Part of his problem was that he was a self-described "megalopolitan maniac"; he needed the complexity and variety of the city. On the other hand, the country (or natural world) excited and inspired him, but only temporarily. He had to return to the ugly, blighted modern city for food, company and culture. This duality isn't particularly unusual, of course, but it prevented Miller from finding the one "great good place" he kept looking for.

Miller's second objective, the recreation of total or complete perception as part of a maximum sensory awareness, is at the heart of his erotic obsession. Miller felt that the formalized, regulated life most Americans lived was a severe deterrent to any passionate participation in the world. He often decried his "Prussian" background, and spoke with sorrow and some bitterness about his mother's coldness. The lack of love and warmth in his home overwhelmed him at the beginning of his adolescence, and he noticed the writers he liked at the time (particularly Lawrence and Jean Giono) advocated a life that seemed in sharp contrast to his own.[5] In addition, he realized that the "education" he was getting in the public school system encouraged the same type of rigid, puritanical, repressive "values" he was being forced to accept by his family. He began to feel that everyone in this country was being taught to eradicate or suppress what was most vital. As Laurens Van der Post has said, "the rational, calculating, acutely reasoning and determined human being that Western man has made of himself has increasingly considered the dark side of himself not as a brother but as an enemy, capable, with his upsurges of rich emotion and colorful impulses, of wrecking conscious man's carefully planned and closely reasoned way of existence."[6] The socially acceptable manner of responding to the world, Miller saw, was actually a barrier between man and the environment, or between one man and another person, or between man and a knowledge of himself. Miller felt that the "way of seeing" that he possessed as a child could never be recaptured within the "rational, calculating, acutely reasoning" society he began to see as his enemy. As he remarks in the essay "Creative Death," meaning, of course, the "death" of a too closely planned and reasoned world, "Strange as it may seem today to say, the aim of life is to live and to live means to be aware, joyously, drunkenly, serenely, divinely *aware*. In this state of god-like awareness one sings; in this realm the world exists as a poem."[7]

Miller intuitively came to the conclusion that one way to confront the restrictions of a repressive society was to thrust himself, in a sense, into that body, the needs of which he was encouraged to deny. Although Miller was generally inclined to try to please people even in terms of unreasonable requests (as a young man, he would actually write in the closet, hidden from his mother's disapproving friends), he also had a point beyond which he instinctively would not yield, and when he was pushed to and past that point, he tended to recoil back far beyond the line he chose to draw. The desperate sexuality of Miller and his friends in *Cancer*, *Capricorn* and *Sexus* is both an expression of the twisted, inhuman attitudes toward sex which society encouraged by repression and ignorance, and an example of Miller overreacting to this repression in an excess of self-indulgence.

It is very difficult to maintain anything like the Lawrentian body-consciousness that Miller admired even in the best of circumstances, but Miller's attempts to overcorrect American puritanism led him into brutal sexual encounters which made it impossible for him to live with himself (in his skin, as Charles Olson would say) or with any other human being. The obscene nature of the sexual activity in much of Miller's writing is a product of the loathing and self-disgust the people he describes had for the way they were using their bodies—and for the way they were neglecting their spirit or soul. Indeed, in Miller's work, one can develop a definition of the obscene as any kind of activity in which one feels such loathing for the body that all its desires seem unnatural and ugly. The problem for Miller was to find a way to live comfortably with the instincts which he acknowledged as crucial to his life as an artist and still retain a sense of respect for himself as a human being. Miller knew that unless he could cope with what Mailer calls, simply, lust, he would not be able to understand and appreciate the enormous potential for sensory and spiritual awareness that can be a function of sheer physicality. As Allen Ginsberg writes in his epigram to Robert Creeley's *Pieces*:[8]

> Yes, yes
>   that's what
> I wanted,
>   I always wanted,
> I always wanted
>   to return
> to the body
>   where I was born.

The "return" to the body meant for Miller a return to the natural sensuality of his childhood, but his abandonment of restraint led instead to a desperate groping for physical gratification that clouded rather than cleared his perceptual apparatus. The struggle to reclaim sensuality from the realm of decadence is central in Miller's work.

Miller's third objective, to somehow get "outside" of time, is a familiar one. His desire to find a way to become a part of the "eternal here and now" (as he put it) is very understandably human, and the factors which motivated him led to the development of several crucial elements in his narrative consciousness and to some of the apparently idiosyncratic patterns of structure that inform his writing. His displeasure with the world he lived in was more than just a nostalgic inclination to replace his current existence with the reincarnation of a prior one. Miller often professed his belief that western civilization was headed for apocalyptic catastrophe and consequently, he was convinced that "progress" was a bizarre mockery of actual historical reality. As an artist, he saw himself permanently excluded from any schemes for social improvement or adaptation, and as a social rebel, he regarded almost all politicians as self-aggrandizing charlatans. This led him to confound chronology as a method of organizing narrative and envision the artist as outside of history. As he says:

> In a way, the artist is always acting against the time-destiny movement. He is always a-historical. *He accepts Time absolutely*, as Whitman says, in the sense that any way he rolls (with tail in

mouth) is direction; in the sense that any moment, every moment, may be the all; for the artist there is nothing but the present, the eternal here and now, the expanding infinite moment which is flame and song.[9]

Which is to say that Miller was never comfortable in the actual *present*, but always energized by its tensions as he worked toward some fabulous future.

Consequently, in his auto-novels, Miller fractured the nearly classical beginning-middle-end sequence of traditional chronology and set his fiction against a shifting polychronic background ordered by a cinematic use of time. Temporal flow is expanded, compressed and distorted as the people in Miller's fiction—including the "I" narrator—live simultaneously in different moments in their lives. The reality of their existence is determined primarily by their reaction to the narrator, and they are frozen in the frame in which they are "alive" in the process of the narrator's life. As Miller explained: "I am a man telling the story of his life, a process which appears more and more inexhaustible as I go on . . . It is a turning inside out, a voyaging through X dimensions, with the result that somewhere along the way one discovers that what one has to tell is not nearly so important as the telling itself."[10]

It is crucial to note that the reference points for Miller's mind as he voyages "through X dimensions" are frequently the ideas and creations of other artists. His rejection of the "false" values of his own age (an age which, in turn, was rejecting him) is balanced by an alliance that Miller has formed with a community of artists who live as a sort of universal wisdom beyond the bonds of their temporal existence. Like Yeats in "Sailing To Byzantium," Miller seemed hopeful that he might be gathered "into the artifice of eternity." Miller wanted to make a spiritual connection with the men he admired, to prove somehow to them that he was one of their kind, a member of their company. He spent most of his time in Paris among writers, painters, sculptors and their patrons and hangers-on, but would have liked to go further to join others he could not meet:

I have always felt that I was born twenty or thirty years too late,

always regretted that I had not visited Europe (and remained
there) as a young man. Seen it *before* the First World War, I mean.
What would I not give to have been the comrade or bosom friend
of such figures as Apollinaire, Douanier Rousseau, George Moore,
Max Jacob, Vlaminck, Utrillo, Derain, Cendrars, Gauguin, Modi-
gliani, Cingria, Picabia, Maurice Magre, Léon Daudet, and such
like. How much greater would have been the thrill to cycle along
the Seine, cross and recross her bridges, race through towns like
Bougival, Chatou, Argenteuil, Marly-le-roi, Puteaux, Rambouillet,
Issy-les-Molineaux and similar environs circa 1910, rather than the
year 1932 or 1933! What a difference it would have made to see Paris
from the top of a horse-drawn omnibus at the age of twenty-one!
Or to view the *grands boulevards* as a *flâneur* in the period made
famous by the impressionists.[11]

The tone of this evocative, almost haunting revival of people
and places is designed to show how well Miller's sensibility
corresponds to that of the august company he calls to. What is
most significant about this passage, however, is Miller's desire
to be in a world he knows only through contact with the work
of other men and through the force of his imagination. And it is
also interesting to observe that Miller is expressing regret that
he didn't see Paris *before* he had lost the "child" within and
become corrupted.

Some of Miller's suggestions that he would never die have
disturbed too literal-minded critics, particularly the suggestion
in *The Colossus of Maroussi* with its aura of mystic gravity. What
Miller means, of course, is that his *work* will resist time; will
merge perhaps with the cultural stream that is life-giving and
aesthetically nourishing; that the "Henry Miller" of the autobiographical inventions will live on. How seriously Miller took his
own claims of a kind of immortality is hard to determine, but
they provide a kind of defense against the various kinds of
failure he had to face. As he says: "It is all a conquest of fear.
The question of why leads to the question of *whither* and then
how. Escape is the deepest wish. Escape from death, from the
nameless terror."[12]

Miller's declaration of his own worth as an artist begins in
Cancer, and the narrative voice that speaks there exists as a

figure correlated to artists working in other periods of history. As Miller's writing progressed, crablike, back toward his origins and forward to his future, his points of location through previously unchartered terrain were frequently the words of other men (and sometimes their pictures). The artists who appear again and again were people with whom Miller felt a strong affinity—sometimes he saw them as reflections of himself—and often their work is a focal plane through which he can screen an image or idea. Since Miller wanted to be some kind of an *Artist* from his earliest adult years, his concerns with land, skin and time/space were channeled through and expressed by his evolving artist/hero narrator. It is necessary to see how this narrative consciousness developed in order to understand how it shaped the *objectives* which I have been discussing. Therefore, I will examine the formulation of the central "character" of Henry Miller's autobiographical inventions before turning to the work itself.

2 The Rebel His Own Cause

GEORGE Orwell heard Henry Miller speak in a "friendly American voice, with no humbug in it, no moral purpose."[1] With characteristic penetration, Orwell saw the inescapable evidence that one must confront about Miller—he is an American writer, or more precisely, a writer who was "made in America." As I have noted, during Miller's childhood, his family was moderately prosperous and the neighborhood he lived in generally clean and comfortable. Although that time in his life was exceptional, no one in his family had any sense that they had reached a peak of modest prosperity and that a long decline into despair was about to begin. The Miller family lived cheerfully in the belief that the Chamber of Commerce clichés of progress, virtue, justice and so on represented the present and future. As a child, Miller was exposed to this attitude along with the devotion of his parents—the American Dream was alive for him in his early years. The optimism they all felt when Henry was born is exuberantly expressed in this passage from the beginning of *Black Spring*:

> Sunday morning no one was dressed. If Mrs. Gorman came down in her wrapper with dirt in her eyes to bow to the priest—"Good morning, Father!" "Good morning, Mrs. Gorman!"—the street

was purged of all sin. Pat McCarren carried his handkerchief in the tailflap of his frock coat; it was nice and handy there, like the shamrock in his button hole. The foam was on the lager and people stopped to chat with one another.[2]

By the time he had graduated from high school, economic and social problems had already been undermining this attitude for ten years. Then, from 1909 when he dropped out of City College until 1922 when he began work on his first novel, he struggled with dead-end jobs and the endless pressures of an unhappy marriage and many unsatisfying affairs. From 1922 to 1930, he made very little progress with his writing, never found suitable employment and lived through a convulsive, gut-wrenching relationship with a woman who became the obsessive focus of his life and work. And yet, when he began to write the book that became *Cancer* in 1931, his optimism and confidence were still there, available as a generator for the enormous energy of that book. How Miller maintained this attitude through the almost constant discouragement of his life is hard to explain, but one can understand it to some extent in terms of several characteristically American ideas.

First, when Miller discovered that the promises of the American Dream were false, he felt a kind of relief that he would not be compelled to follow the familiar school–job–family–fossilization pattern that seemed to be ruining his contemporaries. While he had, at first, nothing to replace the orthodoxy he was discarding, he recognized a kind of peace in the emptiness. As the last vestiges of the dream vanished into the wasteland, Miller became gradually aware of one of the essential features of the American land—namely "SPACE," as Charles Olson has so powerfully expressed it: "SPACE . . . the central fact to man born in America, from Folsom cave to now. I spell it large because it comes large here. Large, and without mercy."[3]

The development of Miller's narrative consciousness can be traced from his gradual realization during the 1920s that he was a solitary individual, responsible for his choices. The vastness of America loomed before him—room to act, space to find one's area and develop it. He saw himself at the beginning of Whitman's open road, a traveler about to begin a voyage of discovery. He was not convinced that all of America had been discovered—no American artist ever is—and he sensed that in searching for "America," he might find himself as well. Although he reviled the United States throughout his writing, his attacks stem from a conviction that the real "America" can still be reclaimed. In *The Air-Conditioned Nightmare*, he says:

> Here we are, we the people of the United States: the greatest people on earth, so we think. We have everything—everything it takes to make people happy. We have land, water, sky and all that goes with it. We could become the great shining example of the world; we could radiate peace, joy, power, benevolence. But there are ghosts all about, ghosts whom we can't seem to lay hands on. We are not happy, not contented, not radiant, not fearless.[4]

The optimism, the belief in redemption and in the possibilities of a new beginning without old ghosts are all a part of the psychology of a new world. One wonders how Miller could maintain this outlook, and as a matter of fact, he didn't maintain it continuously. There are moments, like those described in the essay "Sunday After The War," which suggest a kind of despair that one might expect to be overwhelming; but Miller always bounced back. Good food, talk, sex or the inspirational powers of art would revive him again and again. His resilience stems from another aspect of his American heritage, which Wallace Fowlie described as his ability to "interrupt the traditional American treatment of evil."[5] Fowlie does not entirely clarify his perception, but he is basically on the mark. Like Whitman again, Miller has no real vision of evil.

When he started his first book in 1922, a novel he planned to call *Clipped Wings*, he intended to write about common, decent men who had failed, a book Martin calls a sort of reverse Horatio Alger story. Among the reasons for the project going nowhere was Miller's disinclination to write a book in which all of his subjects were destroyed by the world, because in that case, *evil* would be his ultimate subject. As William Carlos Williams notes, evil is no longer a possibility once one is committed to a transcendental vision of human existence. There is a theological thinning in this kind of thinking, and it may well be a product of a kind of new world innocence common in America. How much evil is there in a lousy job or a mundane marriage, compared to the genuine horror that so many nations have faced in this century? But Miller shares with Whitman a fundamental faith in the goodness (even, to use Shelley's term, the *perfectibility*) of man, and while his inability to understand the terror that evil engenders severely hindered him in writing the *Rosy Crucifixion*, it is a central feature of his resilience. In the midst of the most sordid experience, Miller was capable of proclaiming his pleasure in just *being*, and he never lost sight of his initial and final objective: That some day both he and his country would be restored to the Adamic vision of his youth.

Miller's sense of SPACE, his faith in man, his ignorance of evil and his disgust with middle-American cultural values are important components of his narrative consciousness, but the nucleus that holds them together is probably the most distinctly American aspect of his art. Like Whitman, Miller sings a song of himself. His "I" narrator is the voice of his narrative consciousness, and the manner in which it was discovered, designed, refined and eventually reacted to by Miller both consciously and subconsciously is one of the great delights and major problems of his work.

The failure of *Clipped Wings*, and of the "book" he worked on during the late 1920s, the unpublished "Crazy Cock," may be in large part due to the absence of Henry Miller's "I" in them. They are both essentially third person narratives. The weakness of the long and boring *Plexus*, and many of the incidental essays can certainly be attributed to the watering-down of the "I" voice. Even *Maroussi*, with all its strengths, suffers from the reduction in size and scope of that voice. Miller's initial success in *Cancer* can be traced to his decision to write a book about "Paris and Me," and the example of Anaïs Nin's then unpublished multivolume diary helped to convince him that he did not have to imitate the omniscient perspective of the great authors of the nineteenth century.[6] And while Miller was not very interested in their efforts, his decision to construct his books around the reactions of his own consciousness paralleled the development of such epics of the self as Pound's *Cantos*, Williams's *Paterson* and Charles Olson's *Maximus Poems*, which recorded the collision between the poet's mind and the phenomena of the universe.

When *Cancer* was published, most readers thought that it was strictly autobiographical, a literal account of an unusual and sometimes outrageous human being. Even after one is thoroughly familiar with Miller's life and work, it is still difficult not to be struck by the same almost shocking intimacy and authenticity. The "I" narrator of Miller's narrative consciousness reaffirms Whitman's bold declaration, "I was the man; I suffer'd; I was there." But to assume that Miller's artist/hero, the "I" who speaks in a highly personal voice, and Henry Miller the author of the books in which the "I" addresses us, are equivalent entities is to miss much of what Miller has accomplished. To accept the *auto-novels* (Miller's term) as straight autobiography is a mistake because it denies Miller's control as an artist and suggests that any order or form in his work is either chronological or accidental. To describe them strictly as fiction, as Nelson does, is also a mistake because it rejects Miller's intricate, shaping relationship with the materials of his life and psyche.

Miller himself was rather coy about this relationship, afraid perhaps of revealing too much and making his work seem transparent, or concerned that he might lose his touch if he analyzed it too excessively. So, he generally made claims like the one in *Henry Miller on Writing*, where he maintains that he writes expressly to, "reveal myself as openly, nakedly and unashamedly as possible."[7] None of his serious critics accept his claim literally. Widmer chooses to call Miller's work "partly autobiographical."[8] Hassan says, "the prevarications of Miller on this subject amount to a kind of utopian duplicity."[9] Gordon is dubious about the sexual escapades: "as a matter of fact it is doubtful whether the literal content or the manner of narration is true in any acceptable sense of the word."[10] Jane Nelson avoids the issue altogether by deciding that the characters are nonmimetic figures of the mind. Mathieu, since he is discussing a book in which Miller is apparently writing straightforward autobiography, doesn't consider the issue much at all, while Mailer, who might enjoy the idea that Miller is always writing nonfiction novels (especially the sexual escapades), says, "the real Henry Miller, which is to say the corporeal Miller certain writers knew intimately and wrote about well, Anaîs Nin being the first, is not a Henry Miller who is so very different from his work. He is more like a transparency laid over a drawing, copied, and then skewed just a degree. He is just a little different from his work."[11] Miller might have preferred Mailer's position to the others, because in another section of his book of essays on writing, he writes to Trygve Hirsch, his attorney in one of his obscenity trials, "Am I also one with the protagonist of these 'autobiographical romances,'" and responds, "My answer is yes," adding as an afterthought, "That is perhaps harder to swallow."[12] Gordon, who developed a most congenial relationship with Miller in the course of his study asked him what he thought of the following approach: "Should one distinguish the Miller who speaks in 'The Enormous Womb' or 'The Wisdom of the Heart' from Miller who speaks in *Tropic of Cancer* or *Capricorn?* My only choice was to take the public figure, Henry Miller, and treat him as an entity based on the works."[13]

Gordon's question is not unreasonable. Miller, who has longed for a "poetic, imaginative interpretation" of his work, gives Gordon a most interesting and revealing reply:

> You ask how is one to distinguish between Miller who speaks in "The Enormous Womb" and the Miller of. . . . This is a problem the reader has to solve for himself, it seems to me. One changes, or evolves, one contradicts himself, one emphasizes now one aspect, now another. All a part of life. We are not made to order, consistent, always recognizable. Take Kazantzakis, for instance. See how Prevelakis handles his many changing attitudes toward life and art. But even if he were a true chameleon one would still recognize Kazantzakis. Life affords most of us little chance to reveal our many-sided soul or psyche. In Tibet, for example, they do not have the same fear of insanity as the Western world has. When a man becomes insane they look upon it as though he were revealing another side of himself. His soul is a fasces—multifold.

And did not Whitman say: "Do I contradict myself? Very well, I contradict myself."[14]

The image of the chameleon is especially evocative. It recalls John Barth's description of one of Jorge Luis Borge's labyrinthian constructs—a place where all of the possibilities of choice are embodied and must be exhausted before one reaches the heart. As Miller has said, he is "a man telling the story of his life, a process which appears more and more inexhaustible as I go on," and it is the task of the critic to show that all of the 'fasces" of the artist's soul are still "recognizable." When Miller insists that the episodes of his auto-novels are "plain descriptions of reality," he does not expect the reader to agree on a fixed notion of *reality:* "The difference lies primarily in the understanding and the use I have made of 'reality.' To get at the nature of this reality which pervades all life, and which *is* life, I have had to grapple with the metaphysical aspects of suffering, freedom, experience."[15] I am reminded here of Andrei Sinyavsky's comment that he is "truthful with the help of 'absurd fantasy,' " or Günter Grass's contention that he reaches for the "precise truth through the grotesque and exotic." Or, as Miller puts it in another version of the same thesis: "There are times when I myself no longer know whether I said and did the things I report or whether I dreamed them up. Anyway, I always dream true. If I lie a bit now and then it is mainly in the interest of truth. What I mean to say is that I try to put together the broken parts of myself."[16]

The vital entity of Miller's fiction—the "I" narrator called alternately the artist/hero (Widmer), artist/seer (Fowlie), protagonist (Mailer)—depends upon Miller's intentions for its birth, but owes its growth to numerous crucial actions which Miller committed but did not entirely plan. The creation developed a life or *Will* of its own which drew from the creator a surge of force originating in normally inaccessible reaches, and it took a shape that startled and delighted him. It caused Miller to say in retrospect: "I'm trying to tell you all the time that the influences were many, many, and from all levels, all directions."[17] In his reflections on his career, Miller refers again and again to his determination to "portray the *whole* man," and in the later works, there is a feeling of a man taking samplings of the volcano's initial explosion (*Cancer*) and analyzing them to determine the scope and power of the eruption. The artist/hero begins with Miller himself; what he has done and what he has been; then the character becomes an amalgam of what Miller thinks *he is* at the time of writing, and goes on to expansion and readjustment in terms of what Miller thinks *he should be,* or should become. Even in *Cancer*, one can sense a reciprocation between Miller's reaction to a situation and a muted concern for the way in which his artist/hero should be responding. As the work progresses, there is an increasing awareness that he is being observed by a growing circle of strangers. He seems anxious to respond to the expectations of his observers, and at the same time, to transcend the world they inhabit. While Miller's artist/hero is determined to become a part of a universal artistic community, Miller is tied to his much more mundane desire to achieve success as a writer in his immediate environment. As he tells Durrell: "I wanted so much, so much, to be a writer (maybe not to write so much as to *be* a writer)."[18] One cannot help but sympathize with the writer who worries about transcendence and eternity, but is honest enough to admit his ambitions as well.

The later books, particularly the second half of *Sexus* and most of *Nexus* (not to mention *Maroussi*) are weakened by Miller's growing tendency to withhold the most interesting, controversial and uncontrollable part of his "I" narrator, and his so-called artist/hero becomes more predictable and much less engaging in the process. The fascinating qualities of the "I" narrator—his unpredictability, invention, brashness, irreverence, honesty, love of words—are crucial to the success of Miller's work, because when we are in his presence, the conditions for a "re-birth of wonder" are developed and maintained. As those qualities which made him exciting are gradually withdrawn, he becomes less recognizable and more commonplace. Mailer believes that as Miller's career progressed, he decided to "put on his good literary suit" to pay "a call on the literary academy."[19] This is probably true to some extent, but how close the "I" narrator comes to the "corporeal Henry Miller" is not, finally, the most important point to consider, although it is certainly an interesting feature. What matters most is that the voice of Miller's narrative consciousness was formed to satisfy Miller's compulsion to penetrate all the fasces of his soul—the "inexhaustible process" referred to earlier. When Miller began to respond to the lure of literary acceptability, he may have been at a stage of his life when it was no longer possible to summon the energy, conviction or irritation that existed when the "I" narrator first took shape. While Miller may have made some accommodations along the way, the initial power and sustained attractiveness of the "I" narration stems from a psychological certainty that goes a long way toward convincing the reader (especially at first contact) that extraordinary phenomena are about to be uncovered. This will become more apparent when specific books are discussed in detail, but at this point I will continue to examine the evolution of Miller's narrative consciousness by considering the range of effectiveness of the "I" narration in terms of the language which Miller fashioned to give it life.

It has been said that a masterpiece either creates or exhausts a language. Benjamin Whorf tells us that, "A change in language can transform our appreciation of the Cosmos." On the other hand, the development of new or transformed conditions of awareness may occur prior to the construction of a language which can articulate and communicate these impulses. If that is the case, then one might assume that whatever the power of the new vision may be, it will not fulfill its greatest potential. This, I believe, has been the case with Miller's work. His "friendly American voice" is a versatile instrument for rendering his versions of experience, but it neither creates a new language nor exhausts a familiar one. Miller's ultimate vision of a man living in a state of heightened awareness (or *altered consciousness* to use the sixties term) is not fully realized in his auto-novels, and one reason for this may be that his language does not succeed in transforming one's way of seeing the universe. Because Miller was interested in extending the boundaries of the contemporary sensibility, he was working in advance of nearly everyone writing in the first half of the twentieth century, except for poets like Pound and Williams, and for all his reading he was just about totally ignorant of what the poets were doing—not that he was alone in that ignorance. This meant that he had to work entirely by himself, and although he did a fairly good job with the means at hand, he was not able to extend the language of his "I" narrator beyond several interesting but familiar strains in American literature.

From his transatlantic perspective, Orwell heard a single "American voice," but it would be more accurate to describe Miller as the creator of *two* distinctly American voices. On the one hand, Miller often speaks in the voice of the unlettered but intelligent man of the street, the well-meaning, no-nonsense, anti-intellectual regular guy celebrated in populist rhetoric. He is straightforward, often bigoted, remarkably candid and full of superstition and bogus folk wisdom. On the other hand, Miller almost as frequently speaks in the voice of the poet, inspired and romantic, in turn lyrically precise and rhetorically bombastic, and eternally responsive to the infinite variety of man and the world. The first voice has its origins in folktales and tall stories, and the consciously nonliterary styles of various early American humorists. It was used effectively by such writers as Mark Twain and Jack London, and it is consistent in its implied or stated mistrust for anybody who was obviously the product of "formal" education. Miller tells Gordon: "As for 'education' the biggest bug-a-boo of all and the root of all evil!—I have to quote Rimbaud once again: 'Tout ce qu'on nous enseigne est farce!' (originally I read *faux* for farce. Amounts to the same thing really—at least for *me*!)"[20] During the years that he was resisting the "miseducation" of the New York public school system, Miller claims that he became interested in the life of the mind through the enlightened, unacademic conversations he shared with his father's friends:

> Grossly untrue that my father's boon companions were without intellect or uninterested in books. Quite the contrary. I used to have long conversations with a number of them about my favorite authors at the time, to wit: Nietzsche, Bergson, Hamsun, Dreiser, Marcus Aurelius, Rabelais, Heraclitus, the European dramatists.

They were not drunken sots, these men. They enjoyed life to the
full. Their conversation was always alive and interesting. Among
them were actors like John Barrymore, Corse Payton, the husband
of Constance Collier (forget his name at the moment—oh yes,
Julian L'Estrange.) With one of them, who liked cheese and farted
a lot, I could talk Goethe, Schiller, Heine, and so on. Or Kant and
Schopenhauer.[21]

Miller often tends to exaggerate the good times of his youth,
but his admiration for a certain type of verbal discourse is clear.
He would have been very much at home in a pub in Dublin, for
instance, or in any country where an oral tradition flourished.
The language of the professional scholar always seemed lifeless
to him ("ultra-sophisticated, analytical, critical of everything"),
and the congenial ambiance of the social gatherings he remembers must have given his "long conversations" an especially
prominent place in his recollections: "My father and his drinking companions could talk humorously and intelligently about
all manner of things. It was just this 'non-intellectual' quality of
the talks which intrigues me still—how refreshing, how much
more interesting than talks with professors, scholars, scien-
tists!"[22] Miller's belief in the *power* of talk led him to one of the
principles of construction which he employs in all of his books
and which he used as the basis for the style of his *first* voice.
This is the presentation of ideas and incidents as if they were
occurring spontaneously in an improvisatory dialogue, in
which the "reader" or "audience" provides a kind of assent
and encouragement in the form of an implied "uh huh" or
"ummmm" at appropriate moments. The reader or listener
must become closely attuned to the rhythms of the conversation, caught up in the mood and rather actively involved in the
development of the *argument.* As Emile Capouya points out,
"Miller relies more heavily than most on the intoxication in-
duced in him by his own language and the insights it provokes
when it has worked him up into a state of creative trance."[23]
The effect on the reader must be something similar, in which he
too is elevated or transported into a state of trancelike absorption.

In accordance with this principle, the thread of Miller's narration often approximates the style of conversation—surges, rapid changes of emphasis and tone, repetition and most significantly, digressions. One of the ways to understand Miller's eccentric arrangements of chronology is to recognize that his "conversational" narrative is often interrupted by a switch to a parallel (or closely related) track in the narrator's mind which is followed for some time before the original or basic narrative line is resumed. Sometimes these digressions consume dozens of pages and threaten to become the subject of the narrative. It is almost as if Miller considers the narrator's consciousness to be the subject of his books (and it is *one* of the essential subjects of all of Miller's writing) and seems only vaguely concerned with the traditional constraints of plot. When Miller quotes Emerson's famous dictum that novels will give way to autobiographies (as an epigraph to *Cancer*), he is not just emphasizing the primacy of the author's *self* but suggesting that the traditional structure of the novel will be altered by an evolution that puts as much importance in the reaction of the "I" narrator of the novel to various events as was once put on the events themselves. Miller knew that Bloom's feelings about his life in Dublin were vastly more significant than any of the very ordinary incidents of that life. What seem like irrelevant flights of fancy in Miller's writing are often aspects of a Joycean stream of consciousness that reveal patterns of the narrator's mind that can be understood only in terms of similar passages in other parts of the same book or in other books altogether. These digressions have their origin in the conversational style of exposition that Miller depended on, and while there is a danger of a solipsistic sameness even for a writer as inventive as Miller, the method was crucial in the development of his style. Miller's commitment to this conversational mode is made quite explicit in his celebration of the great "talkers" of *Maroussi*—Katsimbalis, the colossus himself, as well as Aram Hourabedian and the Nobel laureate George Seferis—and it is effectively illustrated and partially explained in a passage from *Nexus* in which Miller recalls an address he made extemporaneously to a group of strangers at a meeting. His friend O'Mara tells him, "you were marvelous; you never hesitated a moment; the words just

rolled out of your mouth." Miller is sceptical at first. With a
shrewd sense of his own limitations, he asks:

> "Did it make sense, that's what I'd like to know."
>
> "Make sense? Man, you were almost as good as Powys."
>
> "Come, come, don't give me that!"
>
> "I mean it, Henry," he said, and there were tears in his eyes as
> he spoke. "You could be a great lecturer. You had them all spell-
> bound. They were shocked too. Didn't know what to make of
> you, I guess."
>
> "It was really that good, eh?" I was only slowly realizing what
> had happened.
>
> "You said a lot before you launched into that Hamsun
> business."
>
> "I did? Like what, for instance?"
>
> "Jesus, don't ask me to repeat it. I couldn't. You touched on
> everything, it seemed. You even talked about God for a few
> minutes."
>
> "No! That's all a blank to me. A complete blank."
>
> "What's the difference?" he said. "I wish *I* could go blank and
> talk that way."[24]

From this passage, we can get an idea of the language which
Miller wanted to create. The voice of the artist/hero should be
an almost instinctual response in which the wisdom of the
mind and heart fuse in a coherent synthesis of all that the artist
has to offer. In such a state, a *total self*, alert and creatively
active, comes into existence. The verbal artist, the "talker," is
involved in an almost mystical act in which language can satisfy
the Aristotelian precepts of instruction and delight, and can
also elevate the audience (and the artist) to ecstasy, that is, out
of a static condition of partial awareness. As Miller says: "I
believe in language, which is something beyond words, something which words give only an inadequate illusion of. Words
do not exist separately, except in the minds of scholars,
etymologists, philologists, etc. Words divorced from language
are dead things, and yield no secrets. A man is revealed in his
style, the language he has created for himself."[25] The conversa-

tional style has its limitations, of course. As Capouya points out, Miller has (in his "street talk"), "three characteristic styles —the daunting prophetic rant, the high-speed hysterico-comic narrative, and the genuine New York dialect."[26] In each of these variants, something crucial to a real "language" of his own is missing. The "daunting prophetic rant" is often striking in its initial effect, but once the shock of its force is dissipated, the thinness and superficiality of its *argument* becomes apparent. The "hysterico-comic narrative" does not have the capacity to develop a character or to offer the possibility for reflection since it depends on constant forward motion. The rather vaguely characterized "New York dialect" is the most limiting since it assumes a posture of exaggerated toughness that precludes sentiment and excludes a serious consideration of the nature of femininity. This is probably the most drastic defect of Miller's "talk." Millett's accusations are too often substantiated by Miller's adoption of a kind of male street-hip slang, a habit he may have fallen into in his early manhood that he found difficult to break. Because his "audience" for his first descriptions of his sexual adventures was exclusively admiring and male, he was never really able to see the necessity for finding another "voice" to describe his sexual experiences and fantasies. Even as he recognized the necessity for counterbalancing his casual racism by presenting another side of his *self* in later books, he sensed that his method for describing and analyzing erotic experience was not appropriate for a man who was vitally interested in understanding the nature of feminine reality. But in spite of his insistence in many interviews during his old age that he was not a "sexist," street-tough talk to an exclusively male audience remained his primary "voice" for expressing his erotic impulses. As I shall explain in my discussion of *Sexus*, this "voice" was often at odds with his serious attempt to understand the nature of his attitudes toward women and probably was responsible for the partial failure of that book.

But even if Miller was unable to modify the "regular guy" aspect of his "friendly American voice," he was able to develop another aspect of it to present that side of his *self* which was not ruled by the rough code of the street. Just as his "street talk" was designed for a particular audience, his "poetic song" was developed as a response to his need to communicate his child-like sense of wonder at the phenomena of the natural (and sometimes unnatural) world, and to his need to address a kin-dred artistic sensibility that he had discovered in his reading.

In a sense, he *spoke* to his peers, and *wrote* for the artists he admired and respected. When he was in their "presence," Miller became shy and modest, an almost reverent disciple at the foot of a master, and as his cloak of toughness slipped away, the ultraromantic side of his personality gradually became dominant. His celebrations of place (and in his essays, of people) are Whitmanic in their rhythms, their imagery and their outlook. In addition, as Mathieu points out in his com-parison of Miller with the symboliste poets (and Rimbaud in particular), Miller often wrote "heraldic monologues" in which a kind of pure sound is used to "release that evocative form of 'nonobjective thinking'" that is one of the goals of the sym-boliste movement. The use of a chantlike rhythm to induce a trancelike state is familiar in American literature, going back to Poe in formal literature, and further back to pre-Columbian and Native American literature in terms of an oral tradition.[27] Mil-ler's use of poetic techniques in his descriptions of setting and evocations of mood depend to a great extent on the rhythms of his voice, and a rearrangement of some of his lines (see chapter 5) indicates just how close to modernist poetry Miller's writing tended to be. The irony of the situation, of course, is that Miller still thought "poetry" was defined by the traditional meters and stanzas of the great British masters, and knew nothing of what Pound, Williams and Olson were doing until long after his style had been fully developed. Therefore, his "poetic" voice, while employing some of the principles that Pound and Olson discuss, was reserved by Miller for "traditionally" poetic subjects. This meant that he never considered using it for vast areas of his life, and it would never have seemed appropriate for him to blend the two aspects of his "American voice" to-gether. He might, in a romantic rapture, write a prose–lyric comparing June Smith, Mona/Mara of the *Rosy Crucifixion*, to some mythic goddess, but when he started describing their erotic encounters, he shifted back to his street vernacular. Within his self-prescribed limits, though, rhythm and measure are vital components of Miller's poetic voice, and his erratic employment of rhythmic controls is a kind of proof of Pound's contention that poetry deteriorates as it is removed from song. Similarly, Olson's lament about the dangers of "sweetness of meter and rime, in a honeyhead"[28] (dangerous for Olson, anyway) might be used to describe the appeal of sheer musicality that Miller so frequently answered. And although he is speaking about what is generally called prose, Mailer's lavish praise of Miller's style is expressed in terms of poetic devices and is concluded by a comparison with two men who are definitely poets:

> Miller at his best wrote a prose grander than Faulkner's and wilder—the good reader is revolved in a farrago of light with words heavy as velvet, brilliant as gems, eruptions of thought cover the page. You could be in the vortex of one of Turner's ocean holocausts when the sun shines in the center of the storm. No, there is nothing like Henry Miller when he gets rolling. Men with literary styles as full as Hawthorne's appear by comparison stripped of their rich language; stripped as an AP style book; one has to take the English language back to Marlowe and Shakespeare before encountering a wealth of imagery equal in intensity.[29]

In Gregory Corso's phrase, Miller is "a mad man of language," and much of his most impressive and memorable writing is in his "poetic" voice.

Nonetheless, the voice of an extraordinary conversationalist alternating with the voice of an accomplished and intense lyric poet is not sufficient to fully express Miller's narrative consciousness at its widest range. Orwell praised Miller for getting "away from the lies and simplifications, the stylised, marionette-like quality of ordinary fiction, even quite good fiction,"[30] and compliments him for "dealing with recognizable experiences of human beings." For the dour, decent political sociologist that Orwell was, "fiction" required little more. For a writer struggling to capture an almost profound vision of Man, the demands of "fiction" are much greater. As John Barth elo-

quently phrases it, an artist of the first rank is one who combines, in his work, "intellectually profound vision with great
human insight, poetic power, and consummate mastery of his
means."[31]

Miller clearly exhibits "poetic power," but his *vision* is rarely
"intellectually profound"—certainly not when he divides his
descriptions of women into romantic abstractions written in his
"poetic" voice and erotic assaults written in his "street" voice.
Thus, Miller's moments of "great human insight" are not combined with a "consummate mastery of his means," and it is this
last separation that most severely limits Miller's ability to develop a really satisfactory *language* for his "I" narrator, the art-
ist/hero who expresses his narrative consciousness. The
"healthy speech" (Thoreau's definition of good poetry) and
plain talk of the regular guy, the inspired, high-energy poetry
of the ecstatic prophet/mystic, the very American concerns with
land, SPACE and the possibilities of transcendence for the self
—all of these features of Miller's writing do not finally coalesce,
but operate in parallel tracks which are alternately emphasized.
There is a mixing of elements, of course, but not a real blending. Miller's work, taken as a whole, sometimes seems like a
series of interesting experiments without any final conclusion.
Miller may have been betrayed by the scandal his work created
into thinking that he was doing something radically new, but
his skillful use of the various methods of composition he had
absorbed in his prodigious reading does not produce a language that belongs only to Henry Miller. His "I" narrator
sounds alternately like the Rabelais of the gargantuan catalog;
the Whitman of the rhapsodic image; the Emerson of the impassioned sermon of logic; the Rimbaud of the symboliste aesthetic. But while Miller makes these elements his own, he does
not seem to go beyond them entirely to forge a tongue that
belongs exclusively to him. This is not to say that he fails to
generate a distinct, individual style, for Miller does establish
one (although that is a function of the fusion of voice, subject
and stance), but he never really achieves a new *language* that
one must learn before one can really know his work. As Mailer
points out, "Nobody has ever written in just this way before,"

referring to the beginning of *Cancer*, but the expectations of that superb beginning are not fulfilled. In this century, Pound, Joyce, Williams, perhaps Hemingway, certainly Faulkner have devised a language that is completely their own. Miller, I think, must be measured by their accomplishments, for he is in their league, even if his batting average isn't as high. His failure to equal their achievements does not invalidate his work, but it is an important consideration in terms of what Miller was trying to do. The language of his narrative consciousness is vital and honest at its best, often inventive and especially appropriate at expressing passionate appreciation. But the various elements and "voices" which Miller uses are not, finally, integrated into a coherent, unified instrument.

To understand why Miller was unable to accomplish this fusion, one must move beyond Miller's language to examine the most fundamental element of Miller's narrative consciousness. I am referring here to the psychological basis for action, both artistic and experiential, at the core of Miller's motivation when he began the serious writing that became *Tropic of Cancer*. This psychological base or foundation is Miller's own version of the concept of rebellion which Albert Camus discusses so brilliantly in *The Rebel*.

Miller did not know Camus during the 1930s (Camus was still in Algeria) and their contact later was mostly a matter of keeping up with each other's work. Camus joined the *Comité de défense d'Henri Miller* (along with Breton, Sartre and others) in 1946, and about the same time Miller wrote to Anaïs Nin that he was "open" to Camus and liked *The Stranger*.[32] But Miller was actively involved in the intellectual ambiance of Franco-European culture during the same decade that Camus was forming the philosophical tenets which eventually contributed significantly to the transformation of Western man's view of himself and the universe. As Mailer points out, in discussing Miller's interest in surrealism:

> Miller was living in the Paris of the thirties, incubator of Patagonians, the whole womb of surrealism. In that air of Europe, the memory of the old horror of the trenches dissipated less slowly

than intimations of the new horror approached. It was as if the mind of Europe comprehended that the oncoming disproportion of the concentration camps would induce a violence into logic that only surrealism could absorb. One breathed the air of the absurd and labored in the vineyards of the absurd rather than surrender to dread.[33]

Miller was too much the Yankee humanist ever to really consider the ramifications of an absurd universe, but the development of his narrative consciousness is constructed along lines that parallel many of the basic conceptions which Camus explains in *The Rebel*. The central parallel between Miller's position and Camus's classic conception of rebellion is that Miller decided to stop trying to adjust to a world which was rejecting all of his best efforts to get along, and chose instead to construct his life and his art in terms of a personal rebellion that finds meaning in *anything* that the self does. Similarly, Camus's absurd hero repudiates suicide (the admission of failure to find meaning) and chooses to accept the encounter between human inquiry and the emptiness of the universe as a means for creating value. Once Miller discovered that he could transmute his ideas and actions into art, he experienced a feeling of tremendous power that was utterly unlike anything he had known. *Cancer* is written with a conviction that stems from the author's exultation and relief that he has finally found a direction for his art; a method for concentrating his energy, ideas and impulses which actually fed energy and inspiration back to him. The tone of psychological certainty which the book projects is partly a product of Miller's exhilaration, and partly also, a determined effort to maintain a stance that was new, artistically effective, and quite possibly, very precarious. The boldness and arrogance of beginning a book called *Paris and Me*, in which *Me* gets equal emphasis, is paralleled in American letters only by Whitman's proclamations. But Miller's sense of power was so much at variance with his moods of the previous two decades that he could not be sure he would be able to sustain it. To admit any vestige of doubt into this scheme might unsettle the entire structure, and consequently, the voice of Miller's "I" narrator is designed primarily as a response to the basic necessity of supporting the personal rebellion at the core of Miller's new confidence.

The struggle to reach this position of confidence is described later, in the *Rosy Crucifixion* and in *Capricorn*, both written after *Cancer* but devoted to the years immediately preceding its creation. In *Cancer*, then, the "I" narrator is speaking at the end of a journey of discovery, and writing with all of the confidence which that apparently successful journey has engendered. However, since the "factual" background of the journey isn't available, one has to accept that the journey has been successful by implication—primarily through the tone of Miller's narrative voices. Miller's "I" narrator explodes into being seemingly from nowhere, his "song" at full strength (like Whitman's) with no apparent antecedents. The total commitment to the author's strengths, his reliance on the instincts of the battle-hardened self and his almost desperate adherence to the validity of his rebellion are the controlling factors in the formation of the narrative consciousness of *Cancer*. The terms of this rebellion are set quite explicitly in a passage from *Black Spring* which was written at about the same time he was working under full momentum on *Cancer*:

> I am Chancre, the crab, which moves sideways and backwards and forwards at will. I move in strange tropics and deal in high explosives, embalming fluid, jasper, myrrh, smaragd, fluted snot and porcupines' toes. Because of Uranus which crosses my longitudinal I am inordinately fond of cunt, hot chitterlings, and water bottles. Neptune dominates my ascendant. That means I am composed of watery fluid, that I am volatile, quixotic, unreliable, independent, and evanescent. Also quarrelsome. With a hot pad under my ass I can play the braggart or the buffoon as good as any man, no matter what sign he born under. This is a self-portrait which yields only the missing parts—an anchor, a dinner bell, the remains of a beard, the hind part of a cow. In short, I am an idle fellow who pisses his time away. I have absolutely nothing to show for my labors except my genius. But there comes a time, even in the life of an idle genius, when he has to go to the window and vomit up the excess baggage. If you are a genius you have to do that—if for no other reason than to build a little comprehensible world of your own which will not run down like an

eight day clock! And the more ballast you throw overboard the
easier to rise above the esteem of your neighbors. Until you find
yourself all alone in the stratosphere.[34]

The cavalier use of astrological terminology to "explain" his
motivation is part of Miller's method of debunking rational
science as a way of understanding the universe. The focus of
this passage, though, is on building one's own world and believing in one's own self. How similar is the mood of Camus's
passionate proclamation: "I proclaim that I believe in nothing
and that everything is absurd, but I cannot doubt the validity of
my proclamation and I must at least believe in my protest."[35]
When Miller found that he could not even "believe in [his] protest," (at the conclusion of *Sexus*), he literally had *nothing*, and
logically, he had lost his will to survive. I will discuss that fascinating "chapter" in Miller's story later. Here, I want to continue to explore the parallels between the basic tenets of rebellion as Camus defines them and the psychological motivation
of Miller's artist/hero.

Camus opens his essay with a defiantly *positive* description of
the rebel: "What is a rebel? A man who says no, but whose
refusal does not imply renunciation. He is also a man who says
yes, from the moment he makes his first gesture of rebellion."[36]
In other words, the first step in the process is actually the birth
of awareness—an awareness that the rebel has something to
live for. In Miller's case, the "awareness" that marks the beginning of the process is his realization that an artist does not have
to "show anything for (his) labors"; that there is a value in his
reactions and responses to the streets of Paris, the Seine, the
French countryside, all of the people he knows, and so on
through the unfolding adventures of the rest of his life. Logically, then, Miller must be an artist to live, and because the artist
can find fertility and life amidst the sterility and death of a
decaying civilization, Miller can be sure that as long as he is an
artist, the strength of his art will sustain him. In *Cancer*, Miller's
narrative consciousness is expressed by the artist who is the
hero of his own art, and that book is Miller's account of a complete commitment to his own version of an artist's life. As

Camus puts it, rebellion is founded on "the confused conviction of an absolute right which, in the rebel's mind, is more precisely the impression that he 'has the right to . . .' Rebellion cannot exist without the feeling that, somewhere and somehow, one is right."[37] I take Camus's use of the word *confused* to mean an instinctual, rather than a systematically worked out philosophical position. For Miller, after twenty years of disappointment and failure, the necessity to feel justified was of utmost importance.[38] Since he had failed at most of the relatively conventional economic ventures he had tried, Miller needed a way to maintain his confidence in himself as a human being, and his belief in the efficacy of an artist's existence permitted him to confront the world once again, but this time on his own terms. In defiance of the bourgeois economic system he had struggled with from 1909 through the twenties, he presents as the hero of *Cancer* the artist who lives by begging, swindling and cheating—but just to satisfy his basic needs. He has no qualms about his behavior because he feels "he has the right to," and that Paris is the "somewhere . . . one is right." As Miller's artist/hero affirms his worth simply by recording his observations and reactions, "every act of rebellion is extended to something that transcends the individual so far as it withdraws him from his supposed solitude and provides him with a reason to act."[39]

The "solitude" which Camus refers to is a kind of stagnation or discouragement which renders the individual incapable of any kind of action. For Camus's "man in revolt," solitude was brought on by a recognition of the absurdity of existence. For Miller, it was brought on by an inability to accomplish anything, and it was a condition marked by another concept Camus defines—the psychic state called *resentment*. Quoting Scheler, Camus defines resentment as follows: "Resentment is very well defined by Scheler as an autointoxication—the evil secretion, in a sealed vessel, of prolonged impotence."[40] The image of enormous energy trapped in a sealed vessel fits Miller's futile struggle during the 1920s very well, and as Camus explains, "Resentment is always against oneself." The act of rebellion, one can see, was absolutely necessary for Miller to restore some semblance of confidence in himself, to overcome "prolonged impotence" in his attempts to create something satisfying artistically. In Camus's words, rebellion is an act which breaks the "sealed vessel, and . . . allows the whole being to come into play. It liberates the stagnant waters and turns them into a raging torrent."[41] Miller's artist/hero is able to project an aura of great psychic confidence because he has overcome his resentment by choosing to act. Again, as Camus describes the situation:

> But one envies what one does not have, while the rebel's aim is to defend what he is. He does not merely claim some good that he does not possess or of which he was deprived. His aim is to claim recognition for something which he has and which has already been recognized by him, in almost every case, as more important than anything of which he could be envious.[42]

The dominant mode of *Cancer* is Miller's insistence that the world recognize "what he is." The psychological basis for the formation of the narrative consciousness of the artist/hero is Miller's recognition that "something which he is"—that is, his sense of himself as an artist—"is more important than anything of which he could be envious." This realization enabled Miller to overcome resentment, with its twin terrors, of impotence and solitude. After almost twenty years of frustration, Miller was finally able to break the "sealed vessel," and by chosing to act as an artist, Miller's "I" narrator shares with Camus's rebel the ability to influence his own existence, or at least, the illusion of this ability. Because he had been relatively powerless in the most important affairs of his life for so long, this choice had, as Camus points out, the liberating effect of turning "stagnant waters" into a "raging torrent." Miller's exuberance might be compared to Aleksandr Solzhenitsyn's mood when he discovered that he would not die from an untreated malignant tumor. "I deliriously took possession of the life restored to me," Solzhenitsyn recalls.[43] Similarly, when Miller discovered that his strategy for *Cancer* was working, he was able to generate enormous energy and to speak from a position of daunting psychological confidence. "Why rebel if there is nothing permanent in oneself worth preserving," Camus asks, and Miller's rebellion is a demonstration of what he had decided to preserve; his untidy, rough-edged, multistranded protoartistic consciousness itself. And once he had decided to "claim recognition" for it, he discovered that the decision now made it possible for him to use it as the basis for his writing. The process of rebellion was extremely fortuitous, because Miller might never have found a narrative base without it. However, the pleasure that Miller experienced in the power which he had finally directed into his writing also tended to narrow his vision. He began to concentrate his attention so completely on its maintenance that he lost sight of several larger considerations that would have ultimately benefited his art. In proceeding to write *Cancer* as a book designed to project and sustain that power, he had not really worked through all of the problems involved in getting the diverse strains of his narrative consciousness to coalesce. This isn't a failure of endurance, for Miller rewrote and reworked the material in *Cancer*, but more of a fragmentation of perception.

In a way, Miller was almost never in "the right place at the right time." He arrived in Paris among the "second generation" of exiles, but by then nearly all of the "lost generation" had already returned to America. He himself says that he would have liked to have been there twenty or thirty years sooner. When he finally settled in Big Sur, he was too old to be anything other than an example to the Beat writers in California. He was too much the humanist and Yankee individualist to really become un homme revolté, but the literary techniques of "realism" and "naturalism" were not sufficient for transcribing his vision.

There is much in Miller that forecasts the direction of American literature after World War II and yet, for all his visionary power, he is essentially leaning backward—his artist/hero has a strong intimation of what the postmodern world will be like, but he is constructed primarily out of familiar materials. He is built out of F. R. Leavis's "Great Tradition" more than one would suspect, and he cannot go far enough back into primitive America or far enough forward into unknown country to stake out his own ground. The concept of a frontier to the West is beyond his imagination, his world is still that of Eliot's "unreal city," and he cannot break on through to the Far East, enchanted as he is by his own concept of an Eastern mythos. The decade he spent in Europe did not prepare him to make the quantum jump into the absurd universe of Camus and Kierkegaard, and thus he only brushed the vast energy that charged the spiritus mundi of the 1930s instead of seizing and controlling it. There are aspects of the eschatological everywhere in Miller, but his instinct for a new age was built on values derived originally from Renaissance humanism, and he was as likely to fall backward into time as to hurtle ahead through a time warp to the future.

I have an image of Miller as an explorer dying on his ship as land is sighted, a figure from the Old World who never quite sets foot in the New one, although he sees it dimly through the mist and imagines its wonders. Miller is a genuinely pivotal figure, writing at the end of an epoch. He is more than slightly aware of his transitional position but he is not really sure how he can make the transition himself. Dostoevski is one of his masters, Lawrence and Joyce almost mentors, Whitman and Emerson compatriots, such contemporaries as Céline and Kenneth Patchen, innovators who interested him.[44] He is tied to the past, tempted by the cutting edge of the present, but afraid to plunge on to the future for fear that his newfound power might be lost. As he begins to create the mind and world of his artist/hero in *Cancer*, the forces that shape the narrative consciousness through which his protagonist speaks are so volatile that Miller contains them in separate channels to avoid being overwhelmed. The language of the artist/hero remains a series of interwoven but still discrete strands, never coalescing but each vibrant in its own form.

And finally, even this limitation might seem trivial if Miller had been successful in finding a suitable form for the entire book, because the context in which the various voices exist could impose a logic or order upon them from a larger perspective. But Miller is caught between the traditional ideas of structure and the visionary experiments in art, music and literature of his own time. Not exactly "novels," nor "autobiography," Miller called his books "auto-novels," or "autobiographical romances," and Philip Rahv understood even in 1957 that Miller's "novels do in fact dissolve the forms and genres of writing."[45] However, this dissolution did not lead to a radical reformation and the experiments without conclusion led some critics to assert that Miller's writing is nothing but amusing juxtapositions and random, disorganized incidents. William Gass notes: "Miller anthologizes well because his completed works are usually shapeless, repetitious and shamelessly self-indulgent; but this is a catastrophic condition when it comes, finally, to estimating Miller's position as an artist, for he is simply not a shaper."[46] Gass summarizes the case for all of those critics who have found Miller inadequate when they tried to find familiar strategies of form and structure in his work. I must disagree, although I have already pointed out that Miller is not the master of a tightly controlled narrative nor the practitioner of a plot that has a discernible beginning-middle-end arrangement. Miller is definitely a "shaper," not only within a particular book, but in terms of a grand design that guided him throughout his work. While it is true that he could not always get his visions into shape, and that sometimes the shape he chose was not ideal for his ambitions, to assume that there is no shape at all to his work, as Gass does, is to miss a very important aspect of Miller's art—both the part that succeeds and the part that fails. Miller would surely have agreed with Robert Creeley who said, "I have felt that to continue form arbitrarily, no matter how pleasant . . . was somehow wrong."[47] Miller's attempts to design a structure appropriate for his way of seeing are a part of an American literary tradition that goes back at least as far as Emerson's ideas on *spontaneous form,* and one can imagine him giving his assent to Allen Ginsberg's complaint about "ghostly academics in limbo screeching about form," because both Miller and Ginsberg took considerable pains to develop a singular form that conveyed the full force of their work. As a starting point, one might approach Miller's work from the position that Charles Olson declared: "There's an appropriate way of saying something inherent in the thing to be said."[48]

3 The Cartography of a Cosmos

Mind is shapely.
Allen Ginsberg

ALMOST from the beginning of his literary career, Henry Miller's friends were anxious to rescue what they felt was Miller's "best" writing from the often forbidding and sometimes frightening mass of words Miller succeeded in publishing. Beginning with Bern Porter's *Henry Miller Miscellanea* in 1945, and culminating with Norman Mailer's *Genius and Lust* (1976), well-intentioned admirers of Miller have made selections from what Karl Shapiro calls "this great amorphous autobiographical novel."[1] Shapiro speaks for them all when he says:

> I wrote to the British poet and novelist Lawrence Durrell last year and said: Let's put together a bible of Miller's work. (I thought I was being original in calling it a bible.) Let's assemble a bible from his work, I said, and put one in every hotel room in America, after removing the Gideon Bibles and placing them in the laundry chutes. Durrell, however, had been working on this "bible" for years; I was a Johnny-come-lately. In fact, a group of writers all over the world have been working on it, and one version has now come out.[2]

Durrell's version managed to work its way around most of the explicitly erotic material (Mailer's revels in it), as did most of the early collections, but each of them works from the principle that Miller wrote too much, repeated himself, and as Mailer says about the *Rosy Crucifixion*, was generally "in need of a great editor."[3] Unable to "help" Miller while he was in the process of writing, these books propose to retroactively perform some of the editing chores now that the author has put down his pen. Except for Mailer who explains his preferences with great flair, the other selectors generally expect the reader to accept their selections and trust their judgment. Instead of ordering the chaos they fear is ruining Miller's writing, they present assorted areas of *chaos* which they consider excellent or exemplary. The attempts to edit the book of Miller's life into chapters containing its most vital and readable components must fail because they ignore for the most part the complex interrelationships of these "chapters." The implication of these selections is that there is no real principle of organization in Miller's material beyond clever titles, whim and accident. As Mailer points out, "There is not one *Henry Miller*, but twenty, and fifteen of those authors are very good."[4] A reader that does not account for this complexity cannot really offer an accurate account of Miller's work. On the other hand, the obstacles to Miller's writing that the selectors have attempted to overcome by reducing the complexity of Miller's structural arrangements still remain to confound the reader.

Although he did not accomplish anything like the gigantic multivolume magnum opus he had envisioned in the late 1920s, Miller worked from that time according to a vast, intricate series of charts which he kept revising throughout his career. As Martin describes it, "he began to produce charts, diagrams, schemes, schedules, journals and notebooks. . . . On the wall beside the typewriter, he tacked two sheets of brown wrapping paper, one by two feet each. He divided these into six columns and headed them 'Words.' "[5] In the book he prepared for Playboy Press in 1971, *My Life And Times*, Miller includes enough of these materials to suggest just how much planning went into his work. There is a list divided into three parts headed, "Ideas," "Characters" and "Descriptive Bits," which he says "[I] told myself I must include when writing my 'autobiographical romances.' " There is a list of "names of places in various parts of the world where mysterious things happened to me." There is a small part of the plan he had for *Capricorn*, showing how it is tied into the material he would later put in the *Rosy Crucifixion*, and there are elaborate charts for books he never got going but which provided ideas that were eventually included in other books.[6] The intention to put something into shape, of course, is not the same thing as being a "shaper," but as Martin points out, Miller was a remarkably systematic person, although not all of his systems worked.

One of the reasons that they didn't always work was that Miller had to struggle so hard to get anything published at all, and that he had to spend a great deal of his energy on some very simple facts of survival. The history of Miller's efforts to get his work into print in even partially acceptable form is instructive. Miller wrote most of the material that appeared in *Tropic of Cancer* and *Black Spring* between 1930 and 1933, and he had already prepared the elaborate chart for *Tropic of Capricorn* by this time. *Cancer* was published in 1934 only after Miller gave up on a 200-plus page manuscript on Lawrence which his publisher, Jack Kahane, wanted to issue simultaneously in a bid for some kind of respectability. *Black Spring* didn't appear until 1938, and underwent considerable alteration, not necessarily for the better, while Miller tried to convince Kahane that the time was propitious for publication. *Sexus* was rewritten four times, finished in 1945 and published in 1949. The manuscript of *Quiet Days in Clichy* was lost for sixteen years. Miller made some fussy, detrimental adjustments on *The World of Sex* seventeen years after it was originally published. *The Colossus of Maroussi*, Mailer thinks, was written in an understandable attempt to woo the literary establishment. *Plexus* did not advance the story of the *Rosy Crucifixion* one inch, and Miller had to begin again in *Nexus* in the late 1950s. The conclusion of *Nexus* ostensibly brought the *Rosy Crucifixion* to its culmination, but Miller spoke from time to time during the 1970s of a *Nexus*, Book 2. There is material in all of the books that is practically unreadable and ought to have been radically revised or altogether excised, material that is interesting on its own terms but superfluous in its context, and material that might logically have appeared in another book entirely, particularly some of the extended essays. Incidents are used more than once, and in some cases, the contents of a "book" have been determined by various accidents of availability rather than any specific plan, although that isn't an isolated phenomenon in publishing. For many of Miller's readers, the books seem like some bizarre, hybrid form of prepop art, all middle without a true beginning or ending, an anti-Aristotelian mockery of linear thinking, more like a television serial or comic strip than any traditional novel.

Whatever misfortunes Miller may have had which prevented him from working according to his most lucid plans for organization, the fact remains that the books exist as they are. Miller had no Pound to throw the chaff out of his *Wasteland*, and Mailer's barely suppressed ambition to make a Borgesian reconstruction of Miller's work, to rewrite it from *within* (almost from *within* Miller's mind!), is not exactly a realistic possibility.[7] The critic has two choices: to call Miller's work chaos as many do, or look closely and carefully to see if Miller made anything of his forty years of writing that doesn't resemble a shapeless mound of words.

In an attempt to get some kind of handle on Miller's output, a consensus of sorts has developed in which commentators generally agree that Miller's auto-novels can be divided into a Parisian trilogy including *Cancer, Capricorn* and *Black Spring*, and an unwieldy three-volume, five-book conglomeration called originally *Fragments from the Rosy Crucifixion*, with the latinate rhyming titles, *Sexus, Plexus* and *Nexus*. Most of Miller's other books are treated as various forms of journalism and generally thought of as entertaining and inventive, with the exception of *The Colossus of Maroussi* which everybody praises but feels somewhat uncertain about. As the chart at the end of this chapter suggests, there is another order of arrangement which I feel is considerably closer to Miller's intentions and accomplishments. In it, I have divided Miller's work into two basic categories. The first might be called a quartet, which I have designated, "The Writer in the World: The Artist as Observer," and in the books in this group, Miller is primarily a spectator and a commentator, presenting his ideas and offering his reactions to the world he lives in. Both his rapturous responses and his vituperative denunciations in these books stem from a position of great confidence in the self, ranging from the defiant rage of *Cancer* to the quieter, more mature strength of *Big Sur*. The second group is a triad called, "The Formation of the Writer: The Artist as Actor," and in this category, Miller tries to demonstrate and explain how he struggled through a series of psychological crises to reach the position of psychic strength and creative insight which he proclaims in the first group. As the chart indicates, there is a circularity to the pattern, and *Cancer* is not only the beginning but also the ultimate returning point and goal of the journey that the books describe. This is a crucial point which must be understood to appreciate the unity, if one might call it that, of Miller's writing.

Fifty years after its publication, *Tropic of Cancer* with its immense energy and wild, violent language still has the power to startle and overwhelm a reader. Nonetheless, once the initial charge has been absorbed, it becomes apparent that the "I" narrator is not so much a participant but a fiercely gleeful spectator commenting on other people's ruin. The immediacy of the language and the very present tense perspective tend to obscure this fact at first, but as Miller rambles and rages cheerfully through the world of *Cancer*, one begins to notice how often he speaks of what he *will* do, what he has recently *done*, and what someone is doing to someone else. He is, curiously, a noncombatant in a combat zone, although he is not an impartial reporter by any means. But his partisan accounts are delivered from a slight distance that is very important. The difference between Miller and the other people in *Cancer* is that his great time of psychic agony has already taken place while most of them are locked in desperate contests for the survival of their mental stability. *Cancer* is Miller's demonstration of his ability to survive, and while it is his first published work, it represents the culmination of a very considerable struggle. Paradoxically, it is this struggle which is the subject of most of the remainder of Miller's writing, and one can chart a progression from the great assurance in *Cancer*, to a position of almost total despair at the conclusion *Sexus*, and then back to what Miller attempts to show is a confidence equal to that of *Cancer* at the conclusion of *Nexus*. There are various detours in the course of this journey, and Miller is nothing if not crablike ("I am Chancre. . . .") in his direction, but at the conclusion of *Nexus*, which was published in 1960, we see the "Henry Miller" of 1930 about to leave for Paris to write *Tropic of Cancer*. This, at least, is Miller's clear intention. Unfortunately, the last sections of *Nexus* do not evoke or account for the singular narrative voice of *Cancer*. Perhaps the act of writing that book drove some of the demons so completely out of his subconscious mind that Miller could never recapture the anger and fierce joy he experienced when he began to see *Cancer* take shape. But even if Miller was not entirely successful in making his journey of psychic discovery and transcendence into a circumpolar cycle (from *Cancer* around and back to *Cancer*), the sense of moving forward and backward in time—back to one's origins, on toward one's destiny—is an essential part of the structural arrangement of his work. This becomes increasingly evident upon examining *Black Spring*.

Cancer is the triumphant assertion of the self, but it is not a description of a world where the self might live, or anyone else either. The confidence that Miller displays in that world is impressive, but without a vision of a better mode of existence, it could easily degenerate into the cynicism of a Céline. *Black Spring* was composed simultaneously with *Cancer*, and it tends to balance the cancerous world of Paris in 1930 with the world of Miller's childhood seen through the idyllic haze of a quarter century of selective nostalgia and imaginative improvement. The title is important. The "spring" Miller speaks of is shadowed: it contains the possibilities of blight; it may become malignant. On the other hand, as the later passages of *Cancer* begin to indicate, amidst the decay of a cancerous world there are signs of a new spring to come.

Miller's recollections connect the "past" with the present in a reciprocal exchange of data which recalls Leibniz's definition of *existenz*, in which "the present is filled with the past and great with the future." To merely proclaim the value of the self, or describe the process by which it becomes vital is not the ultimate goal of art, even if it may be an important way station. As Guy Davenport says, the poet (or artist) in our time "does what poets have always done . . . made a world for the mind (and occasionally the body too) to inhabit."[8] Anaïs Nin told Miller, "In *Tropic of Cancer*, you were only a sex and a stomach. In the second book, *Black Spring*, you begin to have eyes, a heart, hands."[9] *Cancer* was an absolutely necessary first step for Miller, but even while he was writing it he could see the necessity also of describing the world in which his artist/hero hoped to live eventually, and even more important, the world which he hoped to have a hand in making possible through the power of his art. In *Black Spring*, the foundations for that world are set, and because they are set in the past, Miller continues to be an observer.

The first parts of *Black Sping* resemble nothing so much as a description of a mythic America which hardly existed except in the writing of two of Miller's favorite authors—Emerson and Whitman. In the section called "The Fourteenth Ward," Miller tells us that, "In my dreams I come back to the Fourteenth Ward as a paranoiac returns to his obsessions," and describes its inhabitants, his neighbors, as men living in a state of natural grace. They are set in startling contrast to the various specimens of human erosion and damnation Miller introduced us to in *Cancer*. The point is that Miller has not just recreated an Edenic past to lament its loss, but that he is demonstrating that he has the capacity not only to delineate the worst of *Cancer*, but also to describe the crucible in which his own creative consciousness was formed. In a sense, Miller's flight from the United States might be seen partially as a method for saving, while he still could, the spirit of America from the horror of life in an American city. As Mailer points out, "like every other American author, he loved America more than he could ever begin to allow."[10]

The sections about America in *Black Spring* offer a fading vision of a heroic era, a fantastic but familiar place seen by a spectator at a marvelous pageant where the play is "the past" (or the mythologized perpetual present) and the stage is Miller's mind. The sections set in Paris, or in some imaginative landscape, are developed with a surrealistic verve that shows how even Armageddon might be transformed by the eye of the artist into a feast for the imagination rather than a field arrayed in horror.

In the second half of the quartet, both *The Colossus of Maroussi* and *Big Sur and the Oranges of Hieronymus Bosch* are attempts by Miller to show how the artist/hero, combining the confidence of *Cancer* and the memories of *Black Spring*, can live comfortably and creatively in the present. In each book, Miller is interested in the way in which the natural world can inspire a person and restore him to his fullest range of activity.

Maroussi is the better book because it is consistently inventive, while *Big Sur* could be cut by half without losing much, but the conclusion of *Big Sur* is unlike anything Miller wrote elsewhere and it is probably the only work from Miller's later years which expresses a kind of wisdom that is usually the product of maturity. In both books, Miller has tried to make his artist/hero the center of a community, a kind of "great fire source" (as Robert Duncan describes Charles Olson) and pivot point, but in *Maroussi,* it is the poet Katsimbalis who is at the center, while in *Big Sur* Miller himself is placed there. In neither case, unfortunately, is the artist/hero quite like the "I" narrator of *Cancer*.

Katsimbalis, the "Colossus" of the title, is a kind of symbolic life force—the artist as Atlas whose strength leaps from the earth itself. He is constantly associated with the forces of nature, called alternately "the colossus," "the great star fish" and "the whale." He is an artist of the spoken word, Miller's favorite mode of expression, and of him Miller says revealingly, "He talked about himself because he was the most interesting person he knew."[11] As Mathieu explains it, Katsimbalis is a magician who puts man in touch with the limitless world, or an angel (echoing Wallace Stevens) who brings a "message" that does the same thing. Mathieu sees correctly that Miller's Greece is a vision of, as Miller puts it, "the perpetual dawn of man's awakening," and that Miller uses the incredible *light* in Greece as a symbol of this dawn. This is important because during those moments that Miller is trapped in the darkness of an urban hell, a river of light (the Seine in Paris) remains his only contact with the natural world.

In the last section of *Maroussi*, the artist is seen living in a kind of paradise in which he is everyman, the ordinary citizen as seer. The book concludes with a euphoric description that combines the utopia of memory with the actual landscape of Attica. At this juncture, although Miller is still an observer, the act of observation comes very close to total sensory participation, as if Miller is ready at last to move fully into the world. Miller exclaims as the book concludes:

> I see the violet light in which the stiff scrub, the worn rocks, the huge boulders of the dry river beds gleam like mica; I see the miniature islands floating above the surface of the sea, ringed with dazzling white bands; I see the eagles swooping out from the dizzy crags of inaccessible mountain tops, their sombre shadows slowly staining the bright carpet of the earth below; I see the figure of solitary men trailing their flocks over the naked spine of the hills and the fleece of the beasts all golden fuzz as in the days of legend; I see the women gathered at the wells amidst the olive groves, their dress, their manners, their talk no different now than in Biblical Times; I see the grand patriarchal figure of the priest, the perfect blend of male and female, his countenance serene, frank, full of peace and dignity; I see the geometrical pattern of nature expounded by the earth itself in a silence which is deafening. The Greek earth opens before me like the Book of Revelation.[12]

The long, rolling rhythms and measured cadences are like Conrad's marvelous speech in *Youth* when he sees the East for the first time. All that remains is for Miller to write about himself from this perspective, now that the light of Greece has "opened my eyes, penetrated my pores, expanded my whole being"; to write a book in which Miller himself is the artist at the center of a cosmos.

If the last section of *Maroussi* is a portrait of a paradise, the best parts of *Big Sur* are Miller's version of how a paradise of sorts was lost. Although he would have liked to have been able to present himself as the sage of Big Sur, too many intrusions from the rest of his life kept getting in the way. The most interesting intrusion is the arrival of Conrad Moricand, an astrologer and diabolist, and a friend of Anaïs Nin. Miller met him in 1936 in Paris and found him fascinating, partly because Miller saw some of his own less attractive features in Moricand. As Martin points out, the book is like a west coast *Walden*, with Miller's depiction of his friends resembling the chapter "Brute Neighbors,"[13] but only the section on Moricand is written with any sustained power, and only in that part and in isolated, almost random moments is the flickering image of Miller's artist/hero visible. Of course, as he neared seventy and began to enjoy some of the rewards and honors that were long overdue, it is not surprising that he could not (or would not choose to) go back into the psychic state which led to the creation of the narrative consciousness of the "I" narrator. But as the quartet of books about the world, actual and ideal, draws to a close, Miller's "I" narrator has grown steadily further away from the blazing, forceful voice that compelled attention at the beginning of the sequence. The pages on Moricand temporarily recall its best features, but there has been a considerable decline in Miller's ability to, as Mailer put it, write as "nobody had written . . . before."[14]

The diminution in Miller's voice is not just a matter of increasing age. Throughout his career, there are books and fragments of books that are long-winded, dull, vague and uninspired. What marks Miller's work when he is at his best is an intensity that comes from a total involvement with his subject. Miller was never any good at writing about what he felt he should be interested in; he was often enthralling when writing about what he could not escape or avoid. The manufactured *Hamlet* dialogues with Michael Fraenkel are an example of Miller's failure when he tried to write on an "important" theme, as is his finally published book on Lawrence, and even *Plexus*, the middle volume of the *Rosy Crucifixion*. His collections of essays, even the best ones like *The Air-Conditioned Nightmare* and *Remember To Remember* contain some of Miller's sharpest work hard upon some of his dullest.

Once Miller decided he was a writer, he worked at his trade steadily, undaunted by difficulties in getting his work into print and quite ready to crank up the generator even when he had nothing to really say about a subject. As he told Durrell, "he wanted to *be* a writer," and he saw correctly that this meant he must write regularly. The books in the quartet are among Miller's best because of his determination to express the narrative consciousness of his artist/hero and his deep concern about the world in which an artist (and any human being) might live fully. The weaker sections of the last two are due primarily to the exhaustion of his necessity to deal any further with those areas of his experience.

The second grouping of Miller's work, the triad which I call "The Formation of the Writer: The Artist as Actor," covers the one subject for which Miller is actually most famous, or perhaps one should say, most notorious. The fact that the books in the quartet do not devote a great deal of space to women after the first two hundred pages of *Cancer* is due to Miller's awareness that when he wrote about women he could hardly cover anything else. Even *Cancer* is not really about women, in spite of the frequent passages of graphic sexual activity, as much as it is about a particular male attitude toward woman as an erotic device. The artist/hero of *Cancer* reflects aspects of Miller's attitude in 1930 at the end of his obsessive, shattering marriage to June Edith Smith. Miller took a defensive stance to protect the self he was still in the process of reconstructing through his writing and made his "I" narrator close to the cold, sexist oppressor condemned by Kate Millett and others. However, as Anaïs Nin noted, in that book he is "only a sex and a stomach"; that is, just a part of the whole picture. Nin prophesied: "By and by, with each book, you will create a complete man, and then you will be able to write about woman, but not until then."[15] Perhaps because Miller never did create a "complete man," his writing about women was never completely satisfying to either his friends or enemies, or to himself, but in the second group of books, Miller made a very significant effort to write "the great tragedy of love" that he felt had shaped his own life.

"For a long time *reality* for me was Woman," Miller admits, expressing a sentiment that is probably true for almost all heterosexual men at various times in their lives. In the triad of books consisting of *Tropic of Capricorn, Sexus* and *Nexus*, Miller covers the years of the 1920s in an attempt to account for and understand the artist/hero who writes *Cancer* at the end of that decade. In this grouping, Miller is a participant, fully involved in life in a fascinating but hostile environment, and totally consumed by, first, a force which found its expression in sexual activity of great intensity, and second, a sense of romantic abandonment which threatened to carry him into madness. Mailer sees the *force* as lust, and the romantic abandon as narcissism, but that tends to oversimplify the situation, as I will explain. What is crucial here is that in both cases, Miller was obsessed, like Kafka's Hunger Artist, with his involvement. "If only I could have found the food I liked," the Hunger Artist laments; if only Miller could have settled into quiet domesticity with his first wife way back in 1917—not bloody likely. It took Miller more than twenty-five years to write the books in this triad, and at the end, he had not fully explained his obsessions either to the reader or to himself. He had, however, illuminated them, and in the process, expressed vividly concerns central to the lives of both men and women in this century.

In the first grouping, Miller is a finished product and his experiences do not change him. His perspective as observer keeps him at a remove from the action, even when he seems to be taking part in it. In the books of the second grouping, Miller is the central actor in an unfolding drama. This is an important distinction, because it means that the narrative consciousness of the artist/hero is in a state of flux in these books. For many critics, whether they like his writing or not, there is a tendency to describe the voice of the narrative consciousness as narrowly consistent. While examining his relationships with women, and particularly with the woman he calls Mona or Mara (his name for June Smith), Miller's artist/hero is by turns uncertain, desperate, enraptured, fearful and ecstatic. The range of his moods and his apparent inability to control them is an indication of the tremendous energy which Miller had access to, and the three books in this section have as their broadest subject Miller's willingness (one might say *compulsion*) to let the energy flow freely, to see where it led him and to determine what forms it might take.

Capricorn, as Jay Martin explains, has three discernible parts to it. The first sets the scene for the entire triad. The would-be artist/hero is employed as the personnel manager of the Cosmodemonic Telegraphic Company, Miller's marvelous coinage for the metaphorical conceit he develops to dramatize the bureaucratic insanity of modern "civilization." As the protagonist becomes progressively more numbed by the chaos and bestiality he finds himself drawn to, he retreats into a mental landscape which he calls, with characteristic directness, "The Land of Fuck."[16] Incidents in a kind of present-tense reality are paralleled by excursions into this bleak landscape. In the third part of the book, a particularly amorphous piece of writing, the protagonist meets Mara at a dance hall and becomes what Mailer calls "a prisoner of sex," although he is quite clearly also a prisoner of love in its most romantic form. *Capricorn* is a prologue to the *Rosy Crucifixion*—indeed, in a letter to Anaïs Nin in 1943 Miller says, "You ask if I have begun on *Capricorn*," referring to the whole project by that name.[17] During the course of the book, the nascent artist/hero of *Cancer* gradually reduces his distance from the events he describes, and at the end, he is experiencing what Gordon calls, "the first stirrings of self-discovery." One of the reasons that it took Miller another seven years to get *Sexus* ready for publication was his fear that an exploration of his relationship with June Smith would be a very difficult, trying experience; a reopening of the "wound of memory." The hard-won confidence of *Cancer* might be subject to considerable erosion if its base were too closely investigated, but Miller's concern was balanced by a desire to complete his project (the pivotal central "chapters" of the autobiographical fiction drawn from his own life), by his awareness that *he* was his own best, even only subject, and by the demands of his artistic credo. To stop short, to draw back when it seemed that he might lose the psychic power which was the key to his narrative consciousness, would be a refutation of all that Miller's "rebellion" had been about to that point. In accordance with his original plan, Miller had to confront the book which would deal with his frustrating, painful and unresolved struggle toward self-perception and, ultimately, self-acceptance.

Sexus is a daring book, not just because it contains many passages of extraordinary sexual frankness and not only for its exploration of the author's psychic ordeal. The real risk was in beginning a narrative with no sure idea of its conclusion. Miller revised *Sexus* throughout the war years, putting it aside to work on other projects, and then returning to it to continue the story. Eventually, he decided to omit the conclusion, hoping to pull everything together further along in the *Rosy Crucifixion*. In the heart of the book he is drawn into a sexual vortex that has the potential to obliterate every other aspect of his psychic consciousness. As the narration progresses, Miller slowly begins to realize the terrible paradox which is at the core of his agony, and "agony" is not too strong a word to use because the contradictory demands of sexual satisfaction and artistic enlightenment are placed in violent conflict. To put it succinctly:

1. His sexual energy is destroying his attempts to develop a harmonious relationship with the woman he loves;
2. To curtail his sexual nature would lead to a diminution of his creative energy, the source of his psychic stability even though he was not yet an accomplished writer.

In other words, to understand women, which would make him a more complete artist, he must control his blazing energy, which is the basis for his artistic insight.

The narrator must focus his driving forces, because even if they are at the source of his artistic inclinations, they are going to strangle its possibilities for growth. Without an understanding of the other dimensions of human possibility—without the ability to move beyond his traditional masculine perspective so that he might begin to understand *feminine* capability—the artistic enlightenment and personal transcendence Miller sought would remain beyond his reach.

Sexus ends with an extremely powerful dreamlike episode in which the narrator careens aimlessly through a nightmare landscape stripped of all his methods of defense. Whatever the outcome of this trial by terror, the prospect of seeing the process completed is very important. At this point several basic questions have been posed and some resolution must be provided. At the least, one wants to know:

1. Does the narrator regain his original strength? If so, how? If
   not, what happens to him? And if he is changed, how much
   and to what form?
2. How has this process affected Mara? Is she changed? How
   does she feel about the narrator? What, if anything, will their
   relationship be like in the future?

For a writer who does not usually use *plot* and the development of suspense regarding outcome as a major means of holding attention, the situation at the conclusion of *Sexus* is very
intriguing.

The terrifying vision of mental chaos verging on irreversible
insanity at the end of *Sexus* is a haunting invitation to follow
Miller across the threshold of psychic dissolution into whatever
realm lies beyond. The scene has an added power that derives
from its juxtaposition by implication to the supreme confidence
of the artist/hero in *Cancer*—the man who has emerged from
this experience and is living in Paris several years into the future. Miller has undergone soul-wrenching experience in order
to drastically increase or expand his perception of himself and
his ability to respond to the phenomena of the universe. He has
been guided in this venture by his recollection of a utopian past
and his dreams for a utopian future. From *Cancer* through *Sexus*, Miller's writing has a visionary (although often apocalyptic)
and prophetic strain to it that seems to promise an ultimate
revelation which will consolidate the energy that has been
flashing in random bursts of verbal fire. And the fact that the
specific nature of the "revelation" has been rather vague, even
amorphous does not matter. As Borges points out with exceptional insight, "The aesthetic reality is the *imminence* of revelation" (my italics). Throughout Miller's work, there have been
many moments when one feels that this particular author is
one among the few who can actually deliver the extraordinary.
The terrible disappointment of *Plexus,* and of *Nexus* as well, is
not merely the realization that there will be no cosmic vision
unfolding, but far worse, that the potential for revelation no
longer exists.

Plexus, theoretically the second book of the *Rosy Crucifixion,*
was written in 1948 and 1949 and published in 1953. The dra-

matic psychic reordering which *Sexus* forecast is not only conspicuous by its absence, but the whole book seems to have been written by an entirely different author. The text recounts the endless domestic and commercial ventures of a "Henry Miller" with a woman called "Mona," but she is not recognizable as the woman Miller has previously described and the narrator's voice is dull and without distinction. Perhaps the fact that even such close friends as Lawrence Durrell felt Miller had overdone the erotic aspects of *Sexus* bothered him, but in any event, the energy and compulsion are gone, the passion mostly quiet. *Plexus* might be an accurate picture of Miller's generally amiable, quietly domestic state in 1950, but it is supposed to be an account of the wild days of the mid-1920s when Miller was summoning his strength, concentrating it and preparing the devastating explosion of *Cancer*. The book extends itself episode by episode for six hundred pages instead as Miller substitutes "factual" recollection for insight. I am afraid that the book is a very forgettable distraction.

Miller must have known that *Plexus* was a failure, because in *Nexus*, which he wrote in the late 1950s, the first page of the text literally begins with the same sentence that concluded *Sexus*. But in *Nexus*, Miller has not found a way to emerge from the chaos of the unconscious with a new vision of himself or the world. He has, instead, retreated to the brink where the descent began and turned his back on the abyss as if it never existed. The "revelation" of *Nexus* is that Miller has decided that he (the artist/hero) was not so bad after all, that the world was the cause of most of his troubles, and that he ought to be happy in accepting himself as he was and is. This is actually an acceptance of defeat, because the motivation and singularity of the mind of *Cancer* have not been explored further, and because Miller has avoided writing with real intelligence about any woman, or been unable to do so. The questions which were raised in *Sexus* and in the earlier books have not been answered, which is not devastating in itself since not every question can be answered conclusively, but the process of examination has been discontinued abruptly. In terms of the way Miller started, and in view of his unique talents and absorbing complexity, this is the real failure.

In *Nexus,* Miller suggests that the ongoing quest which has given him the "Book" of his life has been most valuable as *process,* and that his search for the self has been instrumental in shaping, forming and disclosing what is most valuable in the self. This is fair enough, but Miller was reaching, in the beginning, for something quite a bit beyond a reconciliation to his essential nature; he was reaching for some invention of language and sensibility which would permit a new, energizing understanding of the shape of the universe itself. As Martin points out, "Miller was one of the few American writers who by 1932 still preserved the grandiloquent hope of the twenties: to compose works as great as any that have ever been written."[18] This incredible, Promethean ambition has been at the heart of Miller's appeal and it is quite a letdown to learn that the quest has come to an end merely because the explorer has decided to reconsider his goals.

Nexus moves toward the moment when Miller left Brooklyn for Paris and began to write the manuscript of *Cancer.* As Miller looks back from 1960 to the wild, rebellious closet artist of 1928, his approval lends a certain warmth to the conclusion of *Nexus,* but it is not sufficient to evoke a realm of ecstasy that would balance the realm of despair that Miller created for the end of *Sexus.* The balancing ecstasy is in *Cancer* itself, and Miller's journey does not move toward a real culmination in *Nexus* that would compel a connection to its beginning in Miller's first book. The crucial linkage is established only by inference and extraliterary historical information. And Miller seems to have sensed this. He claimed, until sheer age made it impossible, that there would be a second volume of *Nexus.*

The books in the two groups I have been discussing constitute Miller's enduring achievement as a writer. The purpose of this chapter has been to argue that neither the books themselves, nor their relationship with one another, are entirely without shape or form. That they are bloated, excessive and repetitious at times is undeniable. No clever critical strategy will disguise this fact, nor make everything cohere. But beneath and within the sometimes amorphous mass, there is a lean and durable frame.

4 *Tropic of Cancer*

The Journal of a "Year" in the Surreal City

HENRY Miller's first book, *Tropic of Cancer*, remains startling and unique. The radiant spirit and exuberant anger which Miller projected from the opening sentences of *Cancer* are as alive now as the day when they were released. Twenty-five years after its first publication in the United States, and half a century after Miller began his final revisions on the manuscript, *Cancer* is one of the best exemplars of Pound's definition of literature: News that stays news. Many writers have taken advantage of Miller's victories in the war against censorship and suppression, but Miller does not look like a pioneer who is interesting only as a precursor.

In an age when nothing is "outrageous" any more, Miller still has the power to *out* rage almost anyone writing today. As Mailer notes, "a revolution in style and consciousness" was taking place in *Cancer*, and like any real revolution, it has not been entirely absorbed. *Tropic of Cancer* is still threatening and elusive, perhaps more so than works by Miller's famous contemporaries. Miller, in *Cancer*, is still at least a little dangerous, still strangely exciting, still curiously liberating.

The mock invocation with which Miller opens *Cancer* seems

dreadfully timely in the mid-1980s amidst economic uncertainty, international tension, political incompetence and social disintegration—is it the 1930s come back to haunt us in a terrible new form? Instead of cringing in fear, Miller, his own "rebellion" giving him the will to declare himself, snarls: "This then? This is not a book. This is libel, slander, defamation of character. This is not a book, in the ordinary sense of the world. No, this is a prolonged insult, a gob of spit in the face of Art, a kick in the pants to God, Man, Destiny, Time, Love, Beauty . . . what you will." (1)[1] This, indeed, is a declaration of human necessity, a prophetic demand that man must resist all the so-called "solutions"—the neat, packaged answers of the advertising world, the offers of all the salesmen and spokesmen who represent official versions of religion, politics, business and culture. It is an attack on what purports to be scientific rationality (educational *science*, managerial *science*, and so forth) and it leads to a countercommitment to mystery and ecstasy, anticipating and inspiring the social delirium of the 1960s. It is also, in somewhat less obvious terms, an exhortation to preserve the principle of free inquiry and to reject the security of any totalitarian system. Because Miller hardly provides a conventional argument in analytic steps, this is generally overlooked, but what Miller has done is less familiar and more effective. *Cancer* is not a tract but a demonstration, an exhibition of psychic survival.

When he crossed the Atlantic, Miller must have entertained some picture of Paris as an international refuge for the eager artist, but instead of finding a community of kindred spirits, Miller found a city crawling with the detritus of America's spiritual decay. The fabled City of Light was there too, but it took him quite a bit longer to find it. As the book opens, the artist/ hero who is Miller's narrator and protagonist has given up the idea of living in any sort of conventional manner and has become a kind of Dostoevskian underground man. We see him first in *Cancer* prowling through the bottom strata of a civilization in decomposition, recording disasters to which he remains immune. His rage cuts through the lachrymose posturing of his fellow expatriates like a sword, while his dream/vision is drawn around him like a shield. His isolation is his protection, but it has its costs. He has no real friends (how different from the corporeal Henry Miller!), just acquaintances he spends time with, gets drunk with, gets laid with and so on, and his relationship with women is ghastly. But *Tropic of Cancer* is not a cosmos—it is a picture of a time and a place from the perspective of a person who is so delighted to feel and show his strength that everything else is secondary. The book is a product of careful calculation, and some sacrifices have been made. Because Miller knew that *Cancer* was just the beginning, a part of a larger story, he made his artist/hero, as Nin pointed out, mostly sex and stomach, although there is plenty of heart too, if one looks closely. And of course, the book is relentless in its refusal to put a good face on anything.

It is this tone of absolute candor that originally upset so many people. To a world that had shut its ears to all accounts of sexual adventure in fear that it might be reminded of its own inclinations, Miller gleefully raised his voice to sing, just as Allen Ginsberg, to a world deteriorated somewhat further, felt compelled to *Howl*. "I am going to sing for you," Miller boasts, "a little off key perhaps, but I will sing. . . . To sing you must first open your mouth. You must have a pair of lungs, and a little knowledge of music. It is not necessary to have an accordion, or a guitar. The essential thing is to *want* to sing. This then is a song. I am singing" (2). But this is not a "Song of Himself," that will come later, in the *Rosy Crucifixion*. Here, Miller's most active and intense personal reactions are primarily contemplative or fantastic since he is basically an observer. His reverie about Tania, his muse of "chaos," is typical: "I will ream out every wrinkle in your cunt, Tania, big with seed. I will send you home to your Sylvester with an ache in your belly and your womb turned inside out. Your Sylvester! Yes, he knows how to build a fire, but I know how to inflame a cunt. . . . I will tear off a few hairs from your cunt and paste them on Boris' chin. I will bite into your clitoris and spit out two franc pieces" (5). Although there is a sense of the immediate about these promises (or threats), Miller's artist/hero is contemplating what he *will* do (or what he has done), not what he *is* doing. The "song" that runs through the book is a song of the world, and the most erotic verses involve the damaged men and women who live in that world, desperate and weakened creatures who resort to sexual frenzy to reclaim the life they are losing. Passages like the address to Tania are crude and vicious, but they are designed to establish Miller's fierce, defiant stance toward the culture that has been responsible for this human erosion. Unlike Tania, Boris, Sylvester and the others, Miller is not a citizen of this world, although he moves easily there and knows it well. He is more like an explorer, and the bitter humor with which he describes it is a reflection of his disengagement:

> Llona—a wild ass snuffing pleasure out of the wind. On every high hill she played the harlot—and sometimes in telephone booths and toilets. She bought a bed for King Carol and a shaving mug with his initials on it. She lay in Tottenham Court Road with her dress pulled up and fingered herself. She used candles, Roman candles, and door knobs. Not a prick in the land big enough for her . . . *not one.* Men went inside her and curled up. She wanted extension pricks, self-exploding rockets, hot boiling oil made of wax and creosote. She would cut off your prick and keep it inside her forever, if you gave her permission. One cunt out of a million, Llona! A laboratory cunt and no litmus paper that could take her color. She was a liar too, this Llona. She never bought a bed for King Carol. She crowned him with a whiskey bottle and her tongue was full of lice and tomorrows. Poor Carol, he could only curl up inside her and die. She drew a breath and he fell out—like a dead clam. (6)

This is a hard passage to read without experiencing a feeling of uncertainty. Is this the only way Miller's artist/hero sees women? Is it true, as Kate Millett claims, that Miller "is a compendium of sexual neuroses, and his value lies not in freeing us from such afflictions, but in having had the honesty to express and dramatize them."[2] I believe that Millett's comments might be most appropriately applied to a discussion of the books in the triad, "The Formation. . . ," because the distance between author and "character" is considerably narrowed there. In *Cancer*, as I hope will become more apparent, both the *men* and the *women* Miller spends time with are treated with similar harshness. The contempt, disgust and fear which Miller exhibits in the passage on Llona is matched by equally contemptuous descriptions of men throughout *Cancer*. The element of fear is another matter, and it lends credence to Millett's claims. I will refer to this aspect of Miller's attitude while examining the triad, but it should be mentioned here that because of Miller's determination to maintain the tone of great confidence in his "I" narrator, some very significant facets of his life are purposefully excluded.

The point of the passage about Llona and King Carol is that the social landscape is very bleak. The women seem to have magic powers locked in their bodies but the men lack the proper keys. The myth of the fertile, life-giving earth/mother female figure has been distorted so that woman is now an insatiable, self-absorbed, castrating whore. The myth of the male as a noble warrior and a pillar of dignity, integrity, justice and reasoned discourse has been distorted so that man is now a frightened, ego-inflated phallus without feeling or wisdom. The film of *Cancer* by Joseph Strick had Rip Torn play Miller's artist/hero as this kind of man—all cock and no heart. But Miller's "I" narrator is not like these men. He can step out of the cancerous domain at any time. Between the passages on Tania and Llona, the artist/hero, sounding like Joyce Cary's Gulley Jimson, sees another "world" altogether:

Indigo sky swept clear of fleecy clouds, gaunt trees infinitely extended, their black boughs gesticulating like a sleepwalker. Somber, spectral trees, their trunks pale as cigar ash. A silence supreme and altogether European. Shutters drawn, shops barred. A red glow here and there to mark a tryst. Brusque the façades, almost forbidding; immaculate except for the splotches of shadow cast by the trees. Passing the Orangerie I am reminded of another Paris, the Paris of Maugham, of Gauguin, Paris of George Moore. I think of that terrible Spaniard who was then startling the world with his acrobatic leaps from style to style. I think of Spengler and of his terrible pronunciamentos, and I wonder if style, style in the grand manner, is done for. I say that my mind is occupied with these thoughts, but it is not true; it is only later, after I have crossed the Seine, after I have put behind me the carnival of lights, that I allow my mind to play with these ideas. For the moment I can think of nothing—except that I am a sentient being stabbed by the miracle of these waters that reflect a forgotten world. All along the banks the trees lean heavily over the tarnished mirror; when the wind rises and fills them with a rustling murmur they will shed a few tears and shiver as the water swirls by. I am suffocated by it. No one to whom I can communicate even a fraction of my feelings. (5–6)

This is the *Paris* of Henry Miller—a timeless realm of wonder which the artist/hero can share with no one else, except perhaps the eternal company of artists with whom Miller wishes to establish kinship. This Paris is like the prelapsarian America of his imagination, but it is something more at the same time, a place which he can actually observe and enjoy. There is a certain sadness about this Paris too, because he cannot enjoy it with his "friends" ("No one to whom I can communicate. . . ."), but that makes it a kind of sanctuary for him, a refuge from the rot. He is sustained in his pleasure and wonder at this world by his confidence that one day he will be able to join the land of light to the rest of his existence, but in *Cancer*, the two worlds stand apart. And for the moment, that is sufficient, especially since he is comfortable in both of them. With his identity as the man with the most extreme passion staked out and secure, the artist/hero walks through both worlds, one dying and the other "busy being born" (in Bob Dylan's words), his outlook in very sharp contrast to all the inhabitants of the dying land:

> Walking along the Champs-Elysées, I keep thinking of my really superb health. When I say "health" I mean optimism, to be truthful. Incurably optimistic! Still have one foot in the nineteenth century. I'm a bit retarded, like most Americans. Carl finds it disgusting, this optimism. "I have only to talk of a meal," he says, "and you're radiant!" It's a fact. The mere thought of a meal—*another* meal—rejuvenates me. A meal! That means something to go on—a few solid hours of work, an erection possibly. I don't deny it. I have health, good solid, animal health. (45)

Although Miller means "meal" literally, since he often didn't know until it appeared where the next one was coming from, his appetite is clearly for experience itself, and his optimism is based on his belief that any experience will be nourishing for the artist/hero. While *Cancer* describes a world that is perishing, Miller sees beyond it to a time when art ("a few solid hours of work") will give man his soul, and love (unavailable here, only an "erection" is a possibility now) will give him his heart. In order to survive until that time comes, in fact to work to make it happen, the artist/hero needs the strength to live through the cancerous time of his life, and as Martin points out, "at the end of the book the man who can write the book is born."[3] In other words, *Cancer* is a record of Miller's resistance to the squalor which he could easily have slipped into. He is susceptible to the various disorders that have infected the people of *Cancer*—has, as a matter of fact, been infected himself throughout most of the previous decade—and he needs all of his devices (scorn, casual cruelty, the withdrawal of sympathy) to remain relatively healthy ("good solid, animal health"). His relationships with both men and women should be seen in this light. Without this "health" as a base, Miller could never get out of the Villa Borghese, where, as he says on the first page, "We are all alone here and we are dead."

Cancer is divided into fifteen "sections" but they are not *chapters*, just as *Cancer* is definitely not a *novel*. Rahv speaks of the "dissolution of genre" in Miller, but he is not particularly specific about what this amounts to. *Cancer* is really a mutant of sorts, a journal that resembles a diary, a packet of sketches, a rough collection of essays, an assemblage of anecdotes—"what you will," as Miller says. The narrative consciousness of the artist/hero gives it some continuity, but it does not have any real character development, a chronological linear progression, a plot one could outline, or any dramatic denouements or even a "conclusion" that ties things up. The word *novel* confuses the issue and tends to induce expectations that are not satisfied, as Miller may have sensed when he disagreed strongly with Edmund Wilson's review of *Cancer*.[4] I think the word *journal* is most useful, and it might be helpful to call *Cancer* a journal of the surreal city, with its implications of a kind of newspaper that has many departments or features reflecting different concerns and modes of activity, especially if one also recognizes a parallel with the so-called "new journalism" of the 1970s. This journal, however, is not a "daily" in any sense, or regular in its record. The span of time which is covered is very elastic, and the edges are purposely hazy, as are the various divisions. It opens during the "fall of my second year in Paris," which we discover is 1929, and seems to end in the spring of 1931, but those "years" might be months, or decades. The entire concept of a calendar is burlesqued as Miller starts sections by saying, out of nowhere and with no further point, "Easter came in like a frozen hare" (44); or "I think it was the Fourth of July" (168); or "It was close to dawn on Christmas Day" (232). One of the points behind this technique is that the artist/hero has very little to do with the demarcations of a conventional society. There are other rhythms in his life, and they gradually become apparent.

Within each of the fifteen sections, four motifs are repeated with varying emphasis. They are:

1. Rage at "a world crumbling and polished like a leper's skull," expressed sometimes as loathing, sometimes as hilarity.
2. Male bonding, including passages of men together eating, drinking, debating, scheming, fighting and fornicating.
3. Lust, primarily from the point of view of the conventional male narrative consciousness, with women as its object, but also as its inspiration.
4. Quasi-philosophical excursions about art, nature, religion and cosmology, including some fairly powerful lyric "poetry."

These four motifs occur to some extent in each section, and are like four threads interwoven in complementary fashion throughout the book. Whichever one is used to begin the section, the fourth motif is employed in its conclusion in nine of the last ten sections. A systematic analysis of the entire book following this pattern would be possible, but it would become dreary after awhile, just a recitation of the already understood. A brief outline of the fifteen sections, followed by a closer examination of four representative ones, will suffice. The separate sections of *Cancer* are organized in the following manner:

I (1–19):The scene, mood and style of the book are set. Tania, Llona ("a wild ass snuffing pleasure out of the wind"), Carl and Boris, writers like Miller ("They are possessed. They glow inwardly with a white flame. They are mad and tone deaf. They are sufferers"), and Moldorf ("Thyroid eyes. Michelin lips. Voice like pea soup") are introduced. Mona's departure for America is recalled as a cutting of ties, the removal of connections to previous concerns.

II (20–33): Domestic chat; cultural baggage recorded in homes of people where artist/hero cadges meals, a bed, social contact. Attack on America as cause of rot everywhere.

III (34–43): Germaine, the whore the artist/hero finds most compatible.

IV (44–48): Carl and Marlowe, neurasthenic expatriate Americans defeated by life in Paris; Marlowe returning to America directly, Carl looking for a pension or similar sinecure ("I hate Paris! . . . All these stupid people playing cards all day . . . look at them!").

V (49–62): More domestic conversation; the artist/hero finds various households stifling, his distaste for acquaintances is growing, his sense of himself as an artist is clarified ("The artist, I call myself. So be it.").

VI (63–71): He is grateful for help offered by a fellow he meets, but is obliged to reject the companionship of this boring if well-meaning person whose mattress for the artist/hero is "a morgue for lice." Attends a concert, reflects on aesthetic experience of music, its hold on the audience, and what the audience might do if the artist (Ravel) did not hold back at some point.

VII (72–90): A somewhat sympathetic but also destructively comic account of young Hindu man visiting brothel with Miller as guide; parody of Dante, parody of any religious commitment, debunking of blind faith, spiritualism as a solution to the mess and filth of world.

VIII (91–150): Fabulous description of Van Norden, the anti-Colossus of Cancer, a polar-opposite of the Hindu of the previous chapter; the nonspiritual man as mechanical monster and something of a psychic double for Miller's worst impulses.

IX   (151–167): Tentative effort at liaison with Tania—no real relationship develops; he recalls life with Mona through prism of selective nostalgia, and recognizes an irrevocable commitment to the present in Paris and suffers momentary depression.

X   (168–188): He attempts to overcome depression with booze, brawls, broads in company of men—much brutality.

XI   (188–197): No satisfaction with whore who offers interesting persona when dullness beneath mask becomes apparent. Tends to equate unsatisfactory woman with city of Paris, dwelling on disappointment. Fails, momentarily, to see how one's outlook colors incidents and locations.

XII   (199–215): The artist/hero is living with Fillmore, another desperate expatriate. Fillmore's crudity and ugliness point toward dead end inherent in the artist/hero's worst behavior with women.

XIII   (216–233): Grand apostrophe to art and life: A reemergence from chaos, 'the lowest point of *Cancer* now firmly in permanent past.

XIV   (234–259): Visit to Dijon as commitment to art, work, the possibility of viable community. Dijon episode mostly unsuccessful, but effort is worthwhile in itself.

XV   (260–287): Fillmore's pathetic return to America. A man who has been crushed, returning in ruin. Artist/hero helps him on his way, recognizes his own survival, emerges from "year" in world of cancer stronger and fitter.

The four sections I will examine more carefully each concentrate on one of the four motifs I have described, although the others are still present as a kind of muted background. Section III deals primarily with lust, VIII with the male impulse at its worse, XIII is Miller's most serious attempt at a prolonged metaphysical discourse and XIV is concerned with the social order Miller despises.

Kate Millett calls Germaine "the archetypal French prostitute of American tourism," and quotes eight passages out of context in which woman is assigned to a "mindless material capacity."[5] Although I would suggest that the artist/hero and the corporeal Henry Miller are not quite equal entities here, and that all of *Cancer* presents people living under circumstances of considerable nastiness which Miller describes to illustrate things as they ought *not* to be, Millett makes a pretty convincing case that Germaine is treated, like so many other women in Miller's work, with "anxiety and contempt."[6] And yet, there is Norman Mailer arguing that *lust* "takes over the instinct to create life and converts it to a force," and that Miller "captured something in the sexuality of men as it had never been seen before, precisely that it was man's sense of awe before woman, his dread of her position one step closer to eternity (for in that step were her powers) which made men detest women, revile them, humiliate them, defecate symbolically upon them, do everything to reduce them so that one might dare to enter them and take pleasure of them."[7] Although Mailer wrote his essay on lust almost as a direct response to Millett's attack on his thinking in *Sexual Politics*, the two are not listening to or talking to each other at all. Mailer's conclusion is that passages like those that Millett condemns are "screams [of] his barbaric yawp of utter adoration for the power and the glory and the grandeur of the female in the universe."[8] When they are read separately, *both* arguments seem convincing. But "utter adoration" is surely nothing like "anxiety and contempt." A close look at the section in *Cancer* where Germaine appears is in order.

The section begins with the artist/hero pretending not to be hungry so as to avoid disturbing the Cronstadts (actually the family of Walter Lowenfels) who are sitting down at a special meal just as he arrives. He mockingly calls himself *"delicat"* in his pretense, but adds poignantly, "On the way out I cast a lingering glance at the bones lying on the baby's plate—there was still meat on them" (34). As he walks down the Rue de Buci, he notices "The bars wide open and the curbs lined with bicycles. All the meat and vegetable markets are in full swing" (34). The streets are seething with life, "a fresh hive of activity. Long queues of people with vegetables under their arms, turn-

ing in here and there with crisp, sparkling appetites" (35).
Amidst the people rushing to satisfy their appetites, the artist/
hero is both delighted by the motion and color and troubled by
his own persistent hunger. The dual nature of his reaction is
caught by his comparison of the Square de Furstenberg as he
sees it now "at high noon" and as he saw it, "the other night
when I passed by . . . deserted, bleak, spectral" (35). He compares the trees at night to T. S. Eliot's poetry, calling them
"intellectual," trees with their roots in stone, bare branches not
yet in bloom. Images of aridity are overcoming the artist/hero's
delight in the sensuality of the world.

As the day continues and the artist/hero wanders on through
the streets, "guts rattling," it begins to rain and the light and
joy of the city are replaced by images of confusion and disease.
In a bookstore window, he sees the title, *A Man Cut in Slices*
and recognizes its applicability to his life since he is often so
completely occupied with the tasks of finding food, lodging,
good company that he cannot see any larger picture of things.
The title suggests food again, but the food seems to be spoiling
now, less enticing since he can't get it anyhow. The street begins to look like a wax reproduction of organs "eaten away by
syphilis," suggesting the reversal in *Hamlet* where the prince
describes Polonius at supper, but where he is "food" for mag-
gots.

The "beautiful day" has turned 180 degrees, and the artist/
hero pauses "a few minutes to drink in the full squalor of the
scene" (37). Food has become repulsive as he describes "a
clump of decrepit buildings which have so rotted away that
they have collapsed on one another and formed a sort of
intestinal embrace. The ground is uneven, the flagging slip-
pery with slime. A sort of human dump heap which has been
filled with cinders and dry garbage. . . . There is the shrill
squawk of children with pale faces and bony limbs, rickety little
urchins marked with the forceps. A fetid odor seeps from the
walls, . . ." (37). The images here are of rot, starvation, indiges-
tion and waste. But it is not just the visible world that has been
spoiled. The artist/hero turns away from the Place du Combat,
and his mind "reverts to a book I was reading the other day."

The book describes a town in a shambles, "corpses, mangled by butchers and stripped by plunderers, lay thick in the streets; wolves sneaked from the suburbs to eat them" (37). The town is Paris during the days of "Charles the Silly," and the artist/ hero mentions that he has "thought long and ruefully over the sad fate of Charles the Silly. A half-wit, who prowled about the halls of his Hôtel St. Paul, garbed in the filthiest rags, eaten away by ulcers and vermin, gnawing a bone, when they flung him one" (38). A debased monarch, without proper food, eaten away by his own hunger, reminding the artist/hero of *his* need for nourishment. And then, in a typical application of associa- tive logic, the artist/hero mentions the main "diversion" of Charles the Silly, "card games with his 'low-born companion' Odette de Champdivers."

Here, then, is a picture of a man in an ugly world who is a little desperate and very hungry. "It was a Sunday afternoon, much like this, when I first met Germaine," he recalls. Miller has spent several pages showing how one of the most basic of the natural appetites has been perverted. It would be nice to be able to choose one's food, not to have to scramble for it and accept what you can get. It would also be nice to be able to develop a relationship with a woman under ideal conditions, but in the world of *Cancer*, both the men and women Miller knows are operating under less than ideal conditions. Maybe it is arrogant to condemn the behavior of these people from the comfort of an academic cloister. In a landscape where one is either starving or being "eaten," there are different orders of primacy. And even in this setting, Germaine stands out among her "colleagues."

The artist/hero remembers that he was walking on the Rue du Pasteur-Wagner, on the corner "of the Rue Amelot which hides behind the boulevard like a slumbering lizard," when he sees, continuing the image of eating; "a cluster of vultures who croaked and flapped their dirty wings, who reached out with sharp talons and plucked you into a doorway. Jolly, rapacious devils who didn't even give you time to button your pants when it was over" (38). "Germaine was different," he says, although, "There was nothing to tell me so from her appearance" (39). What distinguishes her is the fact that amidst a clearly commercial transaction ("It was not difficult to come to terms"), she notices and responds to those things which make a person distinct as an individual, "she liked the knickerbockers I was wearing. *Très chic!* she thought." Just the sort of statement to make a person feel a bit special, although that could be construed as part of her "job." However, when Germaine presents herself to the artist/hero, he describes her pride in herself as an aspect of a kind of dignity that cannot be demolished by the rude manners of others. "There was something about her eloquence at that moment and the way she thrust that rosebush under my nose which remains unforgettable" (39). Germaine's pride in her sexuality is very sad in that she has nothing else that the world values, but her courage is impressive. And whether it is lust alone, or something more, the artist/hero says, "That Sunday afternoon, with its poisonous breath of spring in the air, everything clicked again" (40). The starving man has found food. After their assignation, the artist/hero is ready to look on her with his cold, discerning eye again, but in spite of his defensive stance, some humane instinct has been ignited in both of them:

> As we stepped out of the hotel I looked her over again in the harsh light of day and I saw clearly what a whore she was—the gold teeth, the geranium in her hat, the run-down heels, etc., etc. Even the fact that she wormed a dinner out of me and cigarettes and taxi hadn't the least disturbing effect upon me. I encouraged it, in fact. I liked her so well that after dinner we went back to the hotel and took another shot at it. "For love," this time. (40)

The artist/hero is not prepared for much more than a satisfying of appetites, but he is forced to admit that he liked Germaine's sexuality and that he liked *her* too. "I liked them separately and I liked them together," he says. When she discovers the artist/hero's "true circumstances," she offers him food and a kind of friendship, and it is at this stage of the narrative that Kate Millett begins to quote Miller's final estimation of Germaine. I would suggest an alternative interpretation. The words which describe Germaine as "a whore from the cradle,"

and refer to "her whore's heart which is not really a good heart
but a lazy one" (41), are an indictment of the artist/hero at this
point in the narrative. He has been rendered unfit to judge the
nuances of a person's motivation because of his own reduced
vision. All he can admire in Germaine are those things which
he values in himself—guts, fire, stamina, courage and cunning.
That she may have more to offer, a complex, caring, sharing
side; possibly a reflective, even philosophic inclination, dis-
tresses the artist/hero because he has become accustomed to
regarding sex as he regards food—the answer to a physical
urge to be satiated however possible. In comparing Germaine
to Claude, another prostitute, the artist/hero mentions to Germaine's "credit" that "she was ignorant and lusty, she put her
heart and soul into her work. She was a whore all the way
through—and that was her virture" (43). Claude troubles the
artist/hero because she "had a soul and a conscience; she had
refinement, too, which is bad—in a whore. Claude always im-
parted a feeling of sadness; she left the impression, unwitting-
ly, of course, that you were just one more added to the stream
which fate had ordained to destroy her" (41). Without any ex-
planatory message, Miller has made it pretty clear that the art-
ist/hero, at this early point in the narrative, has shut down a
vital part of his sensory apparatus because he is not capable of
dealing with a woman beyond certain prescribed, formulaic
rituals of passion-plus-commerce. Millett claims that this is Miller "giving voice to certain sentiments which masculine culture
had long experienced but always rather carefully suppressed."[9]
I would disagree to some extent, and suggest that within the
context of the entire section, Miller is not just "giving voice" to
these sentiments, but criticizing them by showing the narrowness and fear of the person who is delivering them. The dis-
missal of Germaine's qualities as a person at the end of the
section are not the words of a person we can trust on this subject, but of someone who has been temporarily warped by the
accumulated pressures of living "down and out" in an urban
wasteland.

Miller's attitude toward this kind of man becomes more clear
in the section (VIII) that presents the bizarre Van Norden, a

character with many discomforting similarities to the artist/hero at his worst. The long section is one of the most vivid in *Cancer*. What kind of a country, what kind of a civilization could produce such a monster, it almost demands to know? Van Norden is not a murderer in the conventional sense, but he is a killer of the soul, and his homicidal tendencies extend to everyone he meets, including himself. The fact that he goes unpunished, that he is not even discouraged in any way, is a clear indication that something is drastically wrong. This man is, in Millett's words, the one who "yearns to effect a complete depersonalization of woman into cunt," and the one who turns sex into "a game-fantasy of power untroubled by the reality of persons or the complexity of dealing with fellow human beings."[10] The opening paragraphs of the section introduce him and also establish at the outset a separation between him and the narrator:

> At one-thirty I called on Van Norden, as per agreement. He had warned me that if he didn't answer it would mean that he was sleeping with someone, probably his Georgia cunt.
>
> Anyway, there he was, tucked away comfortably, but with an air of weariness as usual. He wakes up cursing himself, or cursing his job, or cursing life. He wakes up utterly bored and discomfited, chagrined to think that he did not die overnight. (91)

The artist/hero often gets angry or discouraged, but he invariably wakes up in high spirits and stays that way until worn down by some problem. He never curses "life."

The first few pages of the section are taken up entirely by a rambling monologue in which Van Norden makes his attitude toward women all too clear. These pages are a masterful example of gruesome comedy, and the comedy is at Van Norden's expense. His pathetic self-centeredness and his simplistic reduction of everything make him a parody of a man. Miller does not have to comment at all as Van Norden is condemned in his own words:

> "My teeth are all rotten," he says, gargling his throat. "It's the fucking bread they give you to eat here." He opens his mouth

wide and pulls his lower lip down. "See that? Pulled out six teeth yesterday. Soon I'll have to get another plate. That's what you get working for a living. When I was on the bum I had all my teeth, my eyes were bright and clear. Look at me now! It's a wonder I can make a cunt any more. Jesus, what I'd like is to find some rich cunt. . . ." (92)

Vain, stupid, consumed by self-pity—and in Paris, he doesn't like the bread! And lacking in both ideals and faith: " 'The married ones! Christ, if you saw all the married cunts I bring up here you'd never have any more illusions. They're worse than the virgins, the married ones. They don't wait for you to start things—they fish it out for you themselves. And then they talk about love afterwards. It's disgusting. I tell you, I'm actually beginning to hate cunt!' " (93). In their basic outlook, Van Norden and the artist/hero are at polar opposites, and even though they share each other's company and go whoring together, this should be apparent immediately. If the tone of Van Norden's whining doesn't get the point across, then his incredible statement, "Would you believe it, I've never been to the Louvre— nor the Comédie-Française. Is it worth going to those joints?" (96), must separate him from Miller whose reactions to the work of painters approaches reverence.

Miller listens to Van Norden rather noncommittally, but when Van Norden starts to invite him to various social engagements, the artist/hero begins to demur ("I can't tomorrow, Joe. I promised to help Carl out . . . "), and when Van Norden proposes they "share" a mother and daughter, his reluctance is apparent ("Listen, Joe, you'd better find somebody else . . . "). At this point, Van Norden becomes almost desperate, practically pleading with the artist/hero for companionship: " 'What do you do with yourself all day? Don't you get bored? What do you do for a lay? Listen . . . come here! Don't run away yet . . . I'm lonely. Do you know something—if this keeps up another year I'll go nuts. I've got to get out of this fucking country. There's nothing for me here. I know it's lousy now, in America, but just the same . . .' " (97). Van Norden's monologue concludes, and during the next few pages, the same theme is played again with minor variations as Carl tells the artist/hero

about his visit to a woman named Irene whom he has been
courting by letter for months. Miller mentions at one point that
as Carl headed for Irene's apartment, "he threw me a last
despairing glance, one of those mute appeals which a dog
makes when you put a noose around its neck. Going through
the revolving door I thought of Van Norden. . . ." (98) Carl's
hesitancy and confusion as he relates the details of their
meeting become steadily more preposterous and then gradually
pitiful:

> "And that's not all. I promised her a letter in the meantime. How
> am I going to write her a letter now? I haven't anything to say. . . .
> Shit! If only she were ten years younger. Do you think I should go
> with her . . . to Borneo or wherever it is she wants to take me?
> What would I do with a rich cunt like that on my hands? I don't
> know how to shoot. I am afraid of guns and all that sort of thing.
> Besides, she'll be wanting me to fuck her night and day . . . noth-
> ing but hunting and fucking all the time . . . I can't do it!" (103)

Both Carl and Van Norden are cases of arrested development,
adolescents who need constant reassurance because they have
so little sense of who they are. Miller is wryly sympathetic,
almost like an older brother ("Maybe it won't be so bad as
you think. She'll buy you ties and all sorts of things. . . ."), but
Carl is a defeated man, and his last words have the stuff of
horror about them: " 'That's it—that's the best solution for a
writer. What does a guy want with his arms and legs? He doesn't need arms and legs to write with. He needs security . . .
peace . . . protection. . . . All I'd want is a good wheelchair and
three meals a day. Then I'd give them something to read, those
pricks' " (106). Obviously, Miller himself does not believe
"that's the best solution for a writer." And similarly, he does
not share Van Norden's view of women, even if there is some
overlapping. The first fifteen pages of this section show plainly
that Miller does not endorse Van Norden's rampant sexism
or Carl's pitiable retreat from life. On the other hand, he does
not quite condemn them either. His attitude is somewhat ambiguous because he has experienced several crises himself that
have brought him, momentarily, rather close to their psychic

states. What interests Miller is the way they behave, and the world which must be partially to blame for this kind of behavior.

As I have noted previously, Miller is an observer in this book. Following Carl's account of his night with Irene, Van Norden tells Miller the whole story again, repeating the details that Carl told him. The next few pages are as imaginatively pornographic as anything Miller has written, and they present an interesting double perspective because Carl is inclined to put a romantic gloss on things while Van Norden has a fixation for specific anatomic detail. Neither man can see the woman herself: In Carl's case she is lost in fantasy, while in Van Norden's she is never more than a collection of erotic accessories. Although Miller does not attempt to psychoanalyze Van Norden, there is one very revealing moment when Van Norden, in a moment of "overwhelming futility," confesses, "I want to be able to surrender myself to a woman. . . . I want her to take me out of myself. But to do that, she's got to be better than I am; she's got to have a mind, not just a cunt. She's got to make me believe that I need her, that I can't live without her" (118). Of course, such a woman will never exist for Van Norden. He does not know how to share any part of himself with anybody, much less "surrender," and he has such an inflated sense of his own "qualities" and such a superficially critical view of all women that he would never admit one is "better" than he is. Miller does not tell us any of these things, but Van Norden's words make it all apparent. (In this section, the artist/hero hardly ever ventures an opinion on anything and rarely explains character except to say why Van Norden cannot write at all.[11]) By the time Van Norden expounds upon the limitations of all women, it is obvious he is not speaking either for the narrator of *Cancer* or for its author, as Millett claims.[12] His "philosophy" is presented as the false gospel of a failure:

> The thing is this—they all look alike. When you look at them with their clothes on you imagine all sorts of things; you give them an individuality like, which they haven't got, of course. . . . Listen, do you know what I did afterwards? I gave her a quick lay and then I turned my back on her. Yeah, I picked up a book and I

read. You can get something out of a book, even a bad book . . .
but a cunt, it's just sheer loss of time. . . . (126–127)

What follows this bit of wisdom is one of the most harrowing
scenes in modern literature, an emblem of an age much like
Chaplin's berserk assembly line in *Modern Times*. Van Norden
has persuaded Miller that they should pick up a whore, and the
artist/hero, once again the observer, watches "with a cool, scientific detachment":

> As I watch Van Norden tackle her, it seems to me that I'm
> looking at a machine whose cogs have slipped. Left to themselves,
> they could go on this way forever, grinding and slipping, without
> ever anything happening. Until a hand shuts the motor off. The
> sight of them coupled like a pair of goats without the least spark
> of passion, grinding and grinding away for no reason except the
> fifteen francs, washes away every bit of feeling I have except the
> inhuman one of satisfying my curiousity. The girl is lying on the
> edge of the bed and Van Norden is bent over her like a satyr with
> his two feet solidly planted on the floor. I am sitting on a chair
> behind him, watching their movements with a cool, scientific de-
> tachment; it doesn't matter to me if it should last forever. It's like
> watching one of those crazy machines which throw newspaper
> out, millions and billions and trillions of them with their meaning-
> less headlines. . . . As long as that spark of passion is missing
> there is no human significance in the performance. The machine is
> better to watch. And these two are like a machine which has
> slipped its cogs. It needs the touch of a human hand to set it right.
> It needs a mechanic. (129–130)

For Miller, the "mechanic" is the artist, the person who can see
the infinite variety of the cosmos, the endless intricacy of the
human heart and mind—what a piece of work is man. After
several more pages commenting on the great richness of Paris
and his almost relentless desire to see, to know, to contemplate
(à la Whitman), Miller concludes the section by showing just how
far from Van Norden he is. If the world of *Cancer* is to be
"drawn back again to the proper precincts of the human
world" (146), then it is artists like Matisse (and Miller himself)
who will be instrumental in the process. Miller describes the
effect of Matisse's work on his own sensibility (an effect that

Van Norden and the other damaged figures in *Cancer* could not feel) in terms of light versus darkness, one of the most prevalent patterns of his writing. The light is a symbol of creative energy, and when it is present, the full range of imaginative possibility of the human mind is brought into play so that everything is seen as marvelous and fascinating. For Matisse, the world could never be boring.

The artist/hero enters the art gallery on the Rue de Sèze as if he were entering a genuinely new world. He has come from what he calls "the world of men and women whose last drop of juice has been squeezed out by the machine—the martyrs of modern progress" (146). The transition from the cancerous world of Van Norden, Carl and the others to "a world so natural, so complete, that I am lost"—the world of Matisse's paintings—is literally staggering: "On the threshold of that big hall whose walls are now ablaze, I pause a moment to recover from the shock which one experiences when the habitual gray of the world is rent asunder and the color of life splashes forth in song and poem" (146). Miller attempts to find verbal equivalents for Matisse's images, knowing that there is no real substitute for seeing the paintings, but trying to capture the spirit behind their creation in his writing. It is the attempt that is most significant, because by his own efforts here he is displaying the active response and total involvement that an artist hopes for but rarely receives from his "public." In doing this, Miller is trying to show that, like Matisse, he can also see a world alive with color and light; and he is also trying to indicate that his own real audience is composed of people who share his knowledge of and appreciation for what Matisse has accomplished. All of these ideas are a part of his strategy to separate himself momentarily from his existence amongst the damaged people he lives with in *Cancer*, the people to whom he can't "communicate even a fraction of" his feeling.

For several paragraphs, Miller engages in what might be called an appreciative participation in Matisse's art: "Vividly now I recall how the glint and sparkle of light caroming from the massive chandeliers splintered and ran blood, flecking the tips of the waves that beat monotonously on the dull gold out-

side the windows. On the beach, masts and chimneys inter-
laced, and like a fuliginous shadow the figure of Albertine gliding through the surf, fusing into the mysterious quick and
prism of a protoplasmic realm, uniting her shadow to the
dream and harbinger of death" (146). Beneath or beyond the
paintings themselves, Miller sees the figure of Matisse, an emblem for the artist as one who is "capable of transforming the
negative reality of life into the substantial and significant outlines of art." "He stands at the helm peering with steady blue
eyes into the portfolio of time. Into what distant corners has he
not thrown his long, slanting gaze? . . . He is a bright sage, a
dancing seer who, with a sweep of the brush, removes the ugly
scaffold to which the body of man is chained by the incontrovertible facts of life" (147). The section concludes with several
images of women in Matisse's work, women who are seen with
an awe and wonder diametrically opposite from Van Norden's
view. It is true that Miller is not writing with sympathy and
understanding of one particular woman, but his evocation of
Matisse is a part of a vision that is as exalting as Van Norden's
is degrading. For the artist/hero, women are never interchangeable, they do not "all look alike":

> But in Matisse, in the exploration of his brush, there is the trem-
> bling glitter of a world which demands only the presence of the
> female to crystallize the most fugitive aspirations. . . . I stumble
> upon the phantom odalisques of Matisse fastened to the trees,
> their tangled manes drenched with sap. . . . Even as the world
> falls apart the Paris that belongs to Matisse shudders with bright,
> gasping orgasms, the air itself is steady with a stagnant sperm,
> the trees tangled like hair. . . . (149)

What is missing from *Cancer* until the Dijon section, the next
to last one, is even the most tentative suggestion that the artist/
hero can operate anywhere between the tremendous extremes
of the hell of "the incontrovertible facts of life" and the heaven
of "the significant outlines of art." This may be seen as a weakness, but *Cancer* has been conceived of as a book of absolutes,
and its lack of a subtle investigation of human relationships in
the middle ground is a part of its character and design. I will

reserve comment on Miller's failure to deal with these matters effectively until I examine those books of the triad, "The Formation . . ." in which they become the central subject. What is important here is to continue to investigate Miller's vision of the world of art as an antidote, or a redemptive force, to be employed against the nightmare of a machinelike people locked into a sterile land. The paean to Matisse is like many of the concluding passages to the separate sections of *Cancer*, a rhapsodic celebration of not only the life-giving powers of art, but also of what Charles Feidelson has called the "symbol-making intelligence" of the human consciousness. It is the ability to see with wonder the endless phenomena of the universe and the desire to try to find language to convey this feeling of "wonder" that marks Miller's sensibility here. It is his relish for naming things and for placing them in bizarre juxtapositions which create new and unusual harmonies that keeps Miller's artist/ hero inviolate in the worst sectors of *Cancer*'s awful blight.

It is in his passages of "impure poetry" that Miller comes closest to actually offering a "philosophy" of existence, and because his writing is much closer to the form of poetry than traditional philosophic discourse, to consider it in terms of philosophic strictures can only lead to misunderstanding and even condemnation. These passages are not logical arguments but attempts to create a mood in which some idea might be seen, or felt or understood. They work, if at all, by the strength and originality of their imagery, by the establishment of a certain ethos through the use of rhythm and structure and by their ability to generate a kindred emotion in the reader. They are, obviously, dependent on the willing participation of a reader with similar sympathies, and as such, their appeal is much more to the mystical than the rational. In other words, they have the very personal, singular and difficult to defend attributes of much contemporary poetry. The section (XIII) which precedes the Dijon trip offers some of this "poetry" at its best and worst.

Miller opens the "poem" with a statement of the conditions that led to its genesis:

And now it is three o'clock in the morning and we have a couple of trollops here who are doing somersaults on the bare floor.
Fillmore is walking around naked with a goblet in his hand, and
that paunch of his is drumtight, hard as a fistula. All the Pernod
and champagne and cognac and Anjou which he guzzled from
three in the afternoon on, is gurgling in his trap like a sewer. The
girls are putting their ears to his belly as if it were a music box.
Open his mouth with a buttonhook and drop a slug in the slot.
When the sewer gurgles I hear the bats flying out of the belfry and
the dream slides into artifice. (222)

The time, the place, the company, the activity, all these are
inducements to shut down the mind and turn up the skin/
senses; but not for Miller. The artist/hero is seemingly inspired
to mental intensity by just those things which encourage sensual abandon for most people, which is a partial explanation of
his "philosophy"—a kind of emotional *reasoning* that parallels a
heightened sensory indulgence; a progression by instinct and a
building of the argument by repetition of related images in increasing intensity.

The subject of this "poem" is woman, and how she contains
the mystery of life. Millett uses it to suggest that Miller is reducing women to sexual apparatus, Mailer to prove that Miller is a
genius.[13] I would suggest that it is an extraordinary series of
images, a catalog of passionate responses like the lists of Rabelais, and in terms of "meaning," a tribute to a sort of Lawrentian life force and a prayer of appreciation for Blake's God of
Energy as Eternal Delight. My temptation is to quote ten full
pages of it, but instead, here are some selections of what I feel
are the most effective "stanzas" with a few comments.

First, blending art, literature, archetype and inspired nonsense, Miller indicates his awe at woman as the living incarnation of some universal power:

I see again the great sprawling mothers of Picasso, their breasts
covered with spiders, their legend hidden deep in the labyrinth.
And Molly Bloom lying on a dirty mattress for eternity. On the
toilet door red chalk cocks and the madonna uttering the diapason
of woe. I hear a wild, hysterical laugh, a room full of lockjaw, and
the body that was black glows like phosphorus. Wild, wild, utter-

ly uncontrollable laughter, and that crack laughing at me too, laughing through the mossy whiskers, a laugh that creases the bright, polished surface of the billiard ball. Great whore and mother of man with gin in her veins. Mother of all harlots, spider rolling us in your logarithmic grave, insatiable one, fiend whose laughter rives me! (223)

Then, like chaos swirling into shape, Miller narrows the focus and makes one mode, the mathematical, the controlling vessel in which to concentrate the rampage:

When I look down into that crack I see an equation sign, the world at balance, a world reduced to zero and no trace of remainder. Not the zero on which Van Norden turned his flashlight, not the empty crack of the prematurely disillusioned man, but an Arabian zero rather, the sign from which spring endless mathematical worlds, the fulcrum which balances the stars and the light dreams and the machines lighter than air and the lightweight limbs and the explosives that produced them. (223)

One wishes that Miller had followed Pound on the principle of *condensare*, because the "poem" is surrounded by sentences of murky theorizing and awkward expostulation. At times, it lapses back into mere argument, and these tend to destroy the mood because, as Mailer pointed out, "his polemical essays read like sludge." But then the poem picks up again, extravagantly extending the image of woman still further:

The earth is not an arid plateau of health and comfort, but a great sprawling female with velvet torso that swells and heaves with ocean billows; she squirms beneath the diadem of sweat and anguish. Naked and sexed she rolls among the clouds in the violet light of the stars. All of her, from her generous breasts to her gleaming thighs, blazes with furious ardor. She moves amongst the seasons and the years with a grand whoopla that seizes the torso with paroxysmal fury, that shakes the cobwebs out of the sky; she subsides on her pivotal orbits with volcanic tremors. (225)

This is a classic apostrophe to great Venus, the goddess of love, and it is very specifically from a male point of view. Perhaps Miller realized that it was a bit superficial, because the next "stanza" describes woman in her sorrow:

And then her sorrow widened, like the bow of a dreadnought and the weight of her sinking flooded my ears. Slime wash and sapphires slipping, sluicing through the gay neurons, and the spectrum spliced and the gunwales dipping. Soft as lion-pad I heard the gun carriages turn, saw them vomit and drool: the firmament sagged and all the stars turned black. Black ocean bleeding and the brooding stars breeding chunks of fresh-swollen flesh while overhead the birds wheeled and out of the hallucinated sky fell the balance with mortar and pestle and the bandaged eyes of justice. (227)

Miller might have actually set this as a poem if he hadn't been bound by the typological barriers of typeset prose. Consider this arrangement:

> And then her sorrow widened
> like the bow of a dreadnought
> and the weight of her sinking
> flooded my ears
>
> Slime wash and sapphires slipping
> sluicing through the gay neurons
> the spectrum spliced and the gunwales dipping
>
> Soft as lion-pad
> I heard the gun carriages turn
> saw them vomit and drool:
>
>> the firmament sagged [and]
>> all the stars turned black
>> black ocean bleeding
>> and the brooding stars breeding
>> chunks of fresh-swollen flesh
>
> Overhead the birds wheeled [and]
> out of the hallucinated sky fell the
> balance with mortar and pestle [and] the
> bandaged eyes of justice

A few "ands" have been removed, but essentially, this is the "stanza" that Miller wrote. It reminds me of Hart Crane, particularly *The Bridge*, which was composed about the same time as *Tropic of Cancer*.

From page 228 through the middle of page 231, the "poem" hovers on a back burner while Miller delivers some more "argument," but then it concludes with some of his best and most powerful writing. Here, he is no longer talking about woman, but about an aspect of women's nature, and about its significance in the world for both men and women. The mood is regenerated by a rhapsody on rivers as the symbolic carriers of life—indeed, the water of life:

> I want a world of men and women, of trees that do not talk (because there is too much talk in the world as it is!) of rivers that carry you to places, not rivers that are legends, but rivers that put you in touch with men and women, with architecture, religion, plants, animals—rivers that have boats on them and in which men drown, drown not in myth and legend and books and dust of the past, but in time and space and history. I want rivers that make oceans such as Shakespeare and Dante, rivers which do not dry up in the void of the past. (231)

Then, Miller shifts from the specific, *water*, to one of its basic properties. Beginning with a generous nod to Joyce (an invocation to the muse?), Miller sings in his most powerful voice of a world at once awful and wondrous; a world in which the artist/ hero can thrive and his art can prosper:

> "I love everything that flows," said the great blind Milton of our times. I was thinking of him this morning when I awoke with a great bloody shout of joy: I was thinking of his rivers and trees and all that world of night which he is exploring. Yes, I said to myself, I too love everything that flows: rivers, sewers, lava, semen, blood, bile, words, sentences. I love the amniotic fluid when it spills out of the bag. I love the kidney with its painful gallstones, its gravel and what-not; I love the urine that pours out scalding and the clap that runs endlessly; I love the words of hysterics and the sentences that flow on like dysentery and mirror all the sick images of the soul. . . . I love everything that flows, everything that has time in it and becoming, that brings us back to the beginning where there is never end: the violence of the prophets, the obscenity that is ecstasy, the wisdom of the fanatic, the priest with his rubber litany, the foul words of the whore, the spittle that floats away in the gutter, the milk of the breast and the bitter honey that pours from the womb, all that is fluid, melting, dissolute and dissolvent, all the pus and dirt that in flowing is purified, that loses its sense of origin, that makes the great circuit toward death and dissolution. (232)

As Mailer says, "No, there is nothing like Henry Miller when he gets rolling."

Cancer concludes with two sections, one almost an interlude and the other as close to a summary of his faith as Miller gets. The interlude (IXV) involves the artist/hero taking a job at a lycée where he is supposed to teach French schoolboys the English language. The section is something of a practical demonstration of how one can actually work toward the realization of a community that has its roots in the life-flow Miller loves. It is set in Dijon, significantly outside Paris, and Miller uses the school as a model for the world he has just left. The dull, oafish, small-minded professors stand for the mind-numbing establishment wisdom which has led to a cultural catastrophe. The boys are still young enough to be saved, and Miller is a guide to and exemplar of an alternative life vision. He attempts to wake the boys up, to make them aware of the world and of themselves. "Here I was," he says, "the emissary of a corpse who, after he had plundered right and left, after he had caused untold suffering and misery, dreamed of universal peace":

> What did they expect me to talk about, I wonder? About *Leaves of Grass*, about the tariff walls, about the Declaration of Independence, about the latest gang war? What? Just what, I'd like to know. Well, I'll tell you—I never mentioned these things. I started right off the bat with a lesson in the physiology of love. How the elephants make love—that was it! It caught like wildfire. After the first day there were no more empty benches. After that first lesson in English they were standing at the door waiting for me. We got along swell together. They asked all sorts of questions, as though they had never learned a damned thing. I let them fire away. I taught them to ask still more ticklish questions. *Ask anything!*— that was my motto. I'm here as a plenipotentiary from the realm of free spirits. I'm here to create a fever and a ferment. (248)

Miller doesn't really save the boys, possibly because he is too busy trying to save himself. Since Dijon offers him no excitement, he must flee back to Paris to stay alive, but he has made his mark and other forays will follow.

On the last pages of *Cancer*, the artist/hero seems to step permanently away from the dying people and the doomed culture of the surreal city and into a landscape of gentle hills rising serenely above a great river. First, Miller helps poor Fillmore onto a boat headed back to England and then America. Fillmore has succumbed and is returning to his home a beaten man. In contrast, Miller has survived, and thus can feel at home anywhere. Although he feels sorry for Fillmore, he can't help noticing that his own strength has been proven in a dangerous combat zone that has produced many casualties. After the dark, depressing winter world in Dijon, "Paris had never looked so good to me," he says (284). With money meant for Fillmore's pregnant mistress divided in two shares so that he might have a reward for his good offices, the artist/hero calls for a cab and magnanimously tells the driver to go "anywhere. . . . Go through the Bois, go all around it—and take your time, I'm in no hurry" (284). The cab cruises around Paris for awhile, and Miller eventually directs it toward the Seine. As he looks at the great river, he experiences a sense of peace that is unlike anything he had known anywhere in *Cancer*. For the first time, he has actually succeeded in transcending the terrors of the immediate present and is able to turn off the tremendous flow of energy that has been driving him. And in doing this, with his defensive network not acting as an impedance, the artist/hero is able to merge for a moment with a much greater energy flow—the river of light from the natural world. The moment may not last, but it augurs well for the future:

> Christ, before my eyes there shimmered such a golden peace that only a neurotic could dream of turning his head away. So quietly flows the Seine that one hardly notices its presence. It is always there, quiet and unobtrusive, like a great artery running through the human body. In the wonderful peace that fell over me it seemed as if I had climbed to the top of a high mountain; for a little while I would be able to look around me, to take in the meaning of the landscape. (286)

5 Black Spring

"As I was young and easy..."

The true paradises are the paradises
we have lost
Marcel Proust

Le Paradis n'est pas artificiel
but is jagged
Ezra Pound

THE artist who is the hero of *Tropic of Cancer* seemed to burst upon the world of that book fully formed, blazing with energy and freed from whatever had been his past. There are some references to an extraordinary affair with a woman called Mona and one can see that his attitude toward women has been molded by that relationship, but otherwise, his origins are a mystery. As one learns about this unusual man and his unique ability to maintain a vision of power amidst a group of people who are marked by weakness and impotence, one cannot help but question the source of his strength—where does it come from and how does he retain it? The book called *Black Spring* which was begun under the title *Self-Portrait* during the years that *Cancer* was being written, helps to answer those questions and by showing another world in which the artist/hero has lived, makes the world of *Cancer* seem even more striking.[1]

Black Spring is divided into ten sections and has three basic settings. First, there is the past, a very distant past in which Miller's childhood in Brooklyn before the turn of the century is recalled. These recollections are presented as "history," but they are rather fantastic in that they recall what Gordon names "a period of almost untrammeled joy, a time when the world was 'forever warm and still to be enjoyed.' "[2] Second, there are several sections which seem like outtakes from *Cancer*. They are set in Paris, and the narrative consciousness of the artist/hero of *Cancer* is the operational voice, but they show a side of the narrator's life that seems to have been quite purposely excluded from the narration in *Cancer*. In these passages, there is evidence of a community of friends who are poor artists but who are also sensible and strong. The artist/hero is one of them, and the conclusion of *Cancer*, as well as other moments of clear vision, creativity and something like compassion which occur briefly and at random throughout that book now begin to make more sense. The third setting is, by and large, the mind of Henry Miller at about the time that he was writing *Tropic of Cancer*. These passages are illuminating in terms of the narrative psychology of that book, and they provide a sense of direction toward the future, including the goals and expectations of the author. The past–present–future arrangement is more casual than it sounds, but it does tend to set *Cancer* itself in the center of a somewhat larger frame. The frame is not as important as the picture, but it does certainly affect the way we see the picture.

The sections of *Black Spring* which detail Miller's life in his first years are sentimental and tend to be heavily weighted with nostalgia. Like so many aspects of Miller's writing, these characteristics work both for and against Miller's aims. Some of what he says is too corny to take seriously and suggests that he has been rather heavily influenced by hack popular versions of similar reminiscences. On the other hand, since nostalgia is only interesting when the past remains vital, at those points where Miller connects this "past" to the present in a reciprocal exchange of parallel perceptions, the narrative consciousness of *Cancer* is amplified by the connection.

In the moment of philosophic reflection that brings *Cancer* to its quite optimistic conclusion, Miller draws himself back from the abyss and muses: "Human beings make a strange fauna and flora. From a distance they appear negligible; close up they are apt to appear ugly and malicious. More than anything they need to be surrounded with sufficient space—space even more than time" (287).[3] The inescapeable implication is that Miller is aware of another "place" or another world in which he has seen human beings when they have adequate "space." This place is the old Fourteenth Ward in downtown Brooklyn, and as Miller begins to describe the locale and its inhabitants, it becomes gradually apparent that these relatively happy, untroubled people are just one generation removed from the human wreckage one sees in *Cancer*, who are direct descendants of these stalwart citizens. But the mode of existence which Miller imagines in *Black Spring*, when "Pat McCarren carried his handkerchief in the tailflap of his frock coat; it was nice and handy there, like the shamrock in his buttonhole. The foam was on the lager and people stopped to chat with one another" (4), has completely vanished in the bleak gutters of *Cancer*. *Black Spring* is an eon away, a recollection of a time when human values were an integral part of a cultural system that appeared to be working:

> . . . we used to congregate in the warm summer evenings and watch the goings-on over the saloon across the street. A coming and going all night long and nobody bothered to pull down the shades. Just a stone's throw away from the little burlesque house called The Bum. All around The Bum were the saloons, and Saturday nights there was a long line outside, milling and pushing and squirming to get at the ticket window. . . . while down below they were scuttling the suds and biting each other's ears off, and such a wild, shrill laughter all bottled up inside there, like dynamite evaporating. (6–7)[4]

Just men and women at their leisure, but how exciting, how

joyful it seemed then. Could it all have been lost in only thirty years? Or is this "Fourteenth Ward" as much a piece of fiction as some of the incredible episodes of sexual endurance which occur in other books? The historical authenticity of Miller's setting isn't really what is at stake here, because the descriptions have an aura of credibility that is designed to support a vision of a mythic America that has, since Shakespeare's time, been as important to most people as the historical facts. As Peter Conrad notes in *Imagining America*, this country has always provided writers (among others) with "an alternative vision of society,"[5] and in Miller's case, the "alternative vision" is a version of "the ideal" as *Cancer* is a version of "the actual."

The "America" of Miller's boyhood is one that had not changed very much since Whitman took the ferry across the East River. It was a land that still offered the promise of freedom to people from all over the western world (Hugh Kenner mentions that in 1877 in Germany, "a tot was christened Hjalmar Horace Greeley Schacht," the name expressing his parent's faith that he would prosper, "a process for which America afforded the world's paradigms").[6] Whether or not this *promise* had any basis in reality is much less important than the fact that at the time, people believed that it did, just as Miller's family believed in the American Dream and inculcated their son with its spirit. The "time" Miller remembers is not just late nineteenth century Brooklyn, but an era of unlimited expectation and faith, and the distance that this world is from *Cancer* is psychic, not chronological. Throughout *Black Spring*, Miller seems determined to recapture or rekindle a kind of spiritual fire that animated everyone on the streets of a city located as much in the New Jerusalem as in the United States. This "land" or "space" is not only a measure of how much mankind has fallen, but also a model of what it must return to.

The power that this vision has for Miller is expressed quite directly: "In my dreams I come back to the Fourteenth Ward as a paranoiac returns to his obsessions" (4). "I am a patriot—of the Fourteenth Ward, Brooklyn, where I was raised," Miller states proudly, and his pride is justified by the social arrangements that exist in this small sector of America. Every man seems to have an appropriate task, a meaningful vocation that makes rebellion unnecessary (and unthinkable). The ironmolder, for instance, is typical. He works with the earth itself, an elemental connection that casts him in a holy light that cannot be dulled by the superficial darkness of his trade:

> I remember the ironworks where the red furnace glowed and men walked toward the glowing pit with huge shovels in their hands, while outside were the shallow wooden forms like coffins with rods through them on which you scraped your shins or broke your neck. I remember the black hands of the ironmolders, the grit that had sunk so deep into the skin that nothing could remove it, not soap, nor elbow grease, nor money, nor love, nor death. Like a black mark on them! Walking into the furnace like devils with black hands—and later, with flowers over them, cool and rigid in their Sunday suits, not even the rain can wash away the grit. All these beautiful gorillas going up to God with swollen muscles and lumbago and black hands . . . (5)

What a difference between these people, marked with the sign of their work but glowing with a kind of honesty and divine innocence, and the people in *Cancer*, polished and shining with the glaze of their decadent veneer, but black at the core. And significantly, it isn't the artist but the "beautiful gorilla" who is walking before God, because in this world, the stuff of divinity is in all men (and perhaps then they are all "artists")—"the gunnersmith, the chemist, the dealer in high explosives, the undertaker, the coroner, the cuckold, the sadist, the lawyer and contender, the scholar, the restless one, the jolt-head, and the brazen faced" (5).

Miller deepens the sense one has of these men by shifting his discussion to one man in particular, Rob Ramsey, a minister's son and seemingly, the son of all men. He is not an artist, or a writer, not even a contemplative thinker—more of a "natural man," instinctively correct, part of his culture:

> I remember that everybody liked Rob Ramsey—he was the black sheep of the family. They liked him because he was a good-for-nothing and he made no bones about it. Sundays or Wednesdays made no difference to him: you could see him coming down the street under the drooping awnings with his coat over his arm

and the sweat rolling down his face; his legs wobbly, with that long, steady roll of a sailor coming ashore after a long cruise; the tobacco juice dribbling from his lips, together with warm, silent curses and some loud and foul ones too. The utter indolence, the insouciance of the man, the obscenities, the sacrilege. Not a man of God, like his father. No, a man who inspired love! His frailties were human frailties and he wore them jauntily, tauntingly, flauntingly, like banderillas. He would come down the warm open street with the gas mains bursting and the air full of sun and shit and oaths and maybe his fly would be open and his suspenders undone, or maybe his vest bright with vomit. Sometimes he came charging down the street, like a bull skidding on all fours. . . .

That was how he was then, Rob Ramsey. A man on a perpetual spree. (5–6)

Underlying this glorious description is Miller's reluctant recognition that such innocent pride is no longer possible for him because his way of seeing is different now; "the great fragmentation of maturity," as he calls it, "when suddenly all seems to be reversed. We live in the mind, in ideas, in fragments. We no longer drink in the wild outer music of the streets—we *remember* only" (9). But because the "perpetual spree" of an earlier time is gone forever, it has grown in importance, and Miller suggests that much of adult life is spent in trying to find some equivalent to compensate for the loss. Mindless sex, uncontrollable rage and a perverted will to power are poor substitutes; art may take us closer to the "wild outer music of the streets."

"The Fourteenth Ward," then, is not just an account of man (and, indeed, women are almost never mentioned) living in an Edenic state (without Eve for the most part), but an attempt to describe the birth of artistic perception as well. The Fourteenth Ward is the caldron in which Miller's artistic consciousness had its genesis. Although the society that the Fourteenth Ward represents is lost forever, it stands in memory as a symbol of a productive and satisfying mode of existence. While the physical circumstances cannot be duplicated, it may be possible to recapture some aspect of the spiritual outlook that made it so attractive. As Miller tells us, describing the moment that he first heard the name of Dostoevski (an *ur*-artist for Miller), art can transform the world and restore it to its former glory:

> And then one day, as if suddenly the flesh came undone and the blood beneath the flesh had coalesced with the air, suddenly the whole world roars again and the very skeleton of the body melts like wax. Such a day it may be when first you encounter Dostoevski. You remember the smell of the tablecloth on which the book rests; you look at the clock and it is only five minutes from eternity; you count the objects on the mantelpiece because the sound of numbers is a totally new sound in your mouth, because everything new and old, or touched and forgotten, is a fire and a mesmerism. Now every door of the cage is open and whichever way you walk is a straight line toward infinity, a straight, mad line over which the breakers roar and great rocs of marble and indigo swoop to lower their fevered eggs. (12–13)

Miller does not necessarily mean writing or painting or any other specific expression of an artistic impulse, but a way of seeing the world. He divides the cosmos into a world like the Fourteenth Ward where "we were whole," and a world after "the great change" when "we walk split into myriad fragments." In the original state, man is open to all the possibilities of experience. To express this condition, Miller says that he lived "in the street." Then, after "the great change," he feels that he "lived in ideas." This concept is a bit barren when stated that simply, but Miller invests it with a characteristic vitality when he likens the street to a river, flowing to and from eternity, its splendor and variety permitting a person to transcend the mundane by becoming a part of its flow: "To be born in the street means to wander all your life, to be free. It means accident and incident, drama, movement. It means above all dream. A harmony of irrelevant facts which gives to your wandering a metaphysical certitude. In the street you learn what human beings really are . . ." (3). On the street:

> . . . there is buried legend after legend of youth and melancholy, of savage nights and mysterious bosoms dancing on the wet mirror of the pavement, of women chuckling softly as they scratch themselves, of wild sailors' shouts, of long queues standing in front of the lobby, of boats brushing each other in the fog and tugs

snorting furiously against the rush of tide while up on the Brooklyn Bridge a man is standing in agony, waiting to jump, or waiting
to write a poem, or waiting for the blood to leave his vessels because if he advances another foot the pain of his love will kill him.
(10)

Throughout Miller's work, "the dream of the open street" appears again and again, often through the metaphor of the river
from a pure source flowing through a sickened city. After the
first few years on this "street," Miller says that his family was
"uprooted from my native soil and removed to a cemetery,"
suggesting both a loss of innocence and the literal disappear-
ance of his world. From that point on, Miller describes his life
as a series of second-hand experiences, claiming "What is not
in the open street is false, derived, that is to say, *literature*" (3).
The exploits and adventures of the next fifty years of his life
and the development of the artistic process through which they
are rendered are both aspects of Miller's desire to "live" again
on the street as he did in his youth. It is interesting to note, too,
that while women are almost entirely absent (except for the
almost ludicrous reference to "mysterious bosoms") in Miller's
picture of his early years, he spent a good deal of the remainder
of his life attempting to reclaim the feeling of his "green and
golden" times in their company, substituting perhaps the romance of a woman's presence for the romance of the open
road.

But the way Miller reacts to women will become a much more
significant factor in the discussion of the second triad. In *Black
Spring*, one could say, with an awareness of Miller's other
work, that they are conspicuous by their absence. His concern
here, in those sections that deal with the "past," is to show
how close his "beautiful gorilla'" of the streets is to the angels;
how man in a prelapsarian state is at one with his environment
and his soul; and to show how the powers of art can permit
man to transcend the sad lessons of experience. Miller is not
quite sure here how "art" performs this miraculous transformation, but in *Black Spring* one can see him recalling his first intimations that it does indeed happen. All of the sections that
follow "The Fourteenth Ward" are a demonstration of this con-

viction as well as a record of Miller's investigations of how the
process works for him.

The next few sections, however, do not require a sustained
examination because, except for an occasional passage, they
cover the same ground as "The Fourteenth Ward" without providing any new insights or images. In these pages, Miller's perspective as an observer becomes a real detriment to holding the
interest of a reader. There is a limit to how long Miller's comments on the passing scene will hold one's attention when
nothing more is offered. The mental activity surrounding a subject becomes stale when it is only an exhibit of its own dexterity. As bizarrely charming as Miller often is, it may not be
enough to say, "I am a man who pisses largely and frequently,
which they say is a sign of great mental activity" (38), even if
one is about to discourse on Parisian urinals. This is a type of
local "color," and unless the local aspires to become the universal, its appeal is somewhat limited. The mental exertion too
often surrounds a subject of insignificant proportions, and
when it is a stand-in for insight, the resulting outpouring is
decorative at best. Even in the famous selection called, "The
Angel Is My Watermark!" (51–67), aside from Miller's high
spirits and some nicely turned satirical comments at the expense of "traditional" notions of painting, there is little said
about either the "creative process" or Miller's own methods of
creativity. Perhaps the difficulty lies in Miller's lack of ability as
a painter—a slightly cruel judgment, but in terms of the standards he himself sets for his writing, an appropriate one. Since
his own work in the area of water color is so ordinary, his
comments on its creation are limited too. A fitting comparison
is his excellent letter to Anaïs Nin from Greece in December
1939, in which he gives an extraordinary picture of creative force
in operation.[7]

The three pieces which follow "The Fourteenth Ward" are
amusing in spots, but they don't have any sustained strength
or special vision. They are primarily tentative entrances into
areas which Miller explores more thoroughly elsewhere. Since
Miller may have been aware of his somewhat uneasy footing
(the manuscript was revised almost to the date of publication),

these sections are filled with bombast, prick waving and invective. The book gains substance and deepens its penetration when Miller returns to the world of the Fourteenth Ward in the section called "The Tailor Shop."

The section opens with sketches of customers in his father's store. The people are seen from the slightly awestruck perspective of a young boy. Each vignette of a customer amidst his possessions and purchases is vivid and unique, and they coalesce to form a picture of a world that is dominated by a sense of abundance. It is all presented with a kind of awe at the infinite ingenuity of God's plans and Miller ticks off each item in a motley catalog as if he were tolling a litany of bounty:

> A merry crew and the table loaded with good things—with red cabbage and green spinach, with roast pork and turkey and sauerkraut, with kartoffelklösze and sour black gravy, with radishes and celery, with stuffed goose and peas and carrots, with beautiful white cauliflower, with apple sauce and figs from Smyrna, with bananas big as a blackjack, with cinnamon cake and Streussel Küchen, with chocolate layer cake and nuts, all kinds of nuts, walnuts, butternuts, almonds, pecans, hickory nuts, with lager beer and bottled beer, with white wines and red, with champagne, kümmel, malaga, port, with schnapps, with fiery cheeses, with dull, innocent store cheese, with flat Holland cheeses, with limburger and schmierkäse, with homemade wines, elderberry wine, with cider, hard and sweet, with rice pudding and tapioca, with roast chestnuts, mandarins, olives, pickles, with red caviar and black, with smoked sturgeon, with lemon meringue pie, with lady fingers and chocolate eclairs, with macaroons and cream puffs, with black cigars and long thin stogies, with Bull Durham and Long Tom and meerschaums, with corncobs and toothpicks, wooden toothpicks which gave you gum boils the day after, and napkins a yard wide with your initials stitched in the corner, and a blazing coal fire and the windows steaming, everything in the world before your eyes except a finger bowl. (91–92)

Surely this is a feast for all the senses, including the auditory. It should probably be read aloud like a poem of Whitman's or Ginsberg's ("with . . . with . . . with"); an international feast of plenty for everyone, and particularly for *you*, with your own "initials" reassuring provided. It is a picture of a world blazing with the fire of life, and it speaks of a time of contentment. Although there are disquieting intrusions of the adult world into Miller's perspective in this essay (especially his seduction of the widow of his father's friend), it is primarily a child's view of existence (95–97). Amidst myriad disasters and plagues, Miller is "jolly in spite of everything." "There was cancer, dropsy, cirrhosis of the liver, insanity, thievery, mendacity, buggery, incest, paralysis, tapeworms, abortions, triplets, idiots, drunkards, ne'er-do-wells, fanatics, sailors, tailors, watchmakers, scarlet fever, whooping cough, meningitis, running ears, chorea, stutterers, jailbirds, dreamers, storytellers, bartenders—" (91). No one is going to worry about the potentially terrible when it is preposterously juxtaposed with the obviously trivial. All of the things mentioned are just more features of the child's world, an astonishing array of phenomena and a cause not for despair but for delight. His motto for this "time" is "Always merry and bright!"

Probably the most striking feature of this dreamlike vision of a heroic past gradually being mythologized is the masculine camaraderie among Miller's father and his friends:

> Paul must have recognized something of a kindred nature in the old man too. Never have I seen two men look at each other with such a warm glow of admiration. Sometimes they would stand there looking into each other's eyes adoringly until the tears came. In fact, neither of them was ashamed of showing his tears, something which seems to have gone out of the world now. I can see Paul's homely freckled face and his rather thick, blubbery lips twitching as the old man told him for the thousandth time what a great guy he was. (83)

This isn't one of Miller's best efforts, much too mushy and overwrought, but the excess of feeling is not altogether out of line and it is the beginning of a eulogy that turns hard and terse at the close:

> The old man's riding around in an open barouche. I envy the bastard his peace of mind. A bosom pal by his side and a quart of rye under his belt. My toes are blistering with malice. Twenty years ahead of me and this thing growing worse by the hour. It's

> throttling me. In twenty years there won't be any soft, lovable
> men waiting to greet me. Every bosom pal that goes now is a
> buffalo lost and gone forever. Steel and concrete hedging me in.
> The pavement getting harder and harder. The new world eating
> into me, expropriating me. Soon I won't even need a name. (111)

As Dylan's song says, "The times they are a'changing," and
Miller not only expresses this change but exhibits it himself: "In
the past every member of our family did something with his
hands. I'm the first idle son of a bitch with a glib tongue and a
bad heart" (110–111). Of course, this is meant to be taken with
considerable irony, but there is a note of guilt too. The wrench-
ing loss that Miller feels is partly for his father, and his father's
world: "The men my father loved were weak and lovable. They
went out, each and every one of them, like brilliant stars before
the sun. They went out quietly and catastrophically. No shred
of them remained—nothing but the memory of their blaze and
glory. They flow now inside me like a vast river choked with
falling stars" (101). But the loss is seen for what it really is
when we realize that these "lovable" men—Tom Moffat, Paul
Dexter, Tom Jordan—have become the pathetic derelicts and
burned out cases of *Cancer*. The difference is not so much a
change in the world, but in one's way of looking at it.

Actually, Miller had a few friends in Paris who were close
enough to him to be called "bosom pals," and in his later writing, he described them with considerable affection and admiration. The first of these portraits, and one of the only ones which
is a part of his "fiction," is the extraordinary caricature of the
poet Walter Lowenfels which is at the center of *Black Spring*.
Lowenfels appeared on the periphery of *Cancer* as the genial
master of a well-fed and remarkably well-balanced menage
which Miller visited from time to time. His good sense and
composure really had no place in a world of hookers and hollow men, and Miller made a wise decision to save him for a
later book. In *Black Spring*, he is introduced as the first example
of a person living a life of value and creative force who is not a
legendary figure from the mythic past or a long-dead writer
now acknowledged as a "classic." He is the beginning of a line
which runs through Katsimbalis and the various artists cele-

brated in *The Air-Conditioned Nightmare* and *Remember To Remember*, and which eventually strains to include Miller himself. Because Miller was still very unsure about how an artist might survive in the mid-1930s, Lowenfels is not seen straight on but at an oblique angle which burlesques the seriousness of his (and Miller's) approach to literature. Beneath the comedy, however, the delightfully named Jabberwhorl Cronstadt is a strong and committed artist.

Lowenfels was working as a writer and renting agent in 1928 when he and his wife met Miller for the first time. "We were very poor," he recalls, "but not as poor as Henry." Lowenfels encouraged Miller and frequently fed him and "loaned" him money, and in a sense, Miller repaid the loans with his evocation of Lowenfels in the euphoric prose of the section of *Black Spring* called "Jabberwhorl Cronstadt." Miller's artist/hero uses the power of his self-confidence as a shield against the incursions of a hostile environment, and in similar fashion, Miller suggests that Lowenfels/Cronstadt uses an antic attitude as a comic masque to keep trouble and perhaps despair at a distance. Even with this playful persona as his most prominent feature, Cronstadt is still depicted with enough depth to stand as a positive argument for the advantages of expatriotism. Mailer feels that "like Dickens, he (Miller) is at his best with the worst" in human beings, but Cronstadt is an illustration of what Miller could do with one of the best people he knew.[9] Cronstadt's high spirits, his delight with the world and its curious inhabitants, and his intoxication with language make him that rare adult who is something like the unspoiled child whose sensibility Miller described in "The Fourteenth Ward." At the same time, the section about him is a definition by example of the mind of an artist and Miller's first hesitant suggestion that an artist might live beyond anger even in the modern world.

The primary difference between Cronstadt and the other Americans Miller has been describing in *Cancer* is that Cronstadt is completely open to experience, a "natural" man (one thinks of Whitman once again) vastly receptive to sensory encounters, and perhaps more important, an artist capable of transforming these encounters into celebrations of existence.

Whereas most of Miller's acquaintances have become cynical and disillusioned—it is hard to imagine that they were ever any other way, one can hardly see them as children, they seem born old—Cronstadt has not only retained his capacity for wonder, but like Miller himself, has given this "capacity" tongue. He is enamored with the symbol-making power of the mind as it shapes and informs the world through the use of language. Miller leaps into the place where Cronstadt lives as if he were springing, without preparation, into a carnival, and the tone of Cronstadt's life is established immediately by the style of his domain:

> He lives in the back of a sunken garden, a sort of bosky glade shaded by whiffletrees and spinozas, by deodors and baobabs, a sort of queasy Buxtehude diapered with elytras and feluccas. You pass through a sentry box where the concierge twirls his mustache *con furioso* like in the last act of Ouida. They live on the third floor behind a mullioned belvedere filigreed with snaffled spaniels and sebaceous wens, with debentures and megrims hanging out to dry. Over the bell-push it says: "JABBERWHORL CRONSTADT, poet, musician, herbologist, weather man, linguist, oceanographer, old clothes, colloids." (115)

Cronstadt has invented and arranged a field of operation that is distinctly his own. He is surrounded with *things* which express and define his life, and these *things*—versions of fantasy and made-up creatures—begin to live too through the energy Cronstadt generates in his considerations. The objects in his quarters are another variant of the Rabelaisian list Miller loves, and taken together, they begin to overwhelm and then absorb literal reality. On Cronstadt's mantlepiece, one finds: "—*The Anatomy of Melancholy*, an empty bottle of Pernod Fils, *The Opal Sea*, a slice of cut plug tobacco, hairpins, a street directory, an ocarina . . . and a machine to roll cigarettes" (116). Beneath the cigarette machine, there are notes for poems written on menus: " 'the opalescent mucus of Michelet' . . . 'defluxions . . . cotyledons . . . phthisical' . . . 'if Easter falls in Lady Day's lap, beware old England of the clap' . . . 'from the ichor of which springs his successor' . . . 'the reindeer, the otter, the marmink, the minkfrog.' " (116) Mailer says parts of this section are a

parody of *Finnegans Wake* "which may as well set the standard
for parodies of Joyce," but Miller is also taking aim at the poetry of Amy Lowell, Edith Sitwell and numerous others.[10] And
Lewis Carroll (and Edward Lear) must have been in Miller's
mind too, because one sees amidst the clutter: "an enormous
epileptoid beast with fungoid whiskers. It is Jocatha the fam-
ished cat, a big, buggerish brute with a taupe fur and two black
walnuts hidden under its kinkless tail. It runs about like a leop-
ard, it lifts its hind leg like a dog, it micturates like an owl"
(117). In Miller's eyes, all of these items are a part of Cronstadt,
just as the cat is suspiciously like his "master" in his manic
behavior:

> He claws the carpet and chews the wallpaper, he rolls into a spiral
> and unrolls like a corolla, he whisks the knots out of his tail,
> shakes the fungus out of his whiskers. He bites clean through the
> floor to the bone of the poem. He's in the key of C and mad clean
> through. He has magenta eyes, like old-fashioned vest buttons;
> he's mowsy and glaubrous, brown like arnica and then green as
> the Nile; he's quaky and qualmy and queasy and teasey; he chews
> chasubles and ripples rasubly. (117)

Miller was always fascinated with the powers of language,
particularly spoken language, to transform and create perception. His verbal dexterity and phonemic badinage here is a part
of a plan to present Cronstadt's world as a realm of excitement
and almost visionary experience. Ostensibly Cronstadt is living
in the Paris of *Cancer*, but the way in which he *sees* the world
transfers him to another place entirely. If there is an alternative
to the dying land which Miller is attempting to flee from and
destroy in his wake, it will be populated by people like Cronstadt who might just find some room for Miller too.

Cronstadt may be a bit zany in his manner, but he is also,
like a zen master, completely capable of dealing with the rou-
tine matters of his life with affability and confidence. In a spirit-
ed monologue, Miller presents him in his capacity as renting
agent speaking on the phone to a prospective client:

> "*Hello!* Oui, c'est le Monsieur Cronstadt. Et votre nom, s'il vous
> plait? *Bimberg?* Listen, you speak English, don't you? So do I . . .

What? Yes, I've got three apartments—to rent or to sell. *What?*
Yes, there's a bath and a kitchen and a toilet too. . . . No, a regular
toilet. No, not in the hall—in the apartment. One you sit down
on. Would you like it in silver or in gold leaf? *What?* No, the toilet!

"*What?* No, I'm serious. Are *you* serious? *What?* Listen, if you
mean business it means cash. . . . *Cash!* You've got to lay out *cash.*
What? Well, that's the way things are done over here. The French
don't believe in checks. I had a man last week tried to do me out
of 750 francs. Yeah, an American check." (119)

The jagged rhythms of the word *What?* squawked every few
sentences nicely express Cronstadt's method of keeping the
world off balance; it is a sharp jab thrown into the face of an
onrushing opponent. After he hangs up, Cronstadt tells Miller
with affectionate irony, "You think literature is everything. You
eat literature. Now in this house we eat goose, for instance."
One can imagine his expression as he says, "Real estate."

Cronstadt's wife and three visiting German girls (refugees
Lowenfels is helping, although he makes nothing out of it) are
a kind of audience and an inspiration for Cronstadt's performance, and Miller joins the gallery while a goose which has
been saved for this occasion is prepared. The meal is quite important, since we know from Miller's accounts in *Cancer* how
hunger affects him, and Cronstadt enters into the revels with
even more gusto than usual. He gets steadily more drunk as it
is cooked, and under the guise of inebriation, he can afford to
be completely foolish, but without making a fool of himself. It
is time for "the wisdom of the heart," and Cronstadt holds
forth: "The poem is the only flawless thing, provided you
know what time it is. A poem is a web which the poet spins out
of his own body according to a logarithmic calculus of his own
divination. It's always right, because the poet starts from the
center and works outward . . ." (119). Of course, Miller's own
idea of literary creation is at one with this statement, and when
Cronstadt gives Miller some advice, it might be Miller counsel-
ing himself: "You're talking about China all the time . . . *this* is
China, don't you see that?" (125) and taking it further: "No
need to write about China. Write about *that!* About what's inside of you . . . the great vertiginous vertebration . . . the zoo-

spores and the leucocytes . . . the wamroths and the holenlin-
dens . . . every one's a poem. The jellyfish is a poem too—the
finest kind of poem" (126).

Again, what Cronstadt is proposing depends upon how one
sees things. Miller sometimes tends to underplay his strategy to
"write what's inside of you" to avoid making his approach too
obvious, but here Cronstadt speaks for Miller; there is no separation. In the mouth of a man Miller obviously admires a great
deal, "wisdom" must be taken at face value.

Cronstadt's behavior tends toward the totally eccentric as he
becomes progressively higher on whiskey and words, but his
power as a poet is steady, and the humor of his discourse does
not diminish its revelation. "He's losing his mind," says Jill, his
wife: "Wrong again," says Jabber. "I've just found my mind,
only it's a different sort of mind than you imagined. You think
a poem must have covers around it. The moment you write a
thing the poem ceases. The poem is the present which you
can't define. You live it" (127). It is hard to imagine an existence
like Cronstadt's, a "present" which one lives, as something
which a person might sustain for more than a short while, but
like a good poem that "present" resonates beyond its moment
in time. Miller is proposing that one accept Cronstadt's ecstasy
as a spiritual ideal, a model for the person who would remain
"open" to all the possibilities of life. The section concludes with
another list, this time a catalog of all creation, as Cronstadt
touches on some of the phenomena in his "open" field:

> No beginnings and no ends. Chaud the alpha and Froid the
> omega. Perpetuity. The Gemini, ruling over life and death. Alpha-
> Chaud running out through all degrees of Fahrenheit and Reau-
> mur, through magnetic filings and comets' tails, through the boil-
> ing cauldron of Mauna Loa into the dry light of the Tertiary
> moon. . . . through the follicles and tentacles of worlds unformed,
> worlds untouched, worlds unseen, worlds unborn and forever
> lost. (127–28)

Cronstadt, "singing loud and clear like a dead and stricken
swan," gives us his world:

> I, Jabberwhorl, sitting at the iron sink am perplexed and exalted,

never less and never more than a poem, an iron stanza, a boiling
follicle, a lost leucocyte. The iron sink where I spat out my heart,
where I bathed my tender feet, where I held my first child, where
I washed my sore gums, where I sang like a diamond-backed ter-
rapin and I am singing now and will sing forever though the
drains clog and the faucets rust, though time runs out and I be all
there is of present, past and future. *Sing*, Froid, sing transitive!
Sing, Chaud, sing intransitive! Sing Alpha and Omega! Sing Hal-
lelujah! Sing out, O sink! Sing while the world sinks . . ." (128–29)

Just as Miller promised to "sing while you croak," in the beginning of *Cancer*, here Cronstadt is singing a song of life that
Miller has composed for both of them. And it is also a song
celebrating the self, which is quite appropriate since Lowenfels
was one of Whitman's earliest champions.

In his "Unpublished Preface to *Tropic of Cancer*," Lowenfels
notes:

> I am glad the book has been written. It's inevitable . . . as far as
> the bowels go, I loathe the material—masturbation of each other's
> deadness that I read through the pages. That anyone accepts this
> as an audience to which to be alive. A corpse diddling itself. Writ-
> ing machine?—Not at all. He's a Miller-machine, a huge, blood-
> sucking Miller-machine. The moment something has to be relived,
> it's gone. Raw stuff, hot from the griddle, a raw ingot, worthless
> unless it's real hot; then it can make an impression. There's sterili-
> ty in its violence.

Miller's friends were his only editors then, and he paid some
attention to their comments. The "sterility" of the physical
world in *Cancer* is counterbalanced by the world of Jabberwhorl
Cronstadt in the center of *Black Spring*—the world of a man who
is enthusiastically alive in a cosmos of perpetual creation. Then,
the section that follows changes the focus drastically.

For an author who left little of his life unexamined, the years
between Miller's "removal" to a cemetery at the age of ten and
the moment when he began to work for the Cosmodemonic
Telegraph Company in his late twenties are barely touched in
his writing. There are occasional references to his first marriage, but very little else about his life and adventures from age
ten on. He may have left this period out of what he called his

"autobiographical romances" because he felt a greater necessity to write about later periods in his life, or his decision may have been primarily aesthetic in that he did not feel that he could transform the "raw stuff" of his life from 1901 to 1920 into literature. Neither Martin's biography nor Miller's own writing provides a satisfactory answer to this question, but there are a few selections which shed some light on the problem. The section which follows the depiction of Cronstadt as an artist of the beautiful is one of these, a protracted experiment in the techniques of surrealism with a title, "Into the Night Life . . ." borrowed from Freud, and a subtitle, "A Coney Island of the Mind," which suggests a juxtaposition between the antic mood of the amusement park in Brooklyn near his home and the stream of images which careens through his mind in this section.[12]

Through the Cronstadt tour de force, *Black Spring* has been divided nearly equally between Miller's early life in Brooklyn and his days in France while *Cancer* was being written. The years between have been crossed without comment. "Into the Night Life . . . " is drawn primarily from the notebook of dreams which Miller was compiling, but in its choice of images and in their arrangement, one can discern Miller gradually working backward from Paris to Brooklyn, through twenty years of trauma. He has chosen powerful images recorded from his subconscious mind after recurring dreams and is examining them in an attempt to understand more completely the artist/ hero of *Cancer*, who he is and how he got that way. The entire sequence is like a chronicle of the fall from innocence to experience, but run in reverse order, so that one begins at the bottom and gradually struggles back to an unsteady perch above the precipice. The location of this piece directly after the exuberant Cronstadt portrait forces a radical change in mood, but it is a logical continuation in style since so much of Cronstadt's speech is a wash of wordplay and a bizarre amalgam of images.

The art produced since Breton's manifesto suggests that surrealism is an aesthetic accomplished most successfully in visual media, most specifically films and painting. Miller, of course, admits no impediments to his pen, but while his familiarity with painting is well known, his avid interest in cinema, especially while he lived in Europe, is not often discussed. In 1938, in his first collection of "essays," he published an article on film called "The Golden Age," in which he discusses the Bunuel–Dali collaboration on *L'Âge d'Or* within a context that indicates he is quite familiar with the development of cinematic art to that time.[13] This piece is followed by what he calls his "Reflections on *Extasy*," a minor example of tame erotica, and by a "Scenario" for a film very loosely based on Anaïs Nin's *The House of Incest*. Miller was intrigued by the possibilities for temporal expansion and compression in films, and was fascinated by the way in which film could adopt the features of surrealism as its own language and grammar. In various passages throughout his writing, cinematic modes of discourse are used (jump-cuts, fades, zooms, etc.), but the sequence "Into the Night Life . . ." is probably the closest he has come to a screenplay, closer than his "Scenario" because the Nin story is seen from outside the action, while in this case, the point of view is exclusively the subjective camera.[14]

"Into the Night Life" begins with an image of the narrator chained to a bed, confronted by "an old hag," her hair "full of rats." Everything is like a dream, but since one never awakens, the dream becomes the only reality. As Borges asks, what if we awake from this dream to another dream? The setting is the modern world, the time, the present. In other words, this is the world of *Cancer* at its worst; here is the artist/hero without the power of his self-confidence and bereft of his ability to exercise control by stepping out of the frame:

> Suddenly the old hag comes dancing in stark naked, her hands aflame. Immediately she knocks over the umbrella stand the place is in an uproar. From the upturned umbrella stand there issues a steady stream of writhing cobras traveling at lightning speed. They knot themselves around the legs of the tables. . . .
>
> Winding a pair of cobras about my arms I go for the old hag with murder in my eyes. From her mouth, her eyes, her hair, from her vagina even, the cobras are streaming forth, always with that frightful steaming hiss as if they had been ejected fresh from a boiling crater. In the middle of the room where we are locked an

immense forest opens up. We stand in a nest of cobras and our
bodies come undone.

I can't tell any more who I am or where I came from or how I
got there. The room is very small and my bed is close to the door.
I have a feeling that some one is standing on the doorsill watching
me. I am petrified with fright. (134–35)

Jane Nelson ascribes considerable significance to the hag as a
version of the terrible mother archetype, and her comments are
quite instructive within the confines of her Jungian analysis.[15] I
would prefer to consider these images within the formulation I
have previously suggested; that this sequence of dreams moves
from the most forbidding moments of the present back (a film
in reverse) to the utopian past. The greatest horror, as we shall
see at the conclusion of the "film," is that the "past" is always
out of reach, receding toward the horizon as we approach it.

The camera cuts to a man ("When I raise my eyes") who is
like an interrogator from Kafka's bureaucratic nightmare.
" 'Speak!' he says, with that cruel, jeering smile." There is a
train rumbling on the sound track, then a sonic match-cut to a
trolley on a bridge, crossing the Brooklyn Bridge. We see the
city stretched out below, as in a picture by George Grosz:

In the heat of the late afternoon the city rises up like a huge polar
bear shaking off its rhododendrons. The forms waver, the gas
chokes the girders, the smoke and the dust wave like amulets.
Out of the welter of buildings there pours a jellywash of hot bodies glued together with pants and skirts. The tide washes up in
front of the curved tracks and splits like glass combs. Under the
wet headlines are the diaphanous legs of the amoebas scrambling
on to the running boards, the fine, sturdy tennis legs wrapped in
cellophane, their white veins showing through the golden calves
and muscles of ivory. (136)

The trolley carries us to a desert, a landscape by Ives Tanguy
perhaps: "The countryside is desolate. No warmth, no snug-
ness, no closeness, no density, no opacity, no numerator, no
denominator. It's like the evening newspaper read to a deaf
mute standing on a hat rack with a palmetto leaf in his hand. In
all this parched land no sign of human hand, of human eye, of

human voice. Only headlines written in chalk which the rain washes away" (137). Then another woman appears, a "woman I used to know." She is younger (the regression in time), an adolescent's vision of a woman who promises sexual excitement, but she is seen as a trap, her physical attributes changing into odd and confusing amalgams of the human and the natural world:

> She stands in the middle of the desert like a rock made of camphor. Her body has the strong white aroma of sorrow. She stands like a statue saying good-by. Head and shoulders above me she stands, her buttocks swoopingly grand and out of all proportion. Everything is out of proportion—hands, feet, thighs, ankles. She's an equestrian statue without the horse, a fountain of flesh worn away to a mammoth egg. Out of the ballroom of flesh her body sings like iron. Girl of my dreams, what a splendid cage you make! Only where is the little perch for your three-pointed toes? The little perch that swung backward and forward between the brass bars? You stand by the window, dead as a canary, your toes stiff, your beak blue. You have the profile of a line drawing done with a meat-ax. Your mouth is a crater stuffed with lettuce leaves. Did I ever dream that you could be so enormously warm and lopsided? Let me look at your lovely jackal paws; let me hear the croaking, dingy chortle of your dry breath. (137–38)

There is something of Max Ernst's work in this description. After a desperate, frenzied coupling with the woman ("I hold her close in the choked spume of the canyons under the locked watersheds twisted with golden sands while the hour runs out") the camera is placed on a train (tracking shot?) which runs to a seashore that turns out to be "A Coney Island of the Mind." The huge, garish amusement park is the ultimate surreal setting, a place where the rational is no longer a factor at all. The unsettling effect of this weird circus ("Everything is sordid, shoddy, thin as pasteboard") leads to a contrasting recollection of a totally different world, one that seemed to make sense, a world of proportion and order: "Where is the warm summer's day when first I saw the green-carpeted earth revolving and men and women moving like panthers? Where is the soft gurgling music which I heard welling up from the sappy roots of the earth?" (140). That image fades, and for the next few pages, the nightmare carnival, with its "trapdoors and grinning skeletons" becomes an extended metaphor for modern civilization. In desperation, another attempt is made to establish a connection with the values of the past. The artist's father appears, but he is not quite the warm old man of "The Tailor Shop." Instead we see:

> . . . him standing at the window shaving, or rather not shaving, but stropping his razor. Never before has he failed me, but now in my need he is deaf. I notice now the rusty blade he is using. Mornings with my coffee there was always the bright flash of his blade, the bright German steel laid against the smooth dull hide of the strop, the splash of lather like cream in my coffee, the snow banked on the window ledge, putting a felt around his words. Now the blade is tarnished and the snow turned to slush; the diamond frost of the window panes trickles in a thin grease that stinks of toads and marsh gas. "Bring me huge worms," he begs, "and we will plough the minnows." Poor, desperate father that I have. I clutch with empty hands across a broken table. (142–43)

Then cut abruptly to another woman, a very young whore, "young and athletic, and best of all, she is ignorant." Although her features are indistinct, her sexual characteristics are placed in sharp relief, and she merges with images of the artist's first wife. Then a child appears, a wounded child (lack of love?) "a girl and she has a slit in the side of her head" (145). The artist rushes her to a doctor, assists with the operation. The child recovers, but the artist's wife is in the corner, whispering at him "Fiend! Fiend!" Cut abruptly to images of outer space, the sound track filled with a kind of monotonous chanting. For the next few pages, the screen is filled with images from various epochs—the Day Book of the great plague, a wolf hunt, a coffin factory. Then a fade, perhaps the dream is ending, but the next image is that of "a wild park such as I had often stumbled through in the dark." Just as Coney Island, which Miller had visited in his youth was transformed into a terrible circus of madness, now Prospect Park, the beautiful oasis in the midst of middle-class Brooklyn, was transformed into a "dark-clustered wood," a dark wilderness replete with horrifying surprises.

Through the park, a stream is seen, "the water rushes down in a thin sheet of glass between the soft white mounds of the banks." It is the familiar river from the natural world, but instead of bringing new life to a blighted landscape, "it rushes below the knees, carrying the amputated feet forward like broken pedestals before an avalanche." And as the camera pans along this stream, it "quickens into tongues of fire," turning into the *open street* of the Fourteenth Ward.

But it is not quite the same street. In one direction it stretches toward the golden past, "A street that slopes gently toward the sun and then forward like an arrow to lose itself in space. . . . I move in golden hum through a syrup of warm lazy bodies" (151). But in the other direction, it moves back to the present, "the street of early sorrows where the flats string out like railroad cars and all the houses flanked with iron spikes." For a moment, the camera is fixed at the crucial point, "the perimeter of the six extremes (where) I have wandered back by devious routes to the hub where all is change and transformation." Everything is still, and the artist wonders, "When down this cold funereal street they drove the hearse which I hailed with joy had I already shed my skin? I was the lamb and they drove me out. I was the lamb and they made of me a striped tiger" (151–52). The answers to this conundrum are very elusive, and while the camera turns toward the past (a golden filter across the lens), it is also in reverse zoom away from what it seeks. Then, as it moves along "the street of early sorrows," toward the present, images of the modern world in hideous decline become more and more numerous. Past a cemetery ("bursting with things to eat"), past moments in American history ("the tomahawk sailing through the air to the sound of familiar bloodcurdling yells"), the sound track droning a litany of Native American names ("Delaware and Lackawanna, Monongahela, the Mohawk, the Shenandoah, Narrangansett, Tuskegee, Oskaloosa. . . . "), the camera sweeps from side to side as it moves smoothly forward. Then the camera stops moving and the focus narrows again to the street, but now it is winter, the gutters choked with snow, the "witch mother stalking the wind." Along the street (the camera now fixed, the image now

of a numbed state of horror) comes a mass of disconnected
images so fragmented as to suggest a final loss of mental stability:

> All through the street the hearses pass up and down, up and
> down, the drivers munching their long whips, their white crapes,
> their cotton gloves.
>
> North toward the white pole, south toward the red heron, the
> pulse beats wild and straight. One by one, with bright glass teeth,
> they cut away the cords. The duck comes with his broad bill and
> then the low-bellied weasel. One after another they come, sum-
> moned from the fungus, their tails afeather, their feet webbed. . . .
>
> East toward the Mongols, west toward the redwoods, the pulse
> swings back and forth. Onions marching, eggs chattering, the
> menagerie spinning like a top. Miles high on the beaches lie the
> red caviar beds. The breakers foam, snap their long whips. The
> tide roars beneath the green glaciers. Faster, faster spins the earth.
> (158)

The film ends in a mass of color and light, the screen a panorama of blurred images spinning without discernible shape and
form, the camera itself wobbling on its axis, probably hand
held. There is a suggestion of some primordial realm that exists
before birth, perhaps after death: "Out of black chaos whorls of
light with portholes jammed. Out of the static null and void a
ceaseless equilibrium. Out of whalebone and gunnysack this
mad thing called sleep that runs like an eight-day clock." (158).
Slow fade to black. Then the words THE END. Perhaps they
should be replaced by the words THE BEGINNING.

The conclusion of this mind-staggering "film" brought Miller's recollections of the distant past to an end, not only in *Black
Spring* but for the next forty years, or until he began to look
back in fondness in his eighties. It also gave him the courage,
or perhaps one might say the momentum to look toward the
future. In the section "Walking Up and Down in China," Miller
picks up Cronstadt's insight *"this* is China," and weaves a series of variations on that theme. What Cronstadt's life signifies,
and what Miller now can claim he understands at least intellectually, is that one's outlook is the determining factor, to a large

extent, of whether or not one will be "happy" or "satisfied" or "productive" or whatever one wants to be. As Miller puts it, "In Paris, out of Paris, leaving Paris or coming back to Paris, it's always Paris and Paris is France and France is China" (161). "China" is not a physical place, but a condition of being. Miller never got near the East until his sixties, but he had formed a conception of "China" from his vast reading just as he had formed a conception of many other places and times, and he felt that "China" was as good a name as any for a "place" where a certain spirituality replaced the greed and lust of the West. Consequently, as he scorned the cancerous West, he reached for the timeless and eternal East:

> I am here in the midst of a great change. I have forgotten my own language and yet I do not speak the new language. I am in China and I am talking Chinese. I am in the dead center of a changing reality for which no language has yet been invented. According to the map I am in Paris; according to the calendar I am living in the third decade of the twentieth century. But I am neither in Paris nor in the twentieth century. I am in China and there are no clocks or calendars here. (166)

The serenity that being in "China" produces enables Miller to believe, for a moment, that he can actually recapture the spirit of the mythic past. As the city of Paris rushes around him, he muses: "Here I sit in the open street composing my song. It's the song I heard as a child, the song which I lost in the new world and which I would never have recovered had I not fallen like a twig into the ocean of time" (167). But he hasn't recovered his song. Instead, he has had a momentary vision of a kind of existence which approximates the unspoiled past but he is still far from merging with the "ocean of time." As if to underscore this harsh truth, the next few pages are like a rerun of portions of "Into the Night Life . . ." with images of horror moving across the screen in relentless succession.

Every time Miller tries to move away from the present, he finds that the spirit of the past is unrecoverable and that the way to a future in "China" is difficult to discern. The final pages of Black Spring suggest that Miller has resolved to con-

front the circumstances of the present and accept the difficulties
of an uncertain, arduous path toward "China." He begins this
process with a kind of rite of exorcism, intoning the names of
places he has visited (top half of page 175) and people who
have "lived" in his consciousness (the middle of page 176 to the
middle of page 177). This rather bloated catalog is like a song of
farewell and a statement of position. It shows something of the
regions that Miller has passed through and some of the figures
in history who have influenced his attitudes. For good measure, Miller also throws in a few familiar names from the Fourteenth Ward, but in this closing section, the people who were
lovingly described in the first part of the book are now seen as
remnants of a world gone sour. There is "old man Ramsey, the
gospel-monger"; there is his old friend Alfie Betcha who, it
turns out, "was a crook"; there is Mrs. Gorman who greeted
the priest, now seen "in her dirty wrapper, her boobies half
out, and muttering 'Tch tch tch!' " Even his old gang, "boys
from the north side and boys from the south side" were slaugh-
tered in World War I, "rolled into a muck heap and their guts
hanging on the barbed wire." The mythic past is not rejected,
but there is a recognition that it cannot ever be relived. At
times, it can be summoned from memory and imagination to
inspire a new song which may be composed in some future
setting. Because this setting, "China," is just beginning to take
shape in Miller's mind, *Black Spring* ends on a note of ambigu-
ity. Paris is still the present, confusing, frustrating, exhilarating. "China" is the chimera of the future. For practical purposes, "the whole past is wiped out" (181). In the last pages of
Black Spring, Miller is still a self-proclaimed "Megalopolitan Maniac," the archetypal urban underground man. His last
thoughts suggest that he realizes that before he can hope to live
in "China," he must be able to live comfortably with himself.
The title *Black Spring* reflects his uncertainty in this area. The
"spring" suggests promise, optimism, new growth; the "black-
ness" suggests that the new growth has within it the potential
for its own annihilation. The self-confidence of the artist/hero of
Cancer is not as deeply rooted as it might be. Miller knows this,
but he is prepared for further scrutiny: "Tomorrow you may

bring about the destruction of your world. Tomorrow you may sing in Paradise above the smoking ruins of your world-cities. But tonight I would like to think of one man, a lone individual, a man without name or country, a man whom I respect because he has absolutely nothing in common with you—MYSELF. Tonight I shall meditate upon that which I am" (208).

6 *The Colossus of Maroussi* and *Big Sur and the Oranges of Hieronymus Bosch*

Journals of life in a clean, well-lighted place

AFTER publishing *Black Spring*, Henry Miller branched out in two directions in his writing. One path led him through lands on two continents and pointed toward a utopian vision of society which he often called "China." The other took him into his own psyche and through the regions of his mind and heart/skin in the direction of another kind of utopia (or euphoria) called woman. In the first case, he was searching for a "good place" to live and work. In the second case, he was searching for a "good feeling" which would permit him to be comfortable in any place. One can see how the twin quests are related, and various sections in *Black Spring* and *Cancer* show Miller attempting to establish this relationship. One of the central obstacles to Miller's success as a writer is his perhaps unfortunate (and perhaps inevitable) decision to divide his two searches. *Cancer* and *Black Spring* contain elements of both, but the books that follow are primarily concerned with one or the other, and I believe that they all suffer, to some degree, from this division. The loss is greatest in the books which are a part of the voyage of geographic exploration, because Miller's attempts to evoke the spirit of place in the lands he wrote about is much less interesting in the absence of the narrative consciousness of the artist/hero. As Mathieu remarks in his extensive study of *The Colossus of Maroussi:* "*The Colossus of Maroussi* is Miller's account of his rediscovery of paradise in Greece and, as such, it is almost totally free of the uninhabited 'demonic' furies of his earlier books. Like Rimbaud's *Illuminations,* it seldom recalls the 'season in hell' which had preceded it and which had been recorded with roars of anguish in earlier books."[1]

Mailer believes that Miller, in a conscious attempt to "take America by storm with an absolutely charming book," made a compromise of sorts and that "he wrote a book which could be published in America."[2] I don't doubt that some such calculation must have entered Miller's mind, but I think that there are other, equally fundamental reasons for Miller's narrative stance in *Maroussi.* Referring back to Mathieu's comment comparing Miller and Rimbaud, it is important to consider whether Miller was capable of imagining a paradise at this or any point in his life which included women. The evidence suggests that while the artist/hero of *Cancer* (who is seen later in the *Rosy Crucifixion* in a developmental stage) experienced "paradisiacal" moments with women, the majority of his relationships or encounters were more frequently of an infernal nature. Because Miller is ultimately optimistic about the destiny of humankind, his vision of a utopian existence always includes men and women living in harmony, but his thinking in this area is almost entirely theoretical. The actual evidence of a harmonious relationship is scanty, and it never seems to include Miller himself. He observes and comments on other satisfactory relationships, but at a kind of distance which makes them pale ghosts of the fiery encounters he fashions for his artist/hero. The resulting effect is that in *Maroussi* and in *Big Sur and the Oranges of Hieronymus Bosch*, everything that takes place is described by what Mailer calls "a different Henry Miller." Miller might counter this by explaining that he is refracting experience through a different facies of his soul or sensibility. It is difficult for a reader who has admired *Cancer* and *Black Spring* not to feel that this facies isn't different but reduced, less interesting. One senses a vital part has been removed and that there has not been a corresponding addition.

In his comprehensive analysis Mathieu claims that there is an elaborate, complex mixture of elements in *Maroussi* that includes all of the things Miller does well, and that, consequently, *Maroussi* is Miller's best work. But while Mathieu argues that *Maroussi* has an inferno to balance its concluding vision of paradise, I believe that those parts of *Maroussi* that in some way resemble an inferno are minor Miller at best, nothing like his great maps of Hell in *Sexus* or *Cancer*. This is at the core of the problem, because it is the lack of a struggle with the demonic that makes *Maroussi* tame and incomplete in many ways. The paradisiacal aspects of the third section are somewhat artificial in that Miller's rapturous praise for Greece is delivered by a man who knows that his boat for America is waiting in the harbor. Were Miller to have stayed in Greece for more than a few months, he probably would have been forced to become involved with life in a foreign land on a day-to-day basis. He would have had to alter his perspective as an observer who can frame each amusing encounter with the philosophical reflection of one who has no real stake in other people's struggles to survive.

Mathieu's assertions, which I will examine shortly, are a little overstated and they may tend to encourage a reader to expect something the book does not actually produce, especially that reader who is familiar with other "chapters" of Miller's work. But instead of judging *Maroussi* in terms of what's missing, as Mailer does, I think that the book is most accurately seen as Miller's first attempt to show how an artist can live successfully as a part of a society which supports him and draws strength from his work. To understand this concept, one might consider

Charles Olson's idea of *polis* which is strikingly similar to what Miller has in mind.

In his *Mayan Letters* to his friend Robert Creeley, Olson wrote about civilization circa 1200 B.C. when the city of Sumer was "ONE CENTER" and its people had such superior force that "all peoples around them were sustained by it, nourished, increased, advanced, that a city was a coherence which, for the first time since the ice, gave man the chance to join knowledge to culture and, with this weapon, shape dignities of economics and value sufficient to make daily life itself a dignity and a sufficiency."[3] One wonders what Miller might have made of Olson's language here and elsewhere, but he would very likely have agreed with Olson on the value of the polis, a crucial word/concept for Olson "because it clusters and proclaims for him the inseparability of such words as politics and citizens."[4] As Sherman Paul points out, Olson's concern with polis "turns on the hero" whose tasks are "the primary ones of civilization (these include the restoration of equality and the protection of the earth . . .)"[5] Modern (post-Dante) man, for Olson, has a "contrary will" to dispersion, to destruction. This man has no place in a polis, although he surely belongs in the city of *Cancer*, and in the Land of Fuck in *Capricorn*. Rather than a city that uses people up, Olson's polis is a place of generation, an organization based on "function, process, change . . . interaction and communication."[6] In a polis, the exchange of energies adds to each person.

Miller saw in Greece a society centered around various artists —most particularly the colossus of the title—and saw these men as both the inspiration and center of knowledge for their culture. He felt that these men knew the natural world in its strength and variety and that they, through their art, enabled the other citizens of their land to see and know it too. However, Miller deliberately located his first "model" for the "China" of his imagination in a relatively primitive land in which he was a visitor, and from several letters he wrote to Durrell, one gets the impression that he might have been able to find some of the qualities he admired in Greece in a variety of settings. On October 25, 1938, he told Durrell that he would have been delighted to spend the winter in the American desert

and that he actually was afraid of the Mediterranean; that its
landscape was degenerate.[7] Then, in September of 1942, he
wrote to Durrell that he was very happy to hear that Durrell
and his family were safe in Palestine and that he wished he
could join them there, or visit some other part of the Mid-East.[8]
In a well-known "Open Letter" which was addressed to his
"Dear friends" in April of 1944, he claimed that he would be
delighted to live in Mexico and stated that he knew that he
would be comfortable in a foreign land; it was only in his native
land that he didn't find good fortune.[9] Perhaps because his
own country was so much the corrupting force of the modern
world, Miller would logically have decided to place his polis in
a country that was conspicuously unlike America. In his reactions to Greece he may well have been spotting things he was
prepared to find, rather than discovering things he had never
dreamed of. Nearing fifty and growing a little tired of combat,
Miller was ready to think about the kind of world he would like
to live in.

Mathieu's analysis does not contradict these ideas but its emphasis is different. Although he is ostensibly writing about
Henry Miller, and concentrating his attention on *The Colossus of
Maroussi*, his title *Orpheus In Brooklyn* indicates that he is going
to draw significant parallels between the myth of Orpheus and
Miller's life and work. His subtitle *Orphism, Rimbaud and Henry
Miller* quite properly emphasizes the fact that his study is almost equally balanced between a discussion of Miller in terms
of Rimbaudian influences and Rimbaud in the light of Miller's
use of his methods. How *Maroussi* is a part of Miller's major
writing is generally given little attention since Mathieu, possibly for purposes of argument, regards most of the remainder
of Miller's writing as simply inferior to *Maroussi*. But as I mentioned, Mathieu's detailed and careful examination of the text
of *Maroussi* is illuminating in terms of Miller's methods of composition and style and the salient features of Mathieu's analysis
are not at variance with the aspects of *Maroussi* which I wish to
discuss. Let me touch on the central points of Mathieu's investigation as a way of entering the world of Katsimbalis, the
colossus of Maroussi.

First, Mathieu feels that *Maroussi,* "an outwardly simple and charming travel book," is actually a collection of *"Symboliste* prose poems" that use many of the illuminist doctrines of Arthur Rimbaud to achieve coherence and unity.[10] Second, the entire book is "an implicit re-enactment of the myth as well as one of the most strikingly original 'Orphic' texts in modern literature!" The book is divided into three sections, according to Mathieu, and "each section represents a different stage in Miller's attempt . . . to resacralize the lot of common humanity and restore the dimension of the 'magical' to everyday life." In Mathieu's view, it is Miller himself who is the magician, while I will argue that Miller is mostly a part of the audience who watches the show. I would agree with Mathieu that at the conclusion, Miller seems ready to "accept himself and his destiny" as a result of his exposure to the "miraculous *topos* of Greece," but Mathieu does not point out how fragile and temporary this "acceptance" is.

Some of Mathieu's ideas seem a bit strained as he works to fit all of the events and excursions of *Maroussi* into his outline. He must resort to calling "rather somber experiences" *luminous* and explain this as a "typically Millerian paradox," and he is too quick to refer to "this descent which is really an ascent," forgetting that sometimes definitions cannot be endlessly stretched to accommodate unruly matters. However, anyone working with a thesis must deal with the untidy edges which tend to squirt off toward the horizon like mercury under a hammer, and Mathieu's arguments are never deceptive or dishonest, merely less convincing than he suggests. I will refer to his book in my discussion of *Maroussi,* particularly when questions of style arise, because Mathieu has given a good deal of thought to Rimbaud's theories and to the characteristics of language in symboliste poetry. But for the most part, it is the colossus himself, the premier artist among an impressive company, who commands one's attention and who Miller must be measured by in terms of spiritual awakening.

Before Miller meets Katsimbalis (like Homer—just one name), *Maroussi* is like any traveler's diary, familiar and predictable; details of invitations, self-congratulatory philosophy, homiletics ("There we were, a Greek and an American, with something in common, but two vastly different beings"), train and boat schedules, and a touristic eagerness to "know" the significance of everything mark the first twenty-five pages. And then Katsimbalis appears. What impresses Miller first and what remains the fundamental strength of the colossus, is his language, the spoken poetry simultaneously invented and delivered, seemingly endless and always interesting. "I didn't have very much to say that first evening," Miller recalls, a rare tribute from a master of words:

> I listened spellbound, enchanted by every phrase he let drop. I saw that he was made for the monologue, like Cendrars, like Moricand the astrologer. I like the monologue even more than the duet, when it is good. It's like watching a man write a book expressly for you: he writes it, reads it aloud, acts it, revises it, savours it, enjoys it, enjoys your enjoyment of it, and then tears it up and throws it to the winds. It's a sublime performance, because while he's going through with it you are God for him—[11]

Right at the beginning, Miller mentions the importance of a receptive audience, what Guy Davenport calls "listening faces."[12] This makes the poet's work part of a reciprocal process and dignifies the audience by providing an essential role for the listener. To qualify for this "audience," more than attention is required. One must be educated to the point that an appreciation of linguistic ingenuity is combined with sufficient cultural experience to share a similar frame of reference with the poet. The key role of the poet–listener relationship in Greek culture becomes more apparent as the book progresses, but here Miller turns to a physical description of the colossus. Because Katsimbalis is often likened to a part of the cosmos, his physical presence is important, and he is seen here as an interesting mixture of human and animal traits:

> . . . he had the general physique of a bull, the tenacity of a vulture, the agility of a leopard, the tenderness of a lamb, and the coyness of a dove. He had a curious overgrown head which fascinated me and which, for some reason, I took to be singularly Athenian. His hands were rather small for his body, and overly

delicate. He was a vital, powerful man, capable of brutal gestures and rough words, yet somehow conveying a sense of warmth which was soft and feminine. (28)

Although Katsimbalis "talked about himself all the time," he was never egoistic, a man with the confidence to realize that he was a natural center of things and that even as a figure of fun, he could not lose his essential dignity. Miller is reminded of an enormous tortoise who has slipped out of its shell, "a creature which was spending itself in a desperate struggle to get back into the shell which it had outgrown. In this struggle he always made himself look grotesque and ridiculous—he did it deliberately. He would laugh at himself, in the tragic way of the buffoon" (29).

Katsimbalis is often seen in a slightly ridiculous posture, but his antics, particularly his overindulgence in nearly everything, contribute to his humanity. He had been damaged during the war, but he has not been slowed down by these irritating ailments: "But despite the bad arm, the dislocated knee, the damaged eye, the disorganized liver, the rheumatic twinges, the arthritic disturbances, the migraine, the dizziness and God knows what, what was left of the catastrophe was alive and flourishing like a smoking dung-heap"(30). In other words, this is a man who has been shaped by some rugged experiences and wounded in the process, but who is more vitally alive than most supposedly "whole" people. And his life is most dynamically expressed by his art, which Miller evokes superbly in one of his best extended descriptions. Only an exceptional critic is able to demonstrate and explicate how or why *art* works, but Miller's writing is equal to the task. His strategy is to begin with powerful metaphoric equivalents for Katsimbalis's oral art, providing tangible equivalents for what is basically an untouchable essence:

> . . . when he described a place he ate into it, like a goat attacking a carpet. If he described a person he ate him alive from head to toe. If it were an event he would devour every detail, like an army of white ants descending upon a forest. He was everywhere at once, in his talk. He attacked from above and below, from the

front, rear and flanks. If he couldn't dispose of a thing at once, for lack of a phrase or an image, he would spike it temporarily and move on, coming back to it later and devouring it piecemeal. (30)

Then, in case anyone could not imagine how *talk* was like eating, Miller goes on to say, "like a juggler, he would toss it in the air and, just when you thought he had forgotten it, that it would fall and break, he would deftly put an arm behind his back and catch it in his palm without even turning his eye" (30). Getting back to food, Miller compares the flavor of his talk to a meal, an appropriate one composed of materials from local soil. Even when talking about Paris, Katsimbalis's speech was flavored with characteristic Attic ingredients, "with thyme, sage, tufa, asphodel, honey, red clay, blue roofs, acanthus trimmings, violet light, hot rocks, dry winds, dust, *rezina,* arthritis and the electrical crackle that plays over the low hills like a swift serpent with a broken spine" (31). And the talk was literally spun out of his body, its motion an integral part of the process:

> With his snake-like tongue which struck like lightning, with fingers moving nervously, as though wandering over an imaginary spinet, with pounding, brutal gestures which somehow never smashed anything but simply raised a din, with all the boom of surf and the roar and sizzle and razzle-dazzle, if you suddenly observed him closely you got the impression that he was sitting there immobile, that only the round falcon's eye was alert, that he was a bird which had been hypnotized, or had hypnotized itself, and that his claws were fastened to the wrist of an invisible giant, a giant like the earth. (31)

The immobile center amidst the flurry of activity suggests a source of power that is awesome and mysterious. Miller chooses to call it magic, and says that Katsimbalis is in touch with this magic in a way that he cannot really explain or control. Only its effect upon the listener (and the poet) gives evidence that it exists at all. What Miller is referring to is the property of art to transform the consciousness of those who are touched by its power: "Many a time, as Katsimbalis talked, I caught that look on the face of a listener which told me that the invisible wires had been connected, that something was being communicated which was over and above language, over and above personality, something magical which we recognize in dream and which makes the face of the sleeper relax and expand with a bloom such as we rarely see in waking life" (31).

After this introduction, Katsimbalis appears at various times throughout the book. Once his ability as an artist has been established, it is his relationship to the culture he dominates that is the central feature of Miller's observations. But in those times when Katsimbalis is not present, *Maroussi* reverts to the manner of its first twenty-five pages as Miller gives a nearly day-by-day account of who he met, what he saw, how he felt and what it all means. While this may be the most directly autobiographical of Miller's major writing, its lack of invention is one of its most conspicuous weaknesses. The best parts of the book consist of those moments when Miller visits some particularly impressive historic landscape, and then his writing seems to catch fire so that one cannot doubt the effect of the location on his sensibility. He is especially good at combining a fairly thorough knowledge of the historic significance of a setting (Knossos, Delphi) with a very sharp eye for its geophysical features. The effect of his descriptions is to transport the reader back through time to the moment when, for instance, the Delphic oracle delivered some portentous proclamation, and some of the excitement of the mythic action is recaptured in Miller's words.

One of the best examples of this is Miller's visit to Phaestos. As is often the case, Miller's preformed opinions about Greece color everything he sees, but these attitudes are generally so exalted that he cannot fail to find something wondrous in each place. Here, he restates his preconceptions as follows:

> Greece is what everybody knows, even *in absentia*, even as a child or as an idiot or as a not-yet-born. It is what you expect the earth to look like given a fair chance. It is the subliminal threshold of innocence. It stands, as it stood from birth, naked and fully revealed. It is not mysterious or impenetrable, not awesome, not defiant, not pretentious. It is made of earth, air, fire and water. It

changes seasonally with harmonious undulating rhythms. It breathes, it beckons, it answers. (153)

In Phaestos, Miller has been told, "the sky is really closer to the air than anywhere else on this globe," and Miller is ready to see terrain which still resembles the land which was once the cradle of a great civilization, one that existed "twenty-five or thirty centuries before the dawn of that blight called Christianity." As the car he has rented for the day surges along, Miller sees "the illusion of vast distances, the reality of great vistas, the sublimity of silence, the revelation of light. On the top of a dizzying crag a tiny shrine in blue and white; in the ravine a cemetery of terrifying boulders. We begin to climb, curving around the edges of precipitous drops; across the gulch the earth bulges up like the knees of a giant covered with corduroy" (157). This is an ascent toward the domain of the gods and their power becomes increasingly evident as the road winds up in the mountains:

> We climb up beyond the cultivated lands, twisting back and forth like a snake, rising to the heights of contemplation, to the abode of the sage, the eagle, the storm cloud. Huge, frenzied pillars of stone, scarred by wind and lightning, grayed to the color of fright, trembling, top-heavy, balanced like macrocosmic fiends, abut the road. The earth grows wan and weird, defertilized, dehumanized, neither brown nor gray nor beige nor taupe nor ecru, the no color of death reflecting light, sponging up light with its hard, parched shag and shooting it back at us in blinding, rock-flaked splinters that bore into the tenderest tissues of the brain and set it whimpering like a maniac. (157-58)

Miller feels that this is a landscape beyond the range of man's deprivations, a place where primal forces clash, where life itself may have begun. It is a landscape fit for revelation, and Miller is ready for anything. "This is where I begin to exult," he says, further describing his intense awareness of himself and his surroundings by declaring that "In Greece one has the desire to bathe in the sky. You want to rid yourself of your clothes, taking a running leap and vault into the blue. You want to float in the air like an angel or lie in the grass rigid and enjoy the cataleptic trance. Stone and sky, they marry here. It is the perpetual dawn of man's awakening" (159).

One is reminded of Dylan Thomas or of D. H. Lawrence. Then Miller reaches Phaestos and walks around the ancient ruins. The archaeological details in the leveled palace don't interest him very much, but the land is unforgettable:

> Below me, stretching away like an infinite magic carpet, lay the plain of Messara, girdled by a majestic chain of mountain ranges. From this sublime, serene height it has all the appearance of the Garden of Eden. At the very gates of Paradise the descendants of Zeus halted here on their way to eternity to cast a last look earthward and saw with the eyes of innocents that the earth is indeed what they had always dreamed it to be: a place of beauty and joy and peace. (162)

And then, the revelation itself, not exactly profound but still meaningful, if for no other reason than the setting in which it occurs and the obvious sincerity of Miller's feelings: "In his heart man is angelic; in his heart man is united with the whole world. Phaestos contains all the elements of the heart; it is feminine through and through. Everything that man has achieved would be lost were it not for this final stage of contrition which is here incarnated in the abode of the heavenly queens" (162). But this is the high point, the incandescent moment, and I don't think that one can really argue that it is absolutely first rate literature. Neither the style nor the structure are that impressive, and while this is certainly good, interesting writing, it is not great poetry. The quality of sincerity is important but it is certainly not a substitute for the things which are missing. Miller tries to present himself (and his mind) as so exceptional that whatever he sees and says acquires a special significance of its own. The narrative consciousness which he develops for the artist/hero begins to actually achieve this effect, but the corporeal Henry Miller whose thoughts we follow in *Maroussi* is not as interesting as his creation, at least not in print, not in this book.

This is primarily why Katsimbalis is so important in *Maroussi*. He *is* the artist/hero and how he lives does matter. Miller and Katsimbalis are caught by a sea storm but even for frightened terrainers, the whole experience is exhilarating, sheer bravado overcoming anxiety, especially for Katsimbalis who is a "highlander and not an islander" (63). Katsimbalis is seen alone at night in a café, so natural and unaffected that Miller, in a lovely and uncharacteristic aside, addresses the reader directly. *"Can you see him?"* he asks, "I see him very clearly. It's warm now in Athens and he's had a grand night of it with his cronies. The last one he said good-night to is already home and writing it all down in his diary" (74). This self-exposed but unselfconscious moment in which Miller's method of composition is alluded to seems to resonate back and forth across time and space. It is an example of one human being leaving an indelible impression upon another one.

When they visit the tomb of Clytemnestra, they peer down with lighted matches, and Miller is afraid to descend. Katsimbalis, who has been there before, "was for crawling down on all fours, on his belly if needs be" (91). He is as excited by the mythic power of the place as the first time he saw it, possibly more so, and he wants Miller to feel everything too. "We don't want to miss this," Katsimbalis pleads. The descent into the earth leads Miller to a reflection about land. "What is vital here is land, just land. I roll it over and over on my tongue—land, land, land. Why yes, *land*, that's it—I had almost forgotten it meant such a simple, eternal thing" (96). Then, in a shift from the abstract to the specific, Miller shows that the sensitive artist is also a man of property, although his holdings in no way contaminate him. As Miller describes his attitude it seems charmingly aristocratic. He is able to avoid the petty tyranny of poverty but he is uncorrupted by his wealth. Perhaps it is just another gift like his ability to talk, something he can share with his friends: "Katsimbalis had received an urgent call to return to Athens owing to the unexpected discovery of a piece of land which his attorneys had overlooked. The news didn't seem to thrill him. On the contrary he was depressed: more property meant more taxes, more debts—and more headaches" (101). And his friends are everywhere. As Miller points out, "Wherever we went we were sure to be joined by his numerous friends." The reason he is at the center of everything is not just his marvelous talk, but his instinct for the gesture of absolute rightness which makes an event memorable. At the temple of Delphi, as "we speculated at length on the exact position of the city itself which is yet undiscovered," Katsimbalis, with unstrained theatricality:

> . . . strode to the center of the bowl and holding his arms aloft delivered the closing lines of the last oracle. It was an impressive moment, to say the least. For a second, so it seemed, the curtain had been lifted on a world which had never really perished but which had rolled away like a cloud and was preserving itself intact, inviolate, until the day when, restored to his senses, man would summon it back to life again. (194)

Just as Katsimbalis, a man with all his senses, has summoned it. When they climb to the great stadium, Katsimbalis becomes an incarnation of the athletes of legend and again stamps the occasion with his presence as he makes the appropriate gesture: "After wandering about amidst the broken columns we ascended the tortuous path to the stadium on high. Katsimbalis took off his overcoat and with giant strides measured it from end to end" (195).

The scene at the temple of Delphi is followed by a scene with a more modern version of an oracle. One morning Katsimbalis is waiting for Miller with "a mysterious smile on his face." It is just a few days before Miller must return to the United States and Katsimbalis, with his nice sense of another person's needs, has arranged a fitting "present" for Miller. He proposes that they visit an Armenian soothsayer, and Miller "consented with alacrity, never having been to a soothsayer in my life" (198). The words of the seer turn out to be the epitome of various impulses Miller had been feeling, and his account of Miller's past provides strong support for Miller's determination to struggle onward as a writer:

> He began by telling me that I was approaching a new and most important phase of my life, that up to the present I had been wandering in circles, that I had created many enemies (by what I had written) and caused much harm and suffering to others. He said that I had led not only a dual life (I believe he used the word schizophrenic) but a multiple life and that nobody really understood me, not even my closest friends. (202)

This is obviously the way that the artist/hero of *Cancer* sees himself, and since *Maroussi* is in many ways a book of taking stock, a pause in the author's progress to weigh the evidence that has accumulated before continuing, Miller has found an interesting way to justify the sum of his previous actions. The most important part of the seer's words, however, consist of his reading of the future. Miller's hopes for the rest of his career are encapsulated in the prophecy he is given: "before dying I would bring great joy to the world, to everybody in the world, he emphasized, and my greatest enemy would bow down before me and beg my forgiveness. He said that I would enjoy before my death the greatest honors, the greatest rewards which man can confer upon man . . . . That on my last visit to the Orient I would never return, neither would I die, but vanish in the light" (203).

Aside from the wish for public acceptance, critical acclaim and a place in the pantheon among the artists he admires, Miller here is expressing a philosophical stance peculiarly connected to his vision of Greece. As has been the case with other visitors from Northern countries, Miller has been overwhelmed by the quality of the light, and his concept of Greek civilization has evolved out of the contrast between the dark blight of modern, urban cityscapes and the dazzling light of the primal Attic countryside. Miller's search for "China" has been transmuted in this book into a desire to live somewhere as a kind of spiritual embodiment of all that is valuable in Greece, and it is the *light* itself that symbolizes this quest.

Throughout the book, Miller has marveled at this light, speaking of it as a physical force in a poetic version of Einstein's theories: "Here the light penetrates directly to the soul, opens the doors and windows of the heart, makes one naked, exposed, isolated in a metaphysical bliss which makes everything clear without being known" (45). At Hydra, he recognizes a religious dimension: "The light is no longer solar or lunar; it is the starry light of the planet to which man has given life. The earth is alive to its innermost depths; at the center it is a sun in the form of a man crucified. The sun bleeds on its cross in the hidden depths. The sun is man struggling to emerge towards another light. From light to light, from calvary to calvary. The earth song . . ." (57). And to a Greek man married to a wealthy Frenchwoman: " 'Yes,' " I said, " 'I'm crazy enough to believe that the happiest man on earth is the man with the fewest needs. And I also believe that if you have light, such as you have here, all ugliness is obliterated. Since I've come to your country I know that light is holy: Greece is a holy land to me' " (133).

Mathieu, in comparing Miller to Rimbaud, says that "Miller's 'light' leads via the eyes to inner awakening. This, after all, is the crucial meaning of *illumination*. The 'light' not only radiates a greater glory *without* but leads to 'life more abundant' within."[13] The soothsayer's prediction that Miller will "vanish in the light" suggests that the ultimate goal of Miller's life (and by implication, his art) is to *see clearly*, to absorb the light from without and to radiate the light from within; to gain strength from the energy/light of the cosmos, and to transmit that strength to others through the illuminations of one's art. Katsimbalis is proof that it can be done. As Mathieu says, speaking about *Maroussi* as a whole, "we see with our own eyes the genesis of a paradise which is inhabitable by anyone because it has been adequately visualized by *some*one."[14] Perhaps this slightly simplifies the situation, especially since Miller himself "visualizes" this paradise from a slight remove, but I think that Katsimbalis is living the "life more abundant" and that he is very much a part of the land of light itself. Just before the book ends, Miller and Katsimbalis are walking through the streets of Athens the night before Miller's departure:

> Walking with him through the streets of Amaroussion I had the feeling that I was walking the earth in a totally new way. The earth became more intimate, more alive, more promising. He spoke frequently of the past, it is true, not as something dead and forgotten however, but rather as something which we carry within us, something which fructifies the present and makes the future inviting. . . .
>
> How can I ever forget that last impression he made upon me when we said farewell at the bus station in the heart of Athens?

There are men who are so full, so rich, who give themselves so completely that each time you take leave of them you feel that it is absolutely of no consequence whether the parting is for a day or forever. They come to you brimming over and they fill you to overflowing. They ask nothing of you except that you participate in their superabundant joy of living. They never inquire which side of the fence you are on because the world they inhabit has no fences. They make themselves invulnerable by habitually exposing themselves to every danger. They grow more heroic in the measure that they reveal their weaknesses. (238)

This effusive summary of the components of Katsimbalis's greatness leads directly to the magnificent conclusion of the book, a prose poem which combines vividness of imagery, powerful and tightly controlled rhythms, invention and imagination in the service of a central idea, and an impressive structure built measure by measure through the poem. Mathieu rightly identifies this passage as one of Miller's finest, calling it "the quintessential *voyant* moment in his entire *oeuvre.*"[15] It is a passage worthy of Whitman, Miller's true mentor in the poetic realm.

The poem follows Miller's last recollection of Katsimbalis, a lingering vision of the colossus "bending over to pick a flower from the bare soil of Attica." Miller acknowledges that this is an ordinary gesture, but that is probably why he remembers it. "During the time I knew him Katsimbalis' life was relatively quiet and unadventurous," Miller tells us, "But the most trivial incident, if it happened to Katsimbalis, had a way of blossoming into a great event" (240). And in Miller's memory, the image of Katsimbalis picking the flower freezes at the moment of touch, and Miller has a revelation of the man connected through the "blossoming" figure of life and beauty to all that is Greece. "When I think of Katsimbalis bending over to pick a flower from the bare soil of Attica the whole Greek world, past, present and future, rises before me. I see again the soft, low mounds in which the illustrious dead were hidden away"; and the poem continues on, as I have quoted it on page 66, to Miller's final declaration: "From that day forth my life was dedicated to the recovery of the divinity of man. Peace to all men, I say, and life more abundant!"(241). If it were only to be so!

Although Miller undoubtedly felt this way on his last day in Greece, the *Exochorda*, bound for America in January, 1940, had barely sailed out of the harbor when he wrote to Anaîs Nin: "And now on the boat, in the midst of the American scene, I feel as though I am living with people who are not yet born, with monsters who escaped from the womb before their time. I am no longer in communication with anything. I am in a world of broken eggshells. . . . Dimly I seem to remember that but a short time ago I was alive, alive in full sunlight."[16]

As he returned to America Miller was already beginning to feel again like the artist/hero who landed in Paris in 1930, but he never forgot what he saw in Greece. *Maroussi* was written in the summer of 1940 when Miller no longer wished "Peace to all men," but his evocation of his Attic experiences remained true to the spirit of the poem which ends the book. The impression that Greece and George C. Katsimbalis made on him became part of his memory to guide him in his life and his art, just as his youth in Brooklyn lived on in his mind and heart. The vision of the land of light became a permanent part of Miller's psyche, because, as he wrote to Nin: "Greece is fading out rapidly, dying right before my eyes. And the last thing to disappear is the light, the light over the hills, that light which I never saw before, which I could not possibly imagine if I had not seen it with my own eyes. The incredible light of Attica!"[17]

Miller traveled around the United States for the next four years, and expressed his displeasure with life in America through the collection of essays, *The Air-Conditioned Nightmare* (1945). Although that volume is a product of a year-long trip Miller took with his friend the artist Abraham Rattner from October 1940 to October 1941, it is a book written by someone who is distinctly separate from his environment. His mind may still be in Greece, because Miller seems like a kind of European visitor, often looking with disdain at the various vulgarities of popular culture and other facets of America. At other times, he sounds like a sententious writer of editorials for a small-town paper putting on airs, or as Mailer says it, "he is full of virtue and dull with bile" because "his authoritative arrogance never deserts him, only his style."[18] Miller is clearly quite ill at ease with his homeland, but this is an indication of his uncertainty about his life and his work as well. The nomadic nature of his existence in the early 1940s paralleled his wandering in his writing, as he had several projects going simultaneously, none really moving under a clear sense of control. Then, in 1944, Miller found a cabin on Partington Ridge in Big Sur, California, that belonged to a man named Keith Evans, once the mayor of the town of Carmel. Evans pretty much gave the house to Miller rent free, and Miller settled into what he calls "my first real home in America." He had just gotten married again and was ready to become a part of his country once more. *Big Sur and the Oranges of Hieronymus Bosch* is an account of the way he lived for the next twelve years.

Miller was nearly 65 when *Big Sur* was published. In *Big Sur* the artist/hero of *Cancer*, after a trip back in time in *Black Spring* and to another land in *The Colossus of Maroussi*, emerges from the underground into the California sun and tries to combine his vision of an ideal setting with his own sense of what he needed to do with his life and his work. *Big Sur*, though, is not a triumphant account of the establishment of a Pacific Paradise because Miller is not Katsimbalis, America is certainly not Greece, and the materials of Miller's best work are not drawn, unfortunately, from the serenity of "pure being" which he praises as the goal of his life here. Instead, the book is a sometimes painfully honest and often mundane report of a continuing struggle to reconcile the actual facts of existence with an occasionally vague and soft-headed sense of the way things should be. In the course of the narrative, the adjustments that Miller makes to circumstances and the accommodations that he is forced to accept in himself produce what Mailer calls a "wise record" which shows Miller "ingathering the scattered, strewn and dissipated fragments of a lost vision."[19] On the other hand, Mailer adds that this "record" must be judged in terms of just "how much each piece of Miller's philosophy has cost the most unregenerate surrealist of them all." The way in which Miller's artist/hero, now older and prepared to make a stand, retains his vitality and tests its durability without the protection of his old shield of rage and scorn, is the subject of the book.

Big Sur is written primarily from the perspective in 1956 of the artist looking back over the preceding dozen years. It retains the excitement that Miller felt when he made an initial discovery about the land and life on it during that time, but it does not have any real suspense to it, except for the Conrad Moricand section. It takes the form of a person musing over events, data, people and points in the landscape, and its attitude is that of a person balancing and weighing the evidence. This gives everything a sense of distance, and makes Miller once again essentially an observer, although in the last section with Moricand, he is forced to act directly. The epigraphs that open the book initiate this primarily reflective mood. There is a comment from Thoreau about the necessity of living "simply and wisely"—a rather ironic choice since it turns out to be difficult to live a simple life. There is a statement from Picasso to the effect that "I put in my pictures everything I like," an echo of the artist/hero's familiar defiance and a reassertion of one of the fundamental precepts of the credo that rules Miller's best work. Then, there is an interesting comment by the Japanese artist Hokusai from *The Art-Crazy Old Man* that "really nothing I did before the age of seventy was of any value at all," in which Miller acknowledges by implication the idea that life must be considered under the scrutiny of art forever![20]

Much of the central section of *Big Sur* is rambling and repetitive as Miller reproduces large chunks of what is probably his diary. The material itself—people he meets, day-by-day necessities, domestic problems with a growing family—is not uninteresting, but it lacks the cutting and shaping and arranging that would give it emphasis or direction. For one who is interested in Henry Miller, it makes fairly entertaining and enjoyable reading, like visiting an old friend, but it doesn't have the compelling pressures of Miller's best writing. The first and last parts of the book, though, have a tone and style which are distinct. The first fifty pages contain most of what Miller has to say about the progress of his journey. The two hundred odd pages that follow are mostly illustrative material that, in many instances, dissipates the energy of Miller's originally spare and condensed prose rather than adding to it. The last section, the one hundred pages called "Paradise Lost," are Miller's final rejection of Europe and his first real acceptance of himself as *he is*.

The first part of the book, including the Preface, sections called "Chronological" and "Topographical" and "In the Beginning," and a section which Miller designates "Part 1: The Oranges of the Millennium," is Miller's declaration of who he is circa 1956. This part has the confidence of *Cancer* without its sense of outrage, and Miller has developed a lean, terse voice to present the "facts" as he sees them. The Preface and the "Chronological" section move toward this voice from a deceptively calm, almost perfunctory series of pronouncements about books Miller has written. Following the epigraphs, the Preface begins with some data on which of Miller's books are in print, and which have been translated into what languages, but then, Miller mentions that "Sexus is at present forbidden to be published—in any language!—in France"(ix), and that "In Japan the Japanese version of this work has been suppressed but not the English, at least not yet." With a combination of resignation and amusement, Miller advises: "As to how and where to get the banned books, the simplest way would be to make a raid on the customs house in any of our ports of entry" (x).

Miller has seen so much ludicrous posturing about his work that he can take in stride most of the gas and bilge spewed out by protectors of public morality, and the publication of everything he wrote in American editions is only five years in the future. The syntactically curious title "Chronological" heads the next brief section, and most of the material there is just a matter of keeping the record straight. There are references to the fact that he "remarried in Denver, and became the father of a daughter, Valentine"; that Conrad Moricand arrived toward the end of 1947 "to last only three months"; and then another almost incidental piece of information mentioning that "Except for a pleasure trip to Europe in 1953, *when I married again,* I have been living on the Ridge ever since February 1947" (2). [my italics] Just how much of this seemingly important material will be covered in the body of the book remains to be seen, and the choices Miller makes about what to exclude eventually reveal a good deal about his sense of what matters.

The "Topographical" section is next, and here Miller begins to develop the setting, so vital a part of this book that one might without exaggeration call the "topography" one of the major "characters." As Charles Olson says in "Letter 27 *(withheld)* of *The Maximus Poems*, "I come back to the geography of it," and for Miller, the geophysical features of the land are a constant factor in his life and work, literally shaping and bending his mind into a new configuration. Just as the Greek landscape seemed crucial in molding what Miller saw as the Greek "character," the rugged land of Big Sur gave Miller an opportunity for the first time to actually experiment with his theories of the redemptive qualities of the natural world; if his megalopolitan sensibility could be enhanced by this rustic near wilderness, who knows what changes might be wrought for the citizens of America's nightmare cities? The topology begins as history, Miller mentioning early visitors to Big Sur (Robinson Jeffers, Jack London), pioneers in literature and explorers of an uncharted land. As Miller recounts the early history of the area, it becomes apparent that he is a pioneer too, that the land rush had not yet begun in 1945. But people would soon be flocking to Big Sur, and some of Miller's references have a strange prophetic note to them. "The only human beings who had been here before were the Esselen Indians," he notes, and suddenly the origin of the *Esalen Institute* grows clearer in one's mind. He explains that the Little Sur River begins as Malpaso Creek, and the name of Clint Eastwood's film company is explained as well. Then, history blends into geology, and finally, the "story" of Miller's life in Big Sur is ready to start. The section called "In the Beginning" is the real beginning of his voice as sage, the man who has been there. The voice is subdued, relaxed but also firm and steady. The frenzy is gone, but energy still pulses through it. The rhythms are longer now, and the cadences less jagged, more the voice of a distance runner than a sprinter. There is something of Lawrence's last days in New Mexico, but without the bitterness, in this voice:

Who lived here first? Troglodytes perhaps. The Indian came late. Very late.

Though young, geologically speaking, the land has a hoary look. From the ocean depths there issued strange formations, contours unique and seductive. As if the Titans of the deep had labored for aeons to shape and mold the earth. Even millennia ago the great land birds were startled by the abrupt aspect of these risen shapes.

There are no ruins or relics to speak of. No history worth recounting. What was not speaks more eloquently than what was.

Here the redwood made its last stand. (7)

Unfortunately, this very promising beginning winds downs quickly into casual chatter and homily, with only an occasional gathering of strength when the sage speaks again. The "Oranges of the Millennium" illustrates the problems Miller had in becoming the colossus of the California coast. In a parody of the reverence that the artists of Greece had for each other, Miller was sought out by a wonderfully bizarre collection of would-be "artists" most of whom never wrote or painted anything—"I came to join the cult of sex and anarchy," one of them says to Miller. The anecdotes that occur one after another for the next two hundred pages are often very funny, but once Miller gets bogged down selling his paintings to tourists, rescuing helpless vagabonds, advising serious but blocked writers and so on, he can rarely rise above this level of discourse to say anything particularly memorable or penetrating. There are some ringing mottos—"Artists never thrive in colonies. Ants do"—and some perceptive comments on old themes: "One's destination is never a place but rather a new way of looking at things"; but Miller doesn't develop or integrate his ideas into an evolving context. And too often, he gets cute and self-protective, coyly offering comments like, "my quaint biographical romances." Perhaps this is meant to be ironic, but its effect is to make Miller seem fussy and self-consciously decorous.

However, the loss of power is partially compensated for by the rather charming and appealingly open picture that Miller has made of his life in *Big Sur*. He is successful as a genial ironist, particularly in passages like the one in which he describes an autograph session with various Washington officials when he discovers that all of his banned books have found their way into the personal libraries of government agents (160–162). His book talk and his references, mostly in footnotes, to a wide variety of obscure books, offers an indication of his very eclectic tastes. Miller may have consciously tried to present himself as a good-humored, generally easy-going and quite patient person with a couple of kids to raise as a challenge to the image most people had of him. By the time one reaches the end of his "Peace and Solitude: a Potpourri" to come upon a table of contents for the preceding fifteen essays, one begins to realize that Miller's "Paradise" in Big Sur was generally a rather middle-class community in an exotic setting, and while Miller often seemed about to run out of money, he had what he needed, as he assures the reader on several occasions. "I have almost grown to rely on various miracles," Miller says when Jean Wharton gives him her house to live in (120–130). *Big Sur*, in its central section, is an informative account of one variant of the literary life, and it is also an interesting record of the devil-may-care artist/hero's transmutation into a family man who can make the best of most situations. Of course, the younger version of this artist managed to survive pretty well too, but in Paris he was responsible only for himself.

Aside from some similarities in landscape ("The light here is almost as electric, the hills almost as bare, the community almost as autonomous as in ancient Greece" [145]), Big Sur did not really resemble the "paradise" Miller glimpsed in Greece, but the substitutions he made are an example of the "philosophy" Mailer mentions. Miller's paradise includes:

1. Friends (see especially 264);
2. Fellow artists defined by their attitude more than by their ability;
3. The natural world;
4. Writing, including correspondence.

Miller reluctantly accepts as inevitable:

1. Visitors, acolytes, groupies, other guests;
2. Clogged toilets and other mechanical failures;
3. Demanding children;
4. Animals (mostly domestic);

5. Gifts arriving constantly;
6. Uninvited correspondence ("picture postcards from the ass-
   holes of creation").

Since Miller is writing the book from the end first, he never
really says what he expected to find, but when a woman who
showed up to purchase one of his watercolors said, "I never
dreamed that Big Sur was like this!" Miller replied under his
breath, "Nor did I!" (45). While Miller clearly fancies himself a
true brother of Katsimbalis when it comes to talk, the great
energy and invention of his voice has lapsed into chatter in *Big
Sur* (*"Where was I?* Oh yes, Jean Wharton and the little house on
Partington Ridge. . . ." [130]), and while this may have worked
wonderfully when he first told these stories to visitors on the
ridge, in print there is almost nothing of the spellbinding magic
of Katsimbalis. It is as if Miller has sacrificed power for congen-
iality, and not too reluctantly forsworn the role of seer for that
of clown. If there is anything sad about this it is that a clown
can be the greatest of seers, but Miller hasn't taken that route.
Still, as Leslie Fiedler notes in calling Miller "a drop-out," "that
is very much the American vs. the European way," and Big Sur
is a distinctly American, pragmatic paradise.

Miller, even in his sixties, had a much too highly developed
sense of his work to be unaware of what he was doing. There
are two elements absent from *Big Sur* which have been quite
consciously excluded. One, of course, is his relationship with
women. At the end of the "Potpourri" it has become apparent
that his very casual references to his two marriages during this
period are not going to be developed at all. His third wife,
Janina Lepska, left with his two children after several years of
war, and Miller refers to his pain at the conclusion of a description of his attempt (pp. 172–190) to raise his children with the
help of a writer named Walker Winslow: "I went back to the
bathroom, as I had the morning they left, and I wept like a
madman. I wept and sobbed and screamed and cursed. I carried on like that until there wasn't another drop of anguish left
in me. Until I was like a crumpled, empty sack" (191).

He had the writing of *Nexus* in front of him and he may have
decided that he would save all of his passionate thought about

the women in his life for that book. Or he may not have been able to write about a paradise of sorts and include a woman in that setting. I will consider this question further in the next chapter, but here it is sufficient to note that the absence of the women in Miller's life from *Big Sur* leaves a pretty big gap through which a good deal of the energy that might have gone into the book probably escaped. Without the presence of a woman who mattered to him, there is not that much in Big Sur that can really reach Miller or that has the possibility of changing him by making him see himself clearly, especially when he would rather turn and look at all the amusing characters in the vicinity. There is, however, one other element which is missing from *Big Sur* until the last section (the one called "Paradise Lost"), and this is the element of menace—a threat to Miller's nicely balanced universe.

Although Miller never really examined anything that might be called evil, his auto-novella, *A Devil in Paradise*, published in 1956 and included as the last section of *Big Sur*, begins to move into that area. It is about the astrologer Conrad Moricand, an old acquaintance courtesy of Anaïs Nin, whom Miller met in 1936 in Paris. From the opening paragraph of "Paradise Lost," a subtle change in tone indicates that Miller is now in a world in which something sinister may happen. Moricand, like many citizens of Europe, has come on hard times after the war, and Miller decides that the only way to keep Moricand alive is to invite him to the United States. First, Miller introduces the man by recalling some of their conversations in Paris, and immediately one can see that Moricand is almost the antithesis of Miller in outlook and even in ethics. He is almost incapable of supporting himself at all, and at the same time, he is vain, supercilious and haughty. Miller finds his astrological obsession fascinating— indeed, he gives astrology some credence at times himself—but Moricand is the ultimate determinist, both mystical and coldly rational according to his own self-centered system of logic. In Paris, where Miller is alone and unencumbered, Moricand is just another fascinating creature in an extraordinary menagerie. In the United States, he is so out of place that his misery moves him to plan diabolical schemes to drag down everyone near him, including his "friend" and host whom he now blames for his misfortunes. It is interesting that only disaster moves Moricand to action, because in Europe he seemed like a benign curiosity amidst astrological embellishments and paraphernalia, remarking "I say nothing against anything. I observe. I analyze. I calculate. I distillate. Wisdom is becoming, but knowledge is the certainty of certitude" (293). For Miller, this type of calculated inscrutability is another detail for delight, but when he has to live with it, his humor turns to disgust and then to rage.

Moricand must have everything absolutely his way. He is like a piece of stone that has sunk into the earth and cannot be moved. He represents the worst side of European tradition, the useless scholasticism of a burned-out world. In disbelief, Miller asks: "Ah, Iamblichus, Porphyry, Erasmus, Duns Scotus, where are we? What elixir are we drinking? What wisdom are we sucking? Define the alphabet, O wise ones! Measure the itch! Flog insanity to death, if you can!" (342). And Moricand has retreated from the physical world. He is a self-described "spiritual" man who is repelled by any contact with other human beings that isn't coldly mental. In a letter before he leaves for America, Moricand tells Miller he has given his landlady "a lay" to avoid paying the rent; "of course he couched it in more elegant terms" (298). It is a very fitting irony that when Moricand is disabled in Big Sur, his malady is a kind of skin disease that makes him constantly aware of his body.

When Moricand arrives, Miller learns that he cannot exist without stationery of a certain size, without Yardley talcum powder, without special foods, without gauloises bleues. "I sensed the leech Anaïs had tried to get rid of. I saw the spoiled child, the man who had never done an honest stroke of work in his life" (301). But Miller tries to accommodate his guest. "I proceeded to give myself what the French call an *examen de conscience*. I tried to reverse the picture, put myself in his boots" (304). Miller decides that had his "name been Moricand," he would have killed himself years ago, and resolves to do what he can to help. His resolve is tested immediately, though, because Moricand's voice is "comparable in effect to the sound of a gong reverberating in the deathlike silence of a vast desert" (306), and to be in his company is like living with a version of melancholy incarnate:

One could see the bird of ill omen perched on his left shoulder. One could feel the moonlight altering his blood, sensitizing his retina, dyeing his skin with the pallor of the prisoner, the drug addict, the dweller on forbidden planets. Knowing him, one might even visualize those delicate antennae of which he was altogether too proud and on which he placed a reliance which overtaxed his intuitive muscles, so to speak. I might go further—why not?—and say that, looking deep into his sorrowful eyes, somber, simian eyes, I could see skull within skull, an endless, cavernous Golgotha illumined by the dry, cold, murderous light of a universe beyond the imaginative bounds of even the hardiest scientific dreamer. (307)

And yet, Miller is not entirely put off by Moricand's spectral presence. He doesn't really turn against him until he discovers aspects of Moricand's personality that he finds not just repulsive but actively evil.

Moricand tries to buy codeine to use as a sleeping draught and when Miller's doctors refuse to write a prescription, he condemns America as a juvenile place ("What a country! What a country!") and writes to a Swiss pharmacist for the drug. Miller is furious, but admits he would have done the same thing were he similarly desperate. This is the first in a series of incidents in which Moricand condemns America for its naive ways, thus engendering a counteraction in Miller who reaches out in a conspicuous embrace of various aspects of American popular culture. When Moricand is annoyed by the attention Miller gives to his daughter Val ("He seemed to have no use for children; they annoyed him, unless they were extremely well behaved. As with most people who stress behavior, being well behaved meant keeping out of sight and reach. He was utterly at a loss to understand my preoccupation with the child, the daily walks we took. . . .") (312), Miller senses something particularly disturbing about Moricand's attitude, partially because throughout *Big Sur*, he has compared Partington Ridge with his "first 'Paradise' . . . there in the old neighborhood" in Brooklyn. To see his own children stare with wonder at the phenomena of Big Sur deeply moves Miller, and he reports his reaction to their discoveries with an unusual fervor:

In my mind I am with them as they return from some distant
shore to gaze upon the old homestead. My eyes are moist with
tears as I watch them moving tenderly and reverently amid a
swarm of golden memories. . . . lucky the father who is merely a
writer, who can drop his work and return to childhood at will!
Lucky the father who is pestered from morn till sundown by two
healthy, insatiable youngsters! Lucky the father who learns to see
again through the eyes of his children, even though he become
the biggest fool there ever was! (21–22)

Moricand's distress with children (he can't be bothered to teach
Val French) marks him as a man who will not "learn to see
again" in any new way, and to separate himself from this attitude, Miller teaches Val to sing her first song, "Yankee Doodle," and asserts proudly, "Yankee Doodle dandy and the
Devil take the hindmost!" (313). The "Devil" pretends not to
notice, but he tells Miller, "She ought to be disciplined," and
that "In Europe the child knows its place" (314). Miller assumes
that this is mostly just a difference in a philosophy of child
rearing, and since he has been having somewhat similar arguments with his wife, he doesn't worry particularly about the
dispute.

Other incidents contribute to Miller's displeasure, but most
of them are more sad than sinister. Moricand can't keep an
Aladdin lamp going because his room is so stuffy there's insuf-
ficient oxygen; he engages Miller in debates regarding theories
of epistemology, and when he claims that man has no choice in
most matters, Miller answers his deterministic arguments by
saying:

> . . . what am I but an American to the core, an American who
> exposes his Americanism like a sore. Like it or not, I am a product
> of this land of plenty, a believer in superabundance, a believer in
> miracles. . . . What you believe I might have learned through a
> deeper knowledge of astrology I learned through experience of
> life. I made all the mistakes that it is possible for a man to make—
> and I paid the penalty. I am that much richer, that much wiser,
> that much happier, if I may say so, than if I had found through
> study or through discipline how to avoid the snares and pitfalls in
> my path. . . . (319)

Miller's friend Gilbert Neiman visits, and Miller expects them to get along well since they have so many interests in common, but Gilbert sees Moricand clearly and advises Miller "Push him over a cliff" (330). This especially concerns Miller since he feels that Neiman is "such a kind, gentle, considerate soul" and "had been through such hell himself," but it is just another omen that Miller decides to disregard.

Then, one final incident reveals Moricand as the truly diabolical, totally self-centered person he is. Earlier, Moricand had tried to sell some erotic drawings to one of Miller's wealthier friends. Miller gets his first look at the drawings, and he is taken aback. Clearly playing on his own reputation as an erotic artist, Miller says:

> It was my first view of his work. I must confess the drawings left a bad taste in my mouth. They were perverse, sadistic, sacrilegious. Children being raped by lubricious monsters, virgins practicing all manner of illicit intercourse, nuns defiling themselves with sacred objects. . . . flagellations, medieval tortures, dismemberments, coprophagic orgies, and so forth. All done with a delicate, sensitive hand, which only magnified the disgusting element of the subject matter. (337)

Perhaps Miller doth protest a bit too much, but even his sophisticated friend is nonplussed. And significantly, the catalog of erotic dementia begins with "children being raped by lubricious monsters," an especially alarming detail for Miller in terms of his own attachment and concern for his children. Then, some time later, Moricand is enraged as Val snatches a piece of bread lying next to Moricand. As Miller tells us: "It was not the gesture of annoyance so much as the look in his eyes which startled me. It was a look full of hatred, the look of a man so beside himself that he might even commit murder. I never forgot it and I never forgave it" (361). An hour or two later, after Val has been put to bed. Moricand begins to tell a story ("the telling of it seemed to take up the entire evening") that involves a girl of eight or nine and her mother. The story is detailed and develops through a veil of ominous implications, but its conclusion is, for Miller, final and full revelation of Moricand's icy egotism,

his total absorption in the satisfaction of his own needs regard-
less of the cost for any other person. As the story builds to a
crescendo, Moricand "pauses in his narration":

> His eyes were positively dancing. I knew he was waiting for me to
> say "Then what?" I struggled with myself not to reveal my true
> feelings. The words he was waiting for got stuck in my throat. All
> I could think of was the little girl sitting on the edge of the bed,
> half-undressed probably, and nibbling at a piece of pastry. *"Reste-
> là, p'tite, je reviens toute de suite,"* the woman had probably said as
> she closed the door behind her.
>
> Finally, after what seemed like an eternity, I heard myself say-
> ing to him: *"Eh bien,* what then?"
>
> "What then?" he exclaimed, his eyes aflame with a ghoulish
> glee. *"Je l'ai eue,* that's what!"
>
> As he uttered these words I felt my hair stand on end. It was no
> longer Moricand I was facing but Satan himself. (363)

Miller, who has been suffering through a stormy, debilitating
relationship with his wife for what he feels is his own child's
sake, is horrified. Moricand has demonstrated that he is capable of doing anything he can get away with, that "he might
even commit murder." For all of his wild antics, Miller has never acted with anything even approaching this kind of coldness.
In his descriptions of life in Paris, his removal from what he is
watching is designed to withhold judgment. Here, his judgment is explicit. At the conclusion of *Big Sur*, Miller, if not quite
a sage, is no longer the narcissistic artist/hero of *Cancer* either.
He has enough confidence in himself now to risk the further
development of his art for the sake of the people he loves. Of
course, his major work is almost completed, but Miller is still
ready to make a sacrifice contingent upon a principle he believes in. As Miller learned later, Moricand died in Europe almost seven years after he left Big Sur. According to Théophile
Briant, the editor of *Le Goéland*, Moricand in his last moments
was *"seul comme un rat, nu comme le dernier des clochards."* In
America, among his family and his friends, Miller will no
longer ever be "alone like a rat," and in Big Sur, he has found
a *home* and will never really be a "vagabond" again.

7 Tropic of Capricorn

Decay and Erosion—Society and the Self

AT the age of eighty, Henry Miller began a book called *Insomnia or the Devil at Large* about his love for a twenty-five-year-old Japanese singer who worked at a piano bar in Hollywood. If, in 1970, Miller was still writing about the women in his life and their tremendous effect upon him, how could he have left women almost entirely out of two of his most important books? The exclusion of any mention of romantic attachment or erotic attraction from *Maroussi* and *Big Sur* is clearly not a matter of absentmindedness. Rather, it is a logical part of Miller's carefully developed plan to explore every aspect of his relationship with women in a series of books designed primarily for that purpose. *Tropic of Capricorn* is the first in this series, while the *Rosy Crucifixion* carries the examination (or "story") toward but not to its conclusion. Just as *Cancer* was the first book in the quartet in which Miller is an observer talking about the world, *Capricorn* is the first book in a triad in which Miller becomes the central actor in an unfolding drama. Miller used the designation "Capricorn" for this project, and it was supposed to continue through the *Rosy Crucifixion*, including two volumes of *Plexus* and two

volumes of *Nexus*. However, *Plexus* turned out to be so complete a failure that Miller discarded it (or chose to act as if it
didn't exist) and took up the story again at the conclusion of
Sexus with what has turned out to be the only volume of *Nexus*
to appear.

The books in this triad cover the period in Miller's life from
1920 when he became an employment manager for Western
Union, through 1923 when he met June Smith, to 1928 when he
and June left for Europe for the first time. The dates are particularly important, because Miller, while working from plans and
charts which he originally formulated around 1930, was trying
to cover a period in his life which was already many years in
the past. *Capricorn* was published in 1938, but *Sexus*, written
from 1942 to 1945, wasn't published until 1949, while *Nexus*
was written intermittently from 1952 to 1959 and published in
1960. It would not be unreasonable to speculate that Miller's
relationships with his third wife, Janina Lepska, and his fourth
wife, Eve McClure, might have found their way in some form
into these books. The other books that Miller wrote between
1942 and 1960 hardly mention love at all, except in the most
abstract and theoretical sense. Perhaps if Miller had been able
to integrate his romantic relationships into the other aspects of
his autobiographically oriented writing, he would have been
able to develop a certain perspective on that part of his life, but
then, he would not have been Henry Miller. The obsessive intensity of his reactions to women is one of the cardinal features
of his life and work, and his decision to write almost exclusively
about his obsession in the triad I have called "The Formation of
the Writer: The Artist as Actor," was a sensible strategy. Were
he to have tried to include his responses to women within his
other work, the balance would have been tipped so sharply
toward woman that everything else would have been of too
little weight to make an impression. Thus, women are absent
from his golden memory of the past *(Black Spring)*, neutral in
the land of light *(Maroussi)* and side stage in "paradise" *(Big
Sur)*.

As Martin says, "When he was in love Henry abused himself
in every possible way, he surrendered everything—except the

relentless will to possess the loved one completely."[1] Miller was not able to maintain any perspective on his relationships while they held him in thrall, and when he attempted to write about them, he was still trapped by the same ultraromantic attitudes that made his affairs so exciting and so difficult both for Miller and for the women in his life. Miller felt that his marriage to June Smith was the story of a "great tragedy of love" and he maintained at times that he became a writer solely to tell this story. He believed that it was important both for its meaning to him as a man and an artist, and also for its implications about men, women, love and society. Kate Millett would agree with the second part of Miller's position, and she argues that the value of Miller's writing is that it is "a compendium of American sexual neuroses," in which Miller articulates the "disgust, the contempt, the hostility, the violence and the sense of filth with which our culture, or more specifically, its masculine sensibility, surrounds sexuality."[2] She goes on to say that Miller "feels free to speak of objects," not persons, and that "personality and sexual behavior is so completely unrelated that, in the sexual episodes where they appear, any other names might be conveniently substituted."[3] Millett's contentions suggest that Miller failed completely when he was trying to write about "love," but Miller's attitude toward women is much more complicated than Millett's arguments indicate. Although Miller certainly has written episodes which exhibit the attitudes Millett describes, he does not advocate them as a matter of principle or even a matter of convenience. He was aware of the forces, demons even, that drove him, and he had a pretty good sense of their effect on him and on the women he knew. He tried to deal honestly if not dispassionately with his compulsions, and he knew quite well that he was not entirely successful either in his life or in his writing in developing a complete relationship with any woman. He recognized, also, that he often settled for sheer erotic experience in his written descriptions of men and women as an unsatisfactory substitute for all that was missing. Mailer feels that Miller's writing about lust is its own justification because Miller is dealing with a primal force rarely mentioned, much less explored, in the history of literature. Miller knew that this force gave him an unusual power and his writing an incredible energy, but he was not as content as Mailer to merely celebrate its existence and exult in its flow. It is the doubt, un-certainty and even fear which Miller brings to his exploration of love and lust that makes his writing more complex than Mailer acknowledges and less limited and self-indulgent than Millett asserts. An examination of the books in the triad must be re-sponsive to Miller's problems because the worth of these books can most accurately be measured by how well Miller dealt with his difficulties.

One of the worst features of Miller's street-realist voice is his old-fashioned, club-car raconteur style of describing sexual en-counters. The strength of Millett's arguments comes from her assemblage of lines quoted from this "voice" when it was at its stupidest. But even when Miller was at his most destructively obnoxious, there are some significant differences between his writing and the assumptions of most pornography. Tradition-ally and currently, pornography, according to Laurie Stone, "is a patriarchal sadomasochistic vision" in which sexual excite-ment depends upon the maintenance of power over others who suffer gratefully and enjoy their suffering.[4] Violence is a major component of this "vision" which "transforms women from human beings into wounded creatures who were born to bleed."[5] In addition, pornography "touches very little of the kind of sex one really has with a loving partner" since the por-nographic vision is a static one "in which nothing exists but sex (and sexual violence) and the empty spaces between sexual ses-sions."[6] As Stone points out, "in reality, of course, sex some-times does *devour* the rest of life, but life always intrudes again."[7] In many ways, pornography is a support system for a society which sanctions male dominance and encourages female submission, while feminism is a "critique of the sexual politics of the way things are," which "advances the belief that things should be otherwise, better, the opposite."[8] Miller's writing shares some of the attributes of this centuries old por-nographic "tradition," but is at variance with almost all of its elements as well. Although he may have forgotten some of his writing when he claimed to be a supporter of feminism in television interviews during the 1970s, Miller was not dissembling or trying to expiate various sins of his earlier years. Consider, for instance, the defining characteristics of pornography as Stone has stated them.

First, Miller is himself an outsider, and has no stake in the "maintenance of power" of a system that has exluded him. Second, his sexuality does not depend upon violence. Third, there is a great deal happening between sexual sessions, and perhaps most crucially, in the one relationship that Miller describes in great depth, the woman (June Smith; called Mara and then Mona) is presented as a challenge to traditional male dominance. She is not submissive in any way, is not "so much tinder in the crucible in which male ego is to be forged," is neither illogical nor perpetually innocent, has as much of a career as Miller does, does not want to be possessed, and is supported by Miller in her needs and desires during the decade that they spent together. On the other hand, Miller does not seem able to write about such feminine experiences as, in Ann Douglas's words, "women liking women . . . aging, so-called sexual abnormality, the long stretches of married life, maternity, the crisis of divorce."[9] The limitations of Miller's writing, then, are not that he is bound by a pornographic vision of society, but that an extensive understanding of feminine reality is beyond his grasp as a writer. And even while this is true, his writing in the triad is at least an attempt to approach some of these areas of experience. How much success he had in these attempts is one of the most important questions that one must answer in assessing Miller's accomplishments as an artist.

To begin with, although Mailer calls Miller a fellow prisoner of sex, it is necessary to see that Miller was also a prisoner of an old-fashioned belief in romantic love. One of the versions of this courtly attitude is the location of woman on a pedestal as a figure fit for worship but unfit for partnership. There is some of this outmoded thinking in Miller, but is is hardly the most important aspect of his sense of the power of sheer romance. Central to his conception of an ideal love is his belief that through a perfect union of man and woman, new doors of perception are opened out toward the cosmos and inward toward the center of the self. It is this extraordinarily utopian (and strangely innocent) vision of love's great potential that was at the heart of Miller's troubles. This may be seen clearly in Miller's comments on H. Rider Haggard's *She* in *The Books In My Life*. Writing about Haggard's fantastic goddess and heroine, Miller says

> That which sustains Ayesha, and at the same time consumes her, is the faith that she will eventually be reunited with her beloved. And what could the beloved be but the Holy Spirit? No less a gift than this could suffice a soul endowed with her matchless hunger, patience and fortitude. The love which alone can transform the soul of Nature is divine love. Time counts for naught when spirit and soul are divorced. The splendor of neither can be made manifest except through union. Man, the only creature possessed of a dual nature, remains a riddle unto himself, keeps revolving on the wheel of life and death, until he pierces the enigma of identity. The drama of love, which is the highest he may enact, carries with it the key to the mystery.[10]

Miller is being a bit mystical here, but when he speaks of "divine love," he means something which can make man feel like a god, some power which enables man to transcend, at least in his expectations and dreams, the confines of a mundane, ordinary existence. Whatever else he may be, Miller says, the way he will know himself most completely is through contact or union with his "beloved." Similarly, the highest goal one might have is to be a partner in a union which helps one's "beloved" to a similar knowledge of self. With this goal, it is no wonder that Miller found most relationships inadequate. In addition, one must also note that Ayesha's love in *She* is not usually a *union*, but a love which enslaves the spirit and captures the soul. If one can match Ayesha's power, then there will be a mutual sharing, a communion of spirits which can "transform the soul of Nature." But if one partner is inferior in some way, the possibility of total absorption of one being by the other is likely. Like "She," Miller overwhelmed most of his "mortal" partners and treated them as inferiors, but when he found an equal of sorts in June Smith the result was not "union" but two powers in collision—the terrible "tragedy" Miller tries to understand through his writing. His behavior with June Smith, the

Mona/Mara of the triad, and with every other woman he wrote about followed a pattern that began with his nearly medieval belief in the transformative powers of romantic love. Then, as each relationship failed to match Miller's lofty expectations, he often lapsed into erotic gangsterism as a compensation for his disappointment. As his disappointment increased, Miller relied on a nearly total sexual orientation toward "women" in a vain attempt to replace all the missing aspects of romance with a kind of orgasmic frenzy. As the orgasmic excitement became more and more difficult to maintain, Miller sought it more and more desperately, until his struggles began to seem obscene even to him. This, in turn, led to a constant search for new partners, new types of experiences and a corresponding, progressive deterioration of his self-esteem. Somehow, he gradually began to realize, the pattern had to be shattered.

The basic structure of the project which was supposed to become the *Rosy Crucifixion* can be seen as a part of the pattern which I have been outlining. In *Capricorn*, the failure of Miller's first marriage catapults him into what he calls the Land of Fuck where he is caught up in the kind of aimless sexual brutality which Kate Millett identifies and rightly condemns. His reentry into what might be called the "Land of Love" occurs when he meets June Smith. Unfortunately, or perhaps inevitably, Miller feels he must literally worship June Smith in the same way he has always worshipped, in theory, an "ideal love" of his imaginative devising. He seems to have learned nothing from his initial difficulties and continues to expect every relationship to conform to his romantic fantasies. His adolescent ideas were probably a part of his attraction for women, but they set him up for a precipitous plunge into despair. In *Sexus*, Miller's last vestiges of innocence are wiped away as both he and June descend into an abyss in a realm even worse than the Land of Fuck. Their futile, frightening struggle to develop an enduring relationship based on respect, sharing, mutual growth and a gradual ripening is a dismal failure. This defeat, brilliantly analyzed by Mailer in his chapter on "Narcissism," staggers Miller (and June as well, although Miller is weak on this point), driving him almost to the brink of madness. *Nexus* shows Mil-

ler's struggle back from the edge of insanity and gradually
away from June's hold on him. At the end of the book, he
claims to be ready to leave for Paris to become the artist/hero of
Cancer. This claim isn't entirely convincing, as I shall explain,
but it is clear that at this point, Miller has finally lost his innocent sense of the possibilities of romance. His rotten treatment
of women in *Cancer* is a part of his defense against further pain
and a method of preserving the newly won confidence that is
so much a part of his narrative consciousness in that book. It is
also a reflection of how much he has been hurt by the loss of
his romantic dreams and the failure of his most serious love.

At both ends of the triad I have called "The Formation of the
Writer. . . ." Miller is responsible for a type of masculine sexual
behavior that is reprehensible. In the center of the triad, the
sexual activity he describes is so distressing that even his
friends (Durrell in particular) felt he had overdone it. But in
these passages, Miller is neither sanctioning nor advocating the
"lust in action" he portrays. In almost every instance, it is the
result of a man reacting to a series of failures—romantic, artistic, economic—by letting his anger and frustration overcome
the wiser and more humane qualities he has shown on other
occasions. Because these passages are presented with a vividness appropriate for the high energy level that the activity generates, they have the excitement of drama and combat, but Miller is not suggesting that high energy alone justifies cruelty.
Because Miller himself was not sure why he acted as he did,
these books are an exploration of sorts, and when the narrator
is selfish or vicious or even inhuman, it becomes part of the
record of the journey. Miller is not pleased with his behavior,
but he is trying to explain and understand why it happened,
and if this "record" showed how weak a man might be, then so
it would be written. But to say that Miller is satisfied or happy
in any way with the events in the triad is to drastically miss the
narrative stance and the structure of these books. And finally,
Miller's relationship with June Smith shows that in spite of all
of the problems they had, Miller encouraged and supported her
in many ways. Their marriage, for all its tension, was a kind of
partnership of equals, and Miller did not want or expect June to

subordinate her ideas or plans to serve his own. He wanted plenty of assistance, but he was also ready to provide what help he could, and he never thought of marriage as an arrangement where one person sacrifices his or her life for the other. In short, Miller's description of his life with June Smith is not, by any means, an expression of "an ancient sentiment of contempt."[11]

Tropic of Capricorn, the first book in the triad, does not cover Miller's relationship with June Smith, but is like a prologue to it. When Miller finally meets June, introduced here as "Mara" at the conclusion of the book, he is very aware of the ugly condition he is in and looks for his redemption in her love. Martin calls *Capricorn* a book Miller wrote to postpone having to write about his life with June, but this is only partly true. Miller felt that June radically changed his life, and that the time he spent with her was crucial in terms of his becoming an artist. Therefore, to show the emergence of his creative consciousness, it was necessary to show what he was like as an embryonic artist, and *Capricorn* does this very well. All of the creative impulses Miller harnesses later are pulsating in a wild and undefined field in *Capricorn*, but his energy is directed almost entirely outward. He knows that he isn't at ease with himself or the world, but doesn't know how to handle the situation as the book opens. When he finally meets June/Mara, he then begins the actual process of introspection which leads to the development of the narrative consciousness of the artist/hero who writes *Cancer*.

But in *Capricorn*, the "Henry Miller" who is the protagonist is not yet an "artist," and not really a "hero." To use the suffix "pre" or even "future" tends toward awkwardness. Let me refer to the character called "Henry V. Miller" as *the author*, to emphasize that it is on his authority that we have the story, and to try to suggest a relationship between the mind that is formed by the experiences of the book, and the mind that shaped these experiences into literature fifteen years later. After all, even though he was not a *writer* in 1920, Miller had already begun to think about everything that happened to him as if his life were a kind of story. In *Capricorn*, although the protagonist is not ready to record and transmute experience into literature, each incident that occurs registers its impact on his mind and soul and contributes to the artist who will be.

In Miller's usual fashion, the text is anticipated by some eccentric subtitling. First, the book is dedicated "To Her," who is in Martin's words, "the magical Ayesha-anima of his psyche, who, like Dante's Beatrice, draws the Henry-hero through the Inferno of civilization and the Purgatorio of sensuality into the Paradiso of the liberated imagination."[12] The dedication was probably designed for the entire triad (or the projected *Rosy Crucifixion*) and it is as a sincere tribute to the ideals of love that June Smith represented for the author when he met her. The sincerity of the tribute is thrown into a different perspective, however, by the lines from Peter Abelard's *Historia Calamitatum* which follow. On the one hand, the author is referring to one of the themes of the book, "the sufferings which have sprung out of my misfortunes," specifically those of the period 1920–1923 which the book covers. On the other hand, the author may also be referring to a desire to be relieved of the burden of lustful energy which has been driving him to ugly and degrading behavior. And in a further variant, there is also an implication that the overpowering love which Miller is struck by when he meets June/Mara tends to unman him in a way that is both frightening and potentially constructive, or reconstructive. Following the Abelard reference is a wonderful phrase which might stand as the motto for the book: "On the Ovarian Trolley." This phrase becomes more clear as the book progresses, but its essential meaning is that the author has two methods for escaping from the squalor of his life as an employment manager for the Cosmodemonic Telegraph Company. One type of escape is an abandonment of the self in a kind of mindless sexuality, a visceral version of life as sexual adventure. The other method of escape is a retreat into the imagination, a ride on a "mental" trolley through the landscape of the mind.

The first few pages of the book are a blunt declaration of the author's stance through most of the book. The tone of the statement is one of despair mixed with anger, as if the author were alternately on the verge of giving up and also on the brink of doing something violent. There is no sense of hope or of a possible improvement in anything: "To want to change the condition of affairs seemed futile to me; nothing would be altered, I was convinced, except by a change of heart, and who could change the hearts of men?"[13] The author is caught in a kind of isolation which prevents him from establishing any contact of an intimate nature with another human being: "From the very beginning I must have trained myself not to want anything too badly. From the very beginning I was independent, in a false way. I had need of nobody because I wanted to be free, free to do and to give only as my whims dictated. The moment anything was expected or demanded of me I balked" (10). The author's troubles are partly a function of the way he sees himself, and partly a result of his family background and the country he lives in. "I was the evil product of an evil soil," he says, "My people were entirely Nordic, which is to say *idiots*." And as for his country: "I have walked the streets in many countries of the world but nowhere have I felt so degraded and humiliated as in America. I think of all the streets in America combined as forming a huge cesspool, a cesspool of the spirit in which everything is sucked down and drained away to everlasting shit" (12). Wisely, Miller offers only a few pages of this kind of writing. The lacerating anger verges toward a bitter numbness, and the free-wheeling condemnation of everything tends toward a generalized self-pity that would lose any reader's interest after more than a few scenes. But the author has established the set of his mind and now he can shift away from his complaints against the universe to his strategies for surviving its worst abuses.

The first third of the book is one of Miller's most brilliant inventions. Among the various unpleasant jobs he had, he chose to write about the one with Western Union, the Cosmodemonic Telegraph Company. His description of the company is a malicious and searing indictment of the bureaucratic coldness of a giant corporation which dehumanizes everyone who works there, a viciously satiric attack that ranks with Upton Sinclair's *The Jungle* or Joseph Heller's *Something Happened*. But the *company* is more than that. It is also a metaphor de-

signed to reflect American society itself, a Kafkaesque symbol
of an entire culture moving along on its own momentum without anyone having any control or even any sense of why things
proceed as they do. The author, in some degree of desperation,
seeks employment as a messenger, "the last job on earth," because he feels he must do something to support his rarely mentioned but always present wife and child. When he is turned
down for this position, his pride drives him into the vice-presi-
dent's office, where his volcanic energy so impresses the officials that they decide to make him an employment manager.
His job is to fill the ranks of the literally thousands of messengers the company needs, and since the turnover is gigantic, the
author must interview, assess and hire hundreds of people
each week. He finds himself facing the whole lower stratum of
America and must confront a complete cross section of its urban population every day. He is both appalled by what he sees
and wildly exhilarated by his chance to undermine the company and by his contact with so many people:

> In a few months I was sitting at Sunset Place hiring and firing like
> a demon. It was a slaughterhouse, so help me God. The thing was
> senseless from the bottom up. A waste of men, material and ef-
> fort. A hideous farce against a backdrop of sweat and misery. . . .
> I did everything they instructed me to do, but in such a way that
> they had to pay for it. When there was a strike I folded my arms
> and waited for it to blow over. But I first saw to it that it cost them
> a good penny. The whole system was so rotten, so inhuman, so
> lousy, so hopelessly corrupt and complicated, that it would have
> taken a genius to put any sense or order into it, to say nothing of
> human kindness or consideration. (19–20)

This is the American equivalent of the urban chaos the artist/
hero raged at in Paris, but now, the author is caught up in the
midst of it. Although his anger acts again as a shield, he is
bound to be infected by the plague if he remains in contact with
it for too long a time:

> From my little perch at Sunset Place I had a bird's eye view of the
> whole American society. It was like a page out of the telephone
> book. Alphabetically, numerically, statistically, it made sense. But
> when you looked at it up close, when you examined the pages

separately, or the parts separately, when you examined one lone
individual and what constituted him, examined the air he
breathed, the life he led, the chances he risked, you saw something so foul and degrading, so low, so miserable, so utterly hopeless and senseless, that it was worse than looking into a volcano.
You could see the whole American life—economically, politically,
morally, spiritually, artistically, statistically, pathologically. It
looked like a grand chancre on a worn-out cock. It looked worse
than that, really, because you couldn't even see anything resembling a cock any more. (20)

The author's good instincts prevail for a while, as he tries to
help everyone he can: "I never had any money in my pocket
but I used other people's money freely. As long as I was the
boss I had credit. I gave money away right and left; I gave my
clothes away and my linen, my books, everything that was
superfluous. . . . Be firm! Be hard! they cautioned me. Fuck
that! I said to myself, I'll be generous, pliant, forgiving, tolerant, tender" (27). Eventually the burden of trying to be a coun-
selor and friend to everyone he meets overwhelms the author,
and his anger begins to burn away his defenses. He realizes
that no matter how many people he helps, there will always be
many more waiting and asking for his aid:

> I had a representative of almost every species under the sun. I had
> two brothers who were still sun-worshipers, two Nestorians from
> the old Assyrian world; I had two Maltese twins from Malta and a
> descendant of the Mayas from Yucatan; I had a few of our little
> brown brothers from the Philippines and some Ethiopians from
> Abyssinia; I had men from the pampas of Argentina and stranded
> cowboys from Montana; I had Greeks, Letts, Poles, Croats, Slo-
> venes, Ruthenians, Czechs, Spaniards, Welshmen. . . . (31–32)

They are men who were, among other things, "mathemati-
cians, mayors of cities and governors of states, prison wardens,
cowpunchers, lumberjacks, . . . dentists, painters, sculptors,
plumbers" (32), and as the author gasps in dismay, "all of them
down and out, begging for work, for cigarettes, for carfare, *for
a chance, Christ Almighty, just another chance!*" And the author
gives them another "chance" of sorts, and sends them out,
"walking the streets of New York in that bloody, degrading

outfit." This is the early 1920s, years before the Great Depression, and Miller presents an interesting variation of the old melting pot idea—the company reducing singularity to a common despair.

Gradually, it becomes too much for the author to stand. His energy has won him the job, but his sensitivity is making it hard for him to do it to anyone's satisfaction: "When I think of some of the Persians, the Hindus, the Arabs I knew, when I think of the character they revealed, their grace, their tenderness, their intelligence, *their holiness,* I spit on the white conquerors of the world, the degenerate British, the pigheaded Germans, the smug, self-satisfied French" (33). Gathering all of his anger together in one burst of venom, the author calls a curse down on all of the people responsible for the world he sees:

> Wait, you cosmococcic telegraphic shits, you demons on high waiting for the plumbing to be repaired, wait, you dirty white conquerors who have sullied the earth with your cloven hoofs, your instruments, your weapons, your disease germs, wait, all you who are sitting in clover and counting your coppers, it is not the end. The last man will have his say before it is finished. Down to the last sentient molecule justice must be done—*and will be done!* Nobody is getting away with anything, least of all the cosmococcic shits of North America. (33–34)

He attempts to focus his anger in a book he writes about twelve of the messengers all of whom were destroyed by the circumstances of their lives. It is a kind of Horatio Alger "as he looks the day after the Apocalypse" story and the author spends his first vacation in three years ("I was so eager to make the company a success!") writing it. This is Miller's first attempt to rescue himself through the powers of art from the spiritual damage his life has inflicted on his psyche. The book was to be called *Clipped Wings* and it was structured by some familiar theological motifs. Throughout the first part of *Capricorn,* Miller presents the author as a sort of fallen angel walking amidst the damned, and in his job at the Cosmodemonic company, he is both a fellow sufferer and would-be redeemer who still possesses the means for a kind of resurrection. Although Miller gives the author a pose of ironic detachment at first, "I took them on in carload lots—niggers, Jews, paralytics, cripples, ex-convicts, whores, maniacs, perverts, idiots, any fucking bastard who could stand on two legs and hold a telegram in his hands . . ." (28), an essential sympathy breaks through. The author posts the familiar "Abandon all hope. . . ." sign over his desk, and writes about his twelve messengers as souls damned by a system they can't control or understand. They are distinguished only by their bland, ordinary lives until they succumb to violent and inexplicable calamity. Miller was thirty-three at the time he tried to write *Clipped Wings,* and his story of twelve men seems to suggest some conscious parallels with another story of twelve other men who carried a powerful and decisive message to mankind—rather than garbled telegrams usually informing the recipient of disaster. As the author mentions bits of what went into *Clipped Wings,* one sees just how much Miller was touched by the plight of these men, but the book was a failure, partly because, as the author tells us, "I didn't dare to think of anything then except the 'facts' " (35). Miller, in retrospect, believes that "to get beneath the facts I would have had to be an artist," and he was ten hard years away from earning or achieving that designation.

The effect of his "failure" as a writer combined with the pressure he felt at his inability to help the people he met day after day who were in dire straits led the author to adopt two methods for psychic survival. Both of them contributed to the further diminution of the author's qualities of humanity and moved him further on his journey to the spiritual nadir, the Land of Fuck, in the second part of the book. The first of these is his increasing tendency to ride on a "trolley" of what Miller calls "trancelike inspiration" (49). The landscape of Brooklyn in the 1920s was crossed by the tracks of electric trolley cars which served as the primary means of transportation for its citizens. The author rode on these cars nearly every day, and on these rides, his mind began to compose "a book of the hours, of the tedium and monotony of my life in the midst of ferocious activity." "But going over the bridge, the sun setting, the skyscrapers gleaming like phosphorescent cadavers, the remembrance of the past set in . . . remembrance of going back and forth over the bridge, going to a job which was death, returning to a home which was a morgue . . ." (50).

The bridge is the Brooklyn Bridge, and this passage recalls one of the "dreams" of the "Into the Night Life" scenario of *Black Spring*. As the author's waking life became more and more like "death," his mind gradually succeeded it as the realm of his primary reality. His mental excursions represented the most vital, creative aspect of his existence, and his rides on the trolley cars gave him a chance to employ this method of retreat from "death" without any distraction. The trolley itself becomes associated with this process, and as he glides smoothly across the bridge, he has this insight:

> Maybe, being up high between the two shores, suspended above the traffic, above life and death, on each side the high tombs, tombs blazing with dying sunlight, the river flowing heedlessly, flowing on like time itself, maybe each time I passed up there, something was tugging away at me, urging me to take it in, to announce myself; anyway each time I passed on high I was truly alone and whenever that happened the book commenced to write itself, screaming the things which I never breathed, the thoughts I never uttered, the conversations I never held, the hopes, the dreams, the delusions I never admitted. If this then was the true self it was marvelous, and what's more it seemed never to change but always to pick up from the last stop, to continue in the same vein. . . .(51)

Unfortunately, this isn't the "true self," just another aspect of it, and when any one aspect is encouraged so strongly that all of the other elements of the self are submerged, the ultimate result is to distort reality dangerously. The author becomes so involved in his mental "trolley rides" that he neglects the other parts of his life, and Miller tells us that the author is plagued by the realization that he is denying matters of great importance while he is embracing the "life" of his agile mind:

> Then, as in the middle of the bridge, in the middle of a walk, in the middle always, whether of a book, a conversation, or making love, it was borne in on me again that I had never done what I

wanted and out of not doing what I wanted to do there grew up inside me this creation which was nothing but an obsessional plant, a sort of coral growth, which was expropriating everything, including life itself, until life itself became this which was denied. . . . (53)

Similarly, the author becomes lost in sexual activity as a means of forgetting the unpleasant circumstances of his life. He and his wife are married in name only, and just as his job has diminished his sense of other people's suffering by offering him a sample of suffering on an unfathomable scale, his "marriage" has left him with an impression of women that is so narrow and limited that he is temporarily incapable of reacting to any woman as more than a sexual opportunity. This is the ovarian aspect of the subtitle of *Capricorn,* a tuning out of all the other senses but the sexual, so that the author and various partners can remove themselves from the world of pain and luxuriate temporarily in an orgasmic delirium. The author isn't trying to exploit any of the women he is involved with, and he recognizes that they are as unhappy as he is, but his sexual escapades are never a part of a more complete relationship. This episode is typical:

The whole thing was cockeyed and we were all laughing hysterically and then we began to drink—the only thing they had in the house was kümmel and it didn't take much to put us under. And then it got more cockeyed because the two of them began to paw me and neither one would let the other do anything. The result was I undressed them both and put them to bed and they fell asleep in each other's arms. . . . When I got home my wife was awake and sore as hell because I had stayed out so long. We had a hot discussion and finally I lost my temper and I clouted her and she fell on the floor and began to weep and sob and then the kid woke up and hearing the wife bawling she got frightened and began to scream at the top of her lungs. The girl upstairs came running down to see what was the matter. She was in her kimono and her hair was hanging down her back. In the excitement she got close to me and things happened without either of us intending anything to happen. We put the wife to bed with a wet towel around her forehead and while the girl upstairs was bending over her I stood behind her and lifting her kimono I got it into her and she stood

there a long time talking a lot of foolish, soothing nonsense.
(74)

There is a flatness and a deadness in the language used in this
incident; nothing like the rapture and poetic fire Miller is capable of. There is "the wife," who is an object; "the girl upstairs"
who is another object; and "it" which is put into her, still another object. This scene, and many others like it, are meant to
show how far from stability and humaneness the author has
come. Miller is definitely not suggesting that these dreary bouts
of copulation are anything but a momentary surcease from an
unpleasant life, the groping of two frightened and lonely
people who, as Miller puts it, wanted the "eye" that sees the
horror of the world "extinguished" (76). There is nothing in
Capricorn that suggests that Miller approves of the objectifica-
tion of women, and the author is pictured as a man who has
lost most of his humanity, who is desperately in need of the
inspiration and redemption that *she* promises at the end of the
book. When the author meets MacGregor, a man who "worried
his head off, or rather he worried the head off his cock," a man
who can think only of sex, one sees a parallel here to Van Norden of *Cancer*. His philosophy is "a good lay will clean your
ballbearings out and leave a good taste in your mouth," but this
ovarian obsession never leads beyond its own compulsion.
There is a sense of a man on a treadmill as the author and
MacGregor and various women meet and part without any contact other than a genital one. As the author says of one of these
meetings:

> And this in the black frenzied nothingness of the hollow of ab-
> sence leaves a gloomy feeling of saturated despondency not un-
> like the topmost tip of desperation which is only the gay juvenile
> maggot of death's exquisite rupture with life. From this inverted
> cone of ecstasy life will rise again into prosaic skyscraper emi-
> nence, dragging me by the hair and teeth, lousy with howling
> empty joy, the animated fetus of the unborn death maggot lying
> in wait for rot and putrefaction.

Miller's phrase, "saturated despondency," describes the futility
of a totally ovarian existence, the energy that might be better

used in untold ways expressed now by a would-be artist "howling with empty joy."

However, the worst part of the "ovarian trolley" ride is still ahead. By escaping into his mind and into mindless sensuality, the author is able to fight a kind of holding action with his job and his marriage. For fifty pages, he digresses into childhood and teenage recollections, offering a few ideas about how he got trapped in the Cosmodemonic world. "I like to dwell on this period when things were taking shape," Miller says (176). But then, the author takes "a flat in the Land of Fuck," and begins to move into a barren, deadly landscape that is the epitome of all the passionless, obscene, resentful versions of sexual activity that occur in *Capricorn* and in *Cancer* before and in *Sexus* still to be written. In *Big Sur*, Miller remarks that by the Land of Fuck he "meant Cockaigne," but if he is serious at all, he must have had an ironic reading of the medieval poem in mind. In the second section of *Capricorn*, Miller develops, through various surrealistic techniques, a metaphysical montage of sex as death, and not just a "little death" in the Elizabethan sense. Here, he is describing the death of the soul and the spirit, so that a man is left with his body and a mind that sees the limits of that body with awful clarity.

Referring to his sexual preoccupations, the author says:

These misadventures happened so frequently that it was impossible not to believe in the reality of a realm which was called Fuck, because that was the only name which might be given to it, and yet it was more than fuck and by fucking one only began to approach it. Everybody had at one time or another planted the flag in this territory, and yet nobody was able to lay claim to it permanently. It disappeared overnight—sometimes in the twinkling of an eye. It was No Man's Land and it stank with the litter of invisible deaths. (191–192)

This section is a comment on all of the passages in Miller's work where some version of "Henry Miller" does *this* or *that* to some nameless woman who dissolves in delight. They are both inhabitants of a "realm which was called Fuck" which is not a country for any human to inhabit. All of Kate Millett's exam-

ples ought to be read in the context of what Miller says in the
pages which reduce the infinite variety of the world to a place
where, in Mailer's words, "one crazy fuck begets another."[14]
But Mailer may not have read this section too carefully (he does
not include it in his reader beyond the first page about "taking
a flat. . . ,") because it goes directly against his argument that
for Miller, writing about fucking is generally exuberant and joyful. What actually happens is that the despoiling of the erotic
muse is completed in an extended description that is one of the
most bitter and graphic Miller ever wrote. At first, the images
Miller evokes are wry and caustic, mock historic notations that
debunk classical learning:

> On page twenty-three you will find a picture of Priapus juggling a
> corkscrew on the end of his weeny; he is standing in the shadow
> of the Parthenon by mistake; he is naked except for a perforated
> jock-strap which was loaned for the occasion by the Holy Rollers
> of Oregon and Saskatchewan. Long distance is on the wire de-
> manding to know if they should sell short or long. He says *go fuck
> yourself* and hangs up the receiver. In the background Rembrandt
> is studying the anatomy of our Lord Jesus Christ who, if you
> remember, was crucified by the Jews and then taken to Abyssinia
> to be pounded with quoits and other objects. The weather seems
> to be fair and warmer, as usual, except for a slight mist rising up
> out of the Ionian; this is the sweat of Neptune's balls which
> were castrated by the early monks, or perhaps it was by the
> Manicheans in the time of the Pentecostal plague. . . . This is the
> flush of dawn on the first day of sexual intercourse in the old
> Hellenistic world, now faithfully reproduced for us in color thanks
> to the Zeiss Brothers and other patient zealots of industry.
> (192)

The jovial tone of this burlesque, which includes some self-
parody (compare this passage with Miller's other references to
Hellenic culture written both before and after *Capricorn*), gradually gives way to a heavy, monotonous and very depressing
incantation on the author's entanglement with this dreadful
realm. When one is discussing history, a comic stance is possible. When the discussion shifts to the immediate present, it is
somewhat more difficult to find anything particularly humor-

ous, and the comic tone is replaced by one of cold, clinical revulsion. Miller's disgust with and separation from his charac- ters often occurs in the passages in which he writes about sex either as a numbed participant or as a spectator; that is, a spec- tator in the sense of listening to a story, not as a voyeur. In these scenes, Miller or the artist/hero or one of his acquaint- ances is so totally consumed by the physicality of the action that he is not interested in its consequences for either party. In the pages dealing with "life" or "death" in the Land of Fuck, Miller stands back from the "Author" depicted in *Capricorn* to comment on the action that took place circa 1923 from his per- spective in 1938. He does not do this again because this is his definitive and inclusive statement on all of the passages that Millett quotes and on many more besides. The author's com- plicity in this activity is condemned as Miller recalls how de- structive it was: "This time I call the realm of the super-cunt, for it defies speed, calculation or imagery. Nor has the penis itself a known size or weight. There is only the sustained feel of fuck, the fugitive in full flight, the nightmare smoking his quiet cigar. Little Nemo walks around with a seven-day hard on and a wonderful pair of blue balls bequeathed by Lady Bountiful. It is Sunday morning around the corner from Evergreen Ceme- tery" (196).

Neither *man* nor *woman* is recognizable, as a version of Lawrentian blood-consciousness at its most bestial overcomes everything. The phrase about "the fugitive in full flight" de- scribes the distance from a society of any kind that the author feels. The reference to "Sunday morning" suggests the failure of religion just as the mock historical references suggested the failure of scholarship and education as a means of rescuing either an individual or restructuring a civilization. The "Ever- green Cemetery" is a kind of oxymoron fusing of "life" (which means an instinctive use of sexual power) and "death" (which describes the withering of the soul) which is the result of living too long in this realm. The author, in this condition, is not far from Van Norden, MacGregor and other cunt-struck men in Miller's writing, but he is gifted (or cursed, perhaps?) with the ability to see what has happened to him, and he has the language to express the horror of his decline. Miller carries the description further, recalling a time when:

> The world of men and women are making merry in the cemetery grounds. They are having sexual intercourse, God bless them, and I am alone in the Land of Fuck. It seems to me that I hear the clanking of a great machine, the linotype bracelets passing through the wringer of sex. Hymie and his nymphomaniac of a wife are lying on the same level with me, only they are across the river. The river is called Death and it has a bitter taste. I have waded through it many times, up to the hips, but somehow I have neither been petrified nor immortalized. I am still burning brightly inside, though outwardly dead as a planet. From this bed I have gotten up to dance, not once but hundreds, thousands of times. Each time I came away I had the conviction that I had danced the skeleton dance on a *terrain vague*. (197)

The "linotype" echoes Miller's description of Van Norden and the woman in *Cancer*, and although sexual intercourse involves two people, one is always "alone in the Land of Fuck." The naming of the river is meant to imply a resemblance to the Styx, of course, but Miller is also working on a variation of his frequent references to a universal flow of energy and to a "river" as a connection to the natural world when one is caught amidst the crumbling wreckage of a modern city. As a kind of summary, Miller says: "This is the Land of Fuck, in which there are no animals, no trees, no stars, no problems. Here the spermatazoon reigns supreme. Nothing is determined in advance, the future is absolutely uncertain, the past is nonexistent" (203).

The author's habitation in this realm is a result of his need to escape from the Cosmodemonic world. His retreats into the mind and into the realm of the senses are satisfactory alternatives until he discovers that it is becoming increasingly difficult for him to emerge from these "sanctuaries." Like the Minotaur, he has been trapped permanently in the labyrinth. Miller has arranged the details of his decline carefully because he wants to show how desperate his life had become when he first met June Smith. He was literally on the verge of losing, possibly forever, those qualities of humanity which he valued very highly; qualities one can see in his portraits of other artists throughout his work. He was nearly resigned to his mutation into another Van Norden, and since his situation was almost hopeless, the entrance of his apparent saviour was dramatically quite impressive. As Miller says, "The interlude which I think of as the Land of Fuck, a realm of time more than space, is for me the equivalent of that Purgatory which Dante has described in nice detail" (208). Miller indicates here that he was not totally damned, but lost in a limbo from which rescue would not be an easy matter. The force required to shatter the walls of his prison came directly from June Smith, and he declares that when he met her at the Amarillo Dance Hall where she worked as a taxi dancer, "all that I had previously been, was, and about to be foundered" (208).

From this point on, *Capricorn* is dominated by the presence of June Smith, and yet she appears in only two sections covering just twenty of the remaining one hundred and fifty pages of the book. Martin maintains (without explaining his position) that the author moves out of the Land of Fuck at this point through the exercise of his "natural sensuality," and thus awakens his artistic imagination. I do not agree with this argument because it overrates a weak part of the book. The last one hundred and fifty pages could have been radically restructured to avoid what is actually needless repetition. Many passages of reminiscence could have been relocated into the area "when things were taking shape" because they cover the same ground. A concentration of the most vital material of this type into the first half of the book where it would have expanded the Cosmodemonic world and explained further how Miller got there would have made the early parts of *Capricorn* tighter and more densely textured. Then, June Smith's appearance would have been an appropriate conclusion and it would have been even more impressive because it would not have been surrounded by digressions, philosophic ramblings, more scenes of sexual activity and anecdotes about the author. However, even amidst what is largely detritus, June Smith's entrance into the author's life is the occasion for some of the most impressive writing of Miller's entire career.

Miller's account of his first version of June Smith is like an extended lyric poem, an inspired tribute and love letter to an extraordinary woman that is written with rhapsody. If Miller had been able to develop, expand and sustain the power of his initial response to June Smith, the woman called Mara and then Mona would surely have been one of the more celebrated creations in literary history, a modern Madame Bovary perhaps, or an American Molly Bloom. Miller has nothing less ambitious than this in mind, as Hassan points out: "She has something here of Lilith, Circe, and La Belle Dame Sans Merci, something also of the terrible White Goddess, and blood-swilling Kali. She may even suggest the shimmering deity of H. Rider Haggard's *She*."[15] Before she is introduced as an actual person, the author, from his perspective as the man who is writing about a moment in the past, describes the way she has remained in his memory as a living force. In this recollection, June Smith is not seen as a real woman but as a kind of mythic goddess, almost a symbol of eros incarnate. His plan is to make June Smith seem extraordinary by showing her power on a universal, even symbolic level, and then presenting her as a very real woman who inhabits the world of the modern city. In his memory, the legendary love goddess is depicted in abstract but still tangible terms. At first, she seems distant, like an archaeological monument in his mind. "In the tomb which is my memory I see her buried now, the one I loved better than all else, better than the world, better than God, better than my own flesh and blood" (231). But then, images of her in action, a female Proteus figure, flood through his remembrances: "she was radiant, jubilant, an ultra-black jubilation streaming from her like a steady flow of sperm from the Mithraic Bull. She was double barreled, like a shotgun, a female bull with an acetylene torch in her womb" (233).

"She had the gift of transformation," the author recalls, and he sees her as a basilisk, a black rose, a panther, a jaguar, a wild heron, "almost as quick and subtle she was as the devil himself." Their life together was marked by sudden, exciting change too, entire generations consumed in an afternoon:

> I remember how the second time I met her she told me that she had never expected to see me again, and the next time I saw her

she said she thought I was a dope fiend, and next time she called
me a god, and after that she tried to commit suicide and then I
tried and then she tried again, and nothing worked except to
bring us closer together, so close indeed that we interpenetrated,
exchanged personalities, name, identity, religion, father, mother,
brother. (237)

And June Smith remained elusive no matter how much Miller
studied her. "She had begun this process of metamorphosis
before I met her," the author says, and then explains how she
"changed her whole manner of speech, her diction, her intona-
tion, her accent, her phraseology" (238). In his memory, she is
the eternal feminine mystery which no man ever unravels,
composed of some primary organic substances that are like the
building blocks of matter itself: "she lay coiled like a sleeping
serpent riveted to the earth. The body, strong, lithe, muscular,
seemed possessed of a weight unnatural; she had a more than
human gravity, the gravity, one might almost say, of a warm
corpse. . . . She lay coiled at the base of a hollow pyramid, en-
shrined in the vacuum of her own creation like a sacred relic of
the past" (243). Even in memory, her access to a vital force
central to life and creation seems immediate and constant. "She
might live on endlessly, like the moon, like any dead planet,
radiating an hypnotic effulgence, creating tides of passion, engulfing the world in madness, discoloring all earthly substances
with her magnetic, metallic rays" (243). From pages 231 to 247,
image follows image as the author talks of this fantastic
woman, part legend and myth, part Earth Mother/Demeter/
Aphrodite. And then, with no transition, the author says,
"suddenly for no reason at all, when I think of her returning to
her nest, I remember Sunday mornings in the little old house
near the cemetery," and she is gone.

The reader's first glimpse of this creature is unsettling but
intriguing. Is she a product of the author's imagination, a com-
posite of various mundane women he has known, one wonders? Her impact on the author is stunning, so unlike any other
woman he has described in *Capricorn*, that one is reminded of
Yeats's famous lines, "Surely some revelation is at hand." As I
have suggested, Miller might well have moved directly to his
first meeting with June Smith at this point, but nearly one hun-

dred pages pass before we see her as the actual person who inspired these mythic images, and by this time, the book is over. Still, her appearance in the "Coda" complements her earlier appearance in the author's memory. Now, she is introduced as an actual person, one singular individual who will reclaim the author from the Land of Fuck and then, in *Sexus*, travel with him to another realm even more dreadful. But first, she appears wrapped in wonder and alive with the promise of love at its most dazzling and joyous.

On the "night in question" when the author "walked right out of the old life and into the new," he describes himself as "depossessed of the past," a man ready for a sea change (339). When he sees *her* for the first time, she is still clothed in the vestiges of legend, but her reality as a person is established with the gradual accumulation of descriptive detail. At a time when Hemingway was stripping this type of picture out of his own writing and out of American literature itself, Miller rivaled Thomas Hardy settling down to a dozen page portrait of Eustacia Vye. And because every other woman in *Capricorn* (and in *Cancer* before that) had been described only in terms of her sexuality, this description stands as a testament to the author's interest in June Smith. "Standing at the edge of the dance floor," the author says:

> I notice her coming toward me; she is coming with sails spread, the large full face beautifully balanced on the long, columnar neck. I see a woman perhaps eighteen, perhaps thirty, with blue-black hair and a large white face, a full white face in which the eyes shine brilliantly. She has on a tailored blue suit of duveteen. I remember distinctly now the fullness of her body, and that her hair was fine and straight, parted on the side, like a man's. I remember the smile she gave me—knowing, mysterious, fugitive —a smile that sprang up suddenly, like a puff of wind. (340)

None of the details is exceptional in itself, but gradually and with no sense of frenzy, the person comes into focus, and then becomes more and more familiar but not common:

> The whole being was concentrated in the face. I could have taken just the head and walked home with it; I could have put it

beside me at night, on a pillow, and made love to it. The mouth
and the eyes, when they opened up, the whole being glowed
from them. There was an illumination which came from some
unknown source, from a center hidden deep in the earth. I could
think of nothing but the face, the strange, womblike quality of the
smile, the engulfing immediacy of it. The smile was so painfully
swift and fleeting that it was like the flash of a knife. This smile,
this face, was borne aloft on a long white neck, the sturdy, swan-
like neck of the medium—and of the lost and the damned. (340–
41)

For the first time, the author is interested in, ready to love, a
"whole being," not just an isolated sex organ. What's more,
she is as involved in the world as the author, who says in delight, "Almost the whole evening we have been talking about
Strindberg." And in addition to her subtlety and intelligence,
she is as independent and energetic as the author, as much a
restless and inquisitive spirit: "Opulence she has, and magnifi-
cence; it's America right or wrong, and the ocean on either
side. For the first time in my life the whole continent hits me
full force, hits me between the eyes. This is America, buffaloes
or no buffaloes, America the emery wheel of hope and disillu-
sionment. Whatever made America made her, bone, blood,
muscle, eyeball, gait, rhythm, poise, confidence, brass and hollow gut" (342). For the author, this is the moment of a lifetime.
He is as keenly alive as he feels he has ever been, as far from
the Land of Fuck as one pole is from another: "One can wait a
whole lifetime for a moment like this. The woman whom you
never hoped to meet now sits before you, and she talks and
looks exactly like the person you dreamed about. But strangest
of all is that you never realized before that you had dreamed
about her" (343). This is an archetypal moment, "common to
experience but uncommon to expression," as Robert Frost puts
it, and in the lines quoted directly above one finds a fairly good
capsule definition of that undefinable concept, *love*.

Unfortunately for the author, *love* seems to be all promise
with no fulfillment. The author probably exaggerates when he
says, "Whenever I try to explain to myself the peculiar pattern
which my life has taken, when I reach back to the first cause, as

it were, I think inevitably of the girl I first loved. It seems to me that everything dates from that aborted affair" (335). The author goes on to say that he had "the pleasure of kissing her two or three times," that he walked past her home every night trying to catch a glimpse of her at the window, and that he never had the courage even to write her or call her up. Finally, he ran off to the Coast to start a "new life." Although the importance of this initial failure is such that it is worth mentioning, something more fundamental is behind the author's difficulties with the "girl (he) first loved" and every other woman he has loved up to and including June Smith. We have seen June Smith described first as a mythic goddess, elevated in the author's mind to a stature that no woman could hope to equal in the course of an everyday relationship (like Daisy in Gatsby's mind during their separation) and then as an extraordinary and exciting woman of the actual world. Between the memory of grandeur and the first rush of wonder, could a conventional and often ordinary relationship be developed? And could it be that the author has entered every relationship with a woman he might love exalted to the degree that any other level would seem like an unbearable fall from a magnificent prominence? By inflating his "love" and her charm way out of proportion, the author has made it impossible for himself to find a way to live with a woman over any length of time without being terribly disappointed. Either he must change his way of seeing himself and the women he meets, or he must suffer the failure of every romantic friendship he begins. Paradoxically, he seems to feel, at the conclusion of *Capricorn*, that he has been so powerfully affected by June Smith that although he is still wildly romantic in his expectations ("It is well that you promise me so much. I need to be promised nearly everything, for I have lived in the shadow of the sun too long" [347]), he will be able to successfully combine (at last) his dreams of romantic excess with a new, clear vision of himself and the world. His confidence is exceptional, momentarily equal to that of the artist/hero of *Cancer*, as he declares that he knows the dangers involved in wanting too much but that he is prepared to risk everything he *is* because there is so much at stake:

I take you as a star and a trap, as a stone to tip the scales, as a
judge that is blindfolded, as a hole to fall into, as a path to walk,
as a cross and an arrow. Up to the present I traveled the opposite
way of the sun; henceforth I travel two ways, as sun and as moon.
Henceforth I take on two sexes, two hemispheres, two skies, two
sets of everything. Henceforth I shall be double-jointed and dou-
ble-sexed. Everything that happens will happen twice. I shall be
as a visitor to this earth, partaking of its blessing and carrying off
its gifts. I shall neither serve nor be served. I shall seek the end in
myself. (347–48)

This passage sounds as if Miller has realized that his exceptionally masculine orientation toward the world and toward
women has been one of his problems, and that now he will try
to be aware of and encourage the feminine aspect of his nature.
Jane Nelson considerably overstates the situation when she
says, "The goal of the *I's* progress is androgyny, the androgynous self of the utopian vision as a symbol of the reconciliation
of opposites," which sounds impressive, but just isn't so.[16]
Even if Miller, circa 1939 had some idea of his blind areas, the
author does not have this insight, and even Miller himself
could never really "reconcile" the opposite impulses of his
psyche in his writing. Nonetheless, the author's avowed willingness to explore new and different modes of existence shows
how much he has been moved by his meetings with June
Smith, and he is in a state of near euphoria at the conclusion of
Capricorn because he feels that he has been finally elevated out
of the Land of Fuck, helped off the "ovarian trolley" and
released from the grip of the "Cosmodemonic bastards." How
could he know that he would have to face something even
worse than all of these horrors before he would begin to realize
any of his goals for himself as a man and as an artist?

8 Sexus

The Journey to the End of the Mind

THE tremendous promise of the conclusion of *Capricorn* is extended into and through the first two volumes of *Sexus*, a six-hundred-page, five-volume book which follows the author from a peak of exhilaration to a depth of despair that exceeds anything he has ever known. The book is organized around the author's efforts to discover if, by discarding many of his assumptions about love, art and life, he can discern aspects of his soul or spirit that have remained hidden; qualities lost to the protective devices he has developed as a means of survival in a Cosmodemonic world. He is anxious to overcome the attitudes which have resulted in the failure of every relationship he has ever had with a woman so that his love for Mara will lead to something more than explosive sex followed by anger and then silence. He is gradually becoming convinced that he does have talent as an artist, but he is not sure why he can't produce anything worthwhile, and he is determined to look at himself as clearly and honestly as he can to see if he is on some level obstructing his own artistic inclinations. Above all, he is beginning to suspect that his art and his strong desire for the company of women are tied together in some way, and that an understanding of him-

self in both areas will be necessary before he can live successfully in either one.

Mara has excited and inspired him to such a degree that he
not only sees himself as liberated from the disasters of *Capricorn,* but feels now that he has the confidence to live without
the protective strategies that have sustained him thus far in his
adult life. As he says on the first page of *Sexus,* "A wholly new
life lay before me, had I the courage to risk all. Actually there
was nothing to risk: I was at the bottom rung of the ladder, a
failure in every sense of the word" (9).[1] Of course, only someone who expects to be a "success" in the future will admit so
readily that he has been "a failure in every sense of the word."
His confidence in the future is a product of his ultraromantic
belief that *love* will, even must, produce something marvelous,
and the author's commitment to not only Mara but the concept
of *love* itself is awesome in its totality. As he says, "To make
absolute, unconditional surrender to the woman one loves is to
break every bond save the desire not to lose her, which is the
most terrible bond of all." (9) There is an awareness already of
the dangers of his attitude, but the author is undeterred, even
excited further by the possibility of a risky choice. There is also
something just a bit abject in his avowals of love: "What ambitions I may have had were gone; there was nothing I wanted to
do except to put myself completely in her hands. Above everything else I wanted to hear her voice, know that she was still
alive" (10).

When one considers just how important his art was for Miller, the author's disavowal of ambition is a further demonstration of the scope of his passion. His complete infatuation is an
indication of how far he has let down his reserves, and serves
as an index of his vulnerability. When, at the conclusion of
Sexus he is brought to a shocking and unprecedented fragility,
his collapse is convincing because we have seen him on a high,
precarious perch and can imagine the effect of a fall from that
altitude.

Like a confessional poet, the author finds ingenious images
for his passion:

I will go directly to her home, ring the bell, and walk in. Here I am, take me—or stab me to death. Stab the heart, stab the brain, stab the lungs, the kidneys, the viscera, the eyes, the ears. If only one organ be left alive you are doomed—doomed to be mine, forever, in this world and the next and all the worlds to come. I'm a desperado of love, a scalper, a slayer. I'm insatiable. I eat hair, dirty wax, dry blood clots, anything and everything you call yours. (14)

The author believes that the mere confession of his passion, albeit in impassioned language, will be sufficient to win his beloved; and he is right. He would never have fallen in love with someone who would not respond to his fierce eloquence. As in D. H. Lawrence's short story, "The Shades of Spring," Mara is moved by a man with whom "the stars are different." But language is not always employed in the service of passionate insight. As in his other books, Miller lapses at times, his "voice" less clear, less strong, less original. "Mara, Mara, where are you leading me? It's fateful, it's ominous, but I belong to you body and soul, and you will take me where you will, deliver me to my keeper, bruised, crushed, broken. For us there is no final understanding. I feel the ground slipping from under me" (20). While passages like this slide toward pronouncements on Valentine's Day cards, the context generally rescues them, at least to some extent. Immediately after the author has these commonplace thoughts, Mara responds: " 'I'll call you to-morrow,' she said, leaning forward impulsively for a last embrace. And then in my ear she murmured—'I'm falling in love with the strangest man on earth. You frighten me, you're so gentle. Hold me tight . . . believe in me always . . . I feel almost as if I were with a god' " (21). This is the first time any woman has spoken to the author after a moment of sexual passion, and the uniqueness of the conversation takes some of the dross off the fairly mundane nature of the sentiments. One might ask how a reader who has picked up Sexus without looking at anything else Miller wrote would feel about these lines, and many others throughout Miller's work. The only answer is that, as I have argued, the best parts of Miller's books need to be read in conjunction with passages from other books and the weaker parts of all of them are going to intrude frequently. Like the reader of Pound's *Cantos* (or most readers, anyway), one has to decide to skip over those sections one doesn't like or understand because there is so much that is worthwhile and accessible.

The essential conflict of the first two volumes of *Sexus* is established in the pages that follow the author's confessions of the rising pitch of his new love. He visits one of his old friends, a man called Ulric, and seems swept back all the way to the old masculine society of *Cancer* and *Capricorn*, a society of tasteless, sexist, racist comments. The author seems untroubled by these attitudes even when they conflict with the things he is learning about himself. Eventually, one realizes that they have been set in a larger frame in Miller's work, and that Miller is not endorsing entirely what he is describing, still, the tone of the incidents is just a bit too jaunty to suggest that he is fully against what he sees either. In *Sexus*, though, these passages serve to show a man torn between the comforts of a familiar style of living and the promises of a new type of relationship altogether. For all the author's protestations of love, there is something so strange and powerful about Mara that he has some doubts and needs reassurance that he is doing the right thing. Later, in Paris, Miller had friends who were sophisticated enough to understand his complex desires, but in Brooklyn in the 1920s this doesn't seem to have been the case. Here was a man in transition amidst people who were burrowing into ruts they had dug all their lives. As the author says, "I needed some one outside the vicious circle of false admirers and envious denigrators. I needed a man from the blue" (38). Since there isn't anyone like this, Ulric will have to do, but in a sad and hilarious dialogue, the author discovers that he has moved way beyond Ulric's ability to understand what has happened:

"Listen, Ulric, do you know what it is to be in love?" He didn't even deign to look up in answer to this. As he deftly mixed his colors in the tin tray he mumbled something about being possessed with normal instincts.

I went on unabashed. "Do you think you might meet a woman some day who would change your whole life?"

"I've met one or two who've tried—not with entire success, as you can see," he responded.

"Shit! Drop that stuff a moment, will you? I want to tell you something . . . I want to tell you that I'm in love, madly in love. I know it sounds silly, but this is different—I've never been like this before. You wonder if she's a good piece of tail. Yes, magnificent. But I don't give a shit about that . . ."

"Oh, you don't? Well, that's something new." (39–40)

Neither the author nor Ulric can even find the right words to discuss the situation, and the author rushes out "riled" by the conversation.

Because Miller likes to present his ideas through the words of people he admires, or through the medium of an analytical discussion of another artist's work, the author meets a woman named Sylvia, "gorgeously beautiful," who "looks Italian," is married to an understanding older man and never is seen in *Sexus* again. This odd femina ex machina is, I think, a portrait of Anaïs Nin oddly transposed back into an earlier time in Miller's life. Here, Sylvia tells him things about himself which the author wants to hear, things which may have been part of Anaïs Nin's comments to Miller in her letters.[2] Touching on the twin necessities of change and risk, Sylvia speaks as follows:

"You couldn't possibly be a failure," she said, after a moment's hesitation in which she seemed to be collecting herself to make some important revelation. "The trouble with you," she said slowly and deliberately, "is that you've never set yourself a task worthy of your powers. You need bigger problems, bigger difficulties. You don't function properly until you're hard pressed. I don't know what you're doing but I'm certain that your present life is not suited to you. You were meant to lead a dangerous life; you can take greater risks than others because. . . . well, you probably know it yourself. . . . because you are protected." (50)

She continues on to say "you are always looking beyond the object of your love, looking for something you will never find. You will have to look inside yourself if you ever hope to free yourself of torment," and concludes her advice with the further admonition, "You will always be trying to dominate yourself; the woman you love will only be an instrument for you to practice on . . . "

The gist of Sylvia's comments reinforces the author's own instinctive belief that he must continue his love affair with Mara, and for the remainder of the first two volumes of *Sexus*, the author alternates moments of extremely intense sex with Mara (74) and incidents in which he introduces her to his friends. Gradually, he learns more about her, her past and her present life, and as his life with her becomes more of a natural flow, a familiar rhythm, he is able to give up many of his previous customs. At the same time, he is still pulled back to his old habits, including a powerful sexual attraction for his wife with whom he is still "living" but hardly speaking to. It is as if he is drawn back again and again to the Land of Fuck whenever he becomes uncertain or troubled. His late night entry into his own house to approach his wife sexually without either of them having to speak at all is typical of this regression (104–105), but the incident is written with so much intensity—a version of a Joycean stream-of-consciousness monologue—that one can feel the author's temptation to continue his familiar exploits even as he is drawn beyond them.

His own most compelling argument for giving up his old ways is his realization that he and Mara are beginning to resemble all the other faceless copulating couples of the world. Mara has just returned to the city after a visit to the northern part of the state with two of her friends. The author is not in a particularly good mood. He is troubled by Mara's "visits" to various places to meet male "friends," usually older men of means. In spite of her assurances that she is just keeping these men company, and in spite of his own sexual adventuring, the author is not happy with Mara's somewhat mysterious existence beyond his life with her. He is showing the first signs of a possessive attitude which is a part of a growing desire for some permanence in his life. He meets Mara at a hotel near the ocean, and for the first time, their passion is forced and contrived. "Mara was struggling frantically to bring on an orgasm. She had somehow become detached from her sexual apparatus; it was night and she was lost in the dark; her movements were those of a dreamer desperately struggling to reenter the body which had begun the act of surrender" (179).

The couple separates, and the author looks at Mara first, then at himself. Neither image is appealing: "Mara lay prone on the bed, panting and sweating; she had the appearance of a battered odalisque made of jagged pieces of mica" (180). And the author, disgusted with himself, sees his body with contempt:

> What surprised me was that it continued to stand up like a hammer; it had lost all the appearance of a sexual implement; it looked disgustingly like a cheap gadget from the five and ten cent store, like a bright-colored piece of fishing tackle minus the bait. And on this bright and slippery gadget Mara twisted like an eel. She wasn't any longer a woman in heat, she wasn't even a woman; she was just a mass of undefinable contours wriggling and squirming like a piece of fresh bait seen upside down through a convex mirror in a rough sea. (181)

Over this whole scene, "the sun was setting in the West as usual, not in splendor and radiance however but in disgust, like a gorgeous omelette engulfed by clouds of snot and phlegm," and all around the author and Mara, the Cosmodemonic world threatens to absorb them: "We stretched ourselves out in the hollow of a suppurating sand dune next to a bed of waving stink weed on the lee side of a macadamized road over which the emissaries of progress and enlightenment were rolling along with that familiar and soothing clatter which accompanies the smooth locomotion of spitting and farting contraptions of tin woven together by steel knitting needles" (182). Even the excitement each has felt in the other's company is gone, "the conversation was thoroughly desultory, spluttering out with a dull thud like a bullet encountering muscle and sinew."

The author feels that this unpleasant encounter is the result of their fugitive and clandestine meetings, and after being harassed by a prying policeman during a tryst in Prospect Park, he takes Mara to his home. His wife is supposedly away for a long vacation of some kind, but she appears in the morning with "the landlord who lived upstairs, and his daughter," and the author's marriage is formally over. As the second volume concludes, the author and Mara have decided to take a flat in the Bronx in the home of one of the author's friends.

The third and fourth volumes of *Sexus* depict the author's struggle to resolve the various forces pulling him in contradictory directions into one controllable channel of energy. As the initial excitement of his relationship with Mara begins to fade, he finds himself tempted by other women once again. By a kind of perverse and very shoddy logic, he tells himself that since he has been spiritually "rescued" by his love for Mara, he can indulge in obscene behavior and then be cleansed by her love. Mara seems willing to overlook his transgressions, but his self-delusion clearly has him heading for some sort of disaster. Mara, too, wants to maintain a relatively independent existence of her own, although she is also interested in making the author feel that he is the primary man in her life. For some couples an arrangement of this sort is possible, but both Mara and the author encounter serious difficulties in their efforts to make it work. And although the "story" is told almost entirely from the author's point of view, there is a probing honesty to the narrative that prevents the account from becoming an apology for the author's actions or an attempt to place blame entirely on Mara's way of living.

The author and Mara's arrival at their home, the house of a Dr. Onorifick, is not at all auspicious because the house is a symbol of domestic disaster similar to every "marriage" mentioned in *Sexus*. The building is roach-ridden, the family eccentric and Mara has decided to change her name to Mona. This change is never really explained, but there is a suggestion here of a chameleon that reflects surfaces without having any fundamental substance of its own. The author is still so dazzled by the surface, though, that he takes the change as evidence of a new beginning, something that he is too eager to believe in. Miller is not always sure of Mona's motives, but shows her trying to make the relationship work as well as she can: "I was not aware, when I first knew Mona, how much she needed me. Nor did I realize how great a transformation she had made of

her life, her habits, her background, her antecedents, in order
to offer me that ideal image of herself which she all too quickly
suspected that I had created" (211). The dialogue on pages 214
and 215 is genuinely tender and convincing, evidence of a talent that Miller exhibits too rarely, and it gives one the impression that here are two people, powerfully attracted to each
other, but almost desperately conscious of their own singularity
and anxious not to lose a unique sense of the self by merging it
with another person. Still, there is a basis for a growing relationship in discussions like the one on pages 214–215, but during the next hundred pages, the author is drawn again and
again back to his most promiscuous ways. There is never a real
analysis of the author's motivation here, just a very powerful
evocation of the forces of lust which drive him, and this is one
of Miller's more serious failings. One can gather by implication
that as long as the author and Mona are getting along well,
what the author does in his "spare" time is not that important.
Monogamy, after all, is not the only basis for an enduring relationship. And from the author's point of view, he is being true
in a fashion to Mona—the old male double standard. His so-
journs with other women involve only his skin, not his soul.
However, it is an unsubtle man who would think that the *skin*
and the *soul* are never connected, and the author is not unsubtle. He has fooled himself by his ingenious and sometimes
devious ways with words, and more significantly, he is an ac-
complice in his own deception, as when he can analyze his wife
Maude's thinking in a way that would seem to shift the blame
for his own lust onto the insatiable sexual appetite of *all*
women. It is as if he is saying that he is a partner in a conspira-
cy with the women he is sexually tied to; that there is an equality of passion that removes any obligations from all of
them:

> If, she may have told herself, if it were possible to be fucked like
> that whenever she wished, it wouldn't matter what claims the
> other one had on me. Perhaps it entered her mind for the first
> time that possession is nothing if you can't surrender yourself.
> Perhaps she even went so far as to think it might be better this
> way—having me to protect her and fuck her and not having to get
> angry with me because of jealous fears. If the other one could hold

on to me, if the other one could keep me from running around
with every little slut that came across my path, if together they
could share me, tacitly of course and without embarrassment and
confusion, perhaps after all it might be better than the old arrangement. (305)

Perhaps. As Jake Barnes said, wouldn't it be nice to think so.

One waits in vain for the author to indicate that he sees what
he is doing. But at this point in the narrative, almost one hundred pages have been devoted to an extended examination of
the joy, excitement and sheer physical sensation of an unbri-
dled sexuality which does not appear to harm any of the parties
involved. This is the realm of the senses, with no irony in the
author's espousals of sexual activity. These aren't a series of
incidents in which one person exploits another, but explicitly
erotic writings—often pornographic by Laurie Stone's definition (orgasm after orgasm)—in which all of the people involved
are pleased by the outcome of their actions. One might call it
fantasy, and the extreme potency of the male plus the extreme
readiness of the female would support this view, but in a sense,
Miller is writing metaphorically in an effort to capture the awe-
someness of sexual arousal at its most consuming. Mailer is
right when he says that Miller writes about lust as no one has
before, but what Mailer overlooks is that this type of activity
does not constitute an entire existence, even if it dominates the
nature of a person's existence for prolonged periods of time.
And in the case of the author, a man of considerable intelligence, some compassion (erratic in its employment) and an artist's sensibility, even the exceptionally satisfying sexual life he
is leading will not be enough to keep him content. However, as
long as he has his "love" for Mona to keep him directed toward
some vague future in which he settles down and begins to
work at his writing, the author is willing to live in a kind of
perpetual present in which "vitality" is its own excuse for being. As his relationship with his once-hated wife takes another
turn, he exults: "To break a habit, establish a new rhythm—
simple devices, long known to the ancients. It never failed.
Break down the old pattern, the worn-out connections, and the
spirit breaks loose, establishes new polarities, creates new tensions, bequeaths new vitality" (307).

What is missing in this formulation, and apparently of little importance to the author at the moment he is speaking, is any kind of lasting commitment to another person; any real giving of the self to fulfill someone else's needs; any kind of important sacrifice involving one's immediate gratification in the service of some future development. The author is behaving, in other words, like a spoiled child. Still, the author's candor, as Mailer notes, is valuable in itself considering the hypocrisy that lies behind much conventional behavior. As the author says, giving tongue to the dumb instincts of many, many men:

> How many hundred women had I pursued, followed like a lost
> , dog, in order to study some mysterious trait—a pair of eyes set far
> apart, a head hewn out of quartz, a haunch that seemed to live its
> own life, a voice as melodious as the warble of a bird, a cataract of
> hair falling like spun-glass, a torso invested with the flexibility of
> rubber. . . . Whenever the beauty of the female becomes irresisti-
> ble, it is traceable to a single quality. (315)

This poetic passage continues for three pages as the author (and surely Henry Miller as well) composes a song of lust, a catalog of attributes which trigger an initial magnetic response in another person. The burden of the song is that both men and women are caught by this "mysterious" power, and the implication is that a female with a similar sensibility might write the same melody from a feminine perspective. And this summarizes the theme of the central section of *Sexus*, which is that both men and women share these desires and impulses and need each other for their expression.

There is, however, the writer Henry Miller beyond the author whose adventures we follow in *Capricorn* and *Sexus*, and while he has tried to make the song of lust as stirring as he can, he has also given more than a little thought to all of the other aspects of human experience that any intelligent adult must consider. Miller is quite clearly aware of the limitations of an existence regulated by lust alone, and of its consequences for most people. Although the author seems to be successful in balancing both the world of lust and the world of love, when he returns to Dr. Onirifick's "establishment" after his joyous visit to Maude's, he is greeted by the words, "She tried to poison herself!" The third volume of *Sexus* ends as the author begins to realize that the "love" he has had for Mona is so much like "worship" that he hasn't really made any effort to make contact with her as a human being. "Then it came to me," he says as he sits next to her bed while she recovers, "only if she were dead could I love her the way I imagined I loved her!" (325). This realization is followed by a further insight: " 'You did love her once, but you were so pleased with yourself to think that you could love another beside yourself that you forgot about her almost immediately. You've been watching yourself make love. . . .' " (325).

Volume four of *Sexus* involves the author's attempt to re-structure his relationship with Mona so that they can both un-derstand and make allowances for each other's individual pecu-liarities. Mona has taken poison because, in spite of her insistence that she trusts the author, she is actually aware of his "weaknesses" and afraid of what she calls "betrayal." The au-thor realizes that each of them has been holding something back: For him, it is the kind of total commitment which Mona wants. For her, it is a complete confession of origins, actions and intentions which the author needs. What they both most want is precisely what the other finds most difficult to relin-quish. Feeding their resistance is the fear that they will have nothing left to hide behind when they have given up their se-cret strengths. And a part of this fear is that the other person will not accept them when they have completely exposed their most essential selves. Had Miller been able to write about how two people struggled with these problems, he might have achieved the "great tragedy of love" he hoped to create, but in the rest of *Sexus*, both Mona and the author try to make accom-modations rather than risk a real change which could make enduring love possible. However, this doesn't mean that the book is a failure. The relationship that Mona and the author are developing is fascinating, and the weakness of *Sexus*, I believe, is in its digressions and superfluous material. Once Miller has made his point, he would have been well advised to move along rather than remaining "true" to the literal events as they

took place. In the fourth volume of *Sexus*, while the reader
waits for the author and Mona to proceed with their life together, Miller wastes the propelling power of the plot by cutting back to his job at what he now calls the "Cosmodemonic
Cocksucking Corporation," and by recalling lost loves from his
past, and by relocating the couple at the home of "my old
friend Arthur Raymond," and by spending pages on windy
philosophical excursions with various friends. There are,
though, some very effective sections which contribute to the
evolving psychological portrait of Mona and the author which
Miller is gradually getting done.

   The author, speaking from the heart and recollecting ideas
from Miller's other books, defines "real marriage" in terms of
talk. "One talks. If you are talking to some one who knows how
to listen he understands perfectly, even though the words
make no sense. When this kind of talk gets under way a marriage takes place, no matter whether you are talking to a man or
a woman. Men talking with other men have as much need of
this sort of marriage as women talking with women have. Married couples seldom enjoy this kind of talk, for reasons which
are only too obvious" (404). Miller may be revealing some of
the limitations of his idea of what a marriage is by his last comment, but his idea that *talk* is an expression of love is quite
reasonable (even charming) and his views on the importance of
communication between people show again the fundamentally
humane side of his psyche:

> Talk, real talk, it seems to me, is one of the most expressive
> manifestations of man's hunger for unlimited marriage. Sensitive
> people, people who feel, want to unite in some deeper, subtler,
> more durable fashion than is permitted by custom and conven-
> tion. . . . When man begins to permit himself full expression,
> when he can express himself without fear of ridicule, ostracism or
> persecution, the first thing he will do will be to pour out his love.
> (404–05)

This passage begins to go soft at the center, but before Miller's
ideas become drowned in a sea of sentimentality, the author
offers a bizarre illustration of how *talk* can literally inflame the

imagination without leading to any kind of real understanding when he encourages Mona to tell him, in very graphic detail, a story about a date she had with a violent, brutal man in the indeterminate "past." Mona is not particularly interested in continuing the narration ("Oh I don't want to talk about it. . . . it was disgusting.") but the author insists she go on, and as Mona continues he finds himself tremendously excited by the narrative. At the same time, he seems totally immune to Mona's discomfort during the recital and oblivious to her pain during what is obviously a filthy, degrading experience. This account is one of the most violently pornographic in Miller's writing (440–444), and it is a textbook illustration of everything that feminist critics have found wrong with Miller's work. The author is clearly aroused and although he claims to be "eager to keep up with her flights" as if he might learn more about her from the story, he is more interested in luxuriating in the vicarious sexual excitement the narrative provokes. What Miller wants to show here is the author's deteriorating moral sensitivity and his lack of fitness for *marriage* in spite of all his theorizing about "unlimited marriage." As the author decides that he must make allowances for Mona's need for a kind of independence (she continues to spend time with wealthy men on "harmless" outings of various sorts), he is also too ready to make allowances for his own impulsive behavior. This decline culminates in yet another sexual encounter with his wife, in which they are joined by Eloise (the daughter of the landlord who lives upstairs) in a pure celebration of the supersensual:

> After a time I turned back to a prone position. Elsie did the same. I closed my eyes, tried to summon sleep. It was impossible. The bed felt deliciously soft, the bodies beside me were soft and clinging, and the odor of hair and sex was in my nostrils. From the garden came the heavy fragrance of rain-soaked earth. It was strange, soothingly strange, to be back in this big bed, the marital bed, with a third person beside us, and the three of us enveloped in frank, sensual lust. (485)

There is certainly a place in American literature for erotic writing, but the problem here is the context, the situation. The author can no longer distinguish between "frank, sensual lust," pornographic violence at its most exploitive, his own base de- sires, other people's needs and even what is at stake in turning himself into a creature of the skin while his soul slides toward oblivion. The author isn't living in the Land of Fuck now be- cause he is so lacking in introspection that he remains relatively free of self-doubt and despair, but he is in the process of losing his spiritual qualities and the effects are going to be every bit as bad for him. "What would it matter if Mona left me? What would it matter three generations hence how I had behaved on the night of the 14th or so. . . ," (490), he says, finding a ra- tionale for his actions. "When you have an inspiration your mind takes a vacation" (499), he tells Arthur Raymond's wife, accounting for his irresponsible behavior.

And at this point in the narrative, the author's relationship with Mona really becomes clear. In the most brilliant part of his essay on Miller, Norman Mailer discusses what he calls "the uncharted negotiations of the psyche when two narcissists take the vow of love."[3] He identifies Mona and the author as "nar- cissists" and defines narcissistic behavior with several very per- ceptive ideas. First, he points out that "it is too simple to think of the narcissist as someone in love with himself."[4] The real test of a narcissist is what Mailer calls "the fundamental relation," which he says, "is with oneself." Describing the author in *Sexus* precisely, Mailer notes that "the inner dialogue never ceases," and while Mona's inner thoughts are never presented (a failing on Miller's part), practically the entire body of Miller's work is an inner dialogue. Mailer goes on to capture the essence of the attraction that Mona and the author have for each other. "They have a passionate affair to the degree each allows the other to resonate more fully than when alone."[5] When Mona returns to their house where the author has been waiting for her with some concern, she is described this way: "Mona returned, wide awake, lovelier than ever, her skin glowing like calcium. She hardly listened to my explanations about the night before; she was exalted, infatuated with herself. So many things had hap- pened since then—she didn't know where to begin" (503–04). Both the author and Mona want to bounce their energy off each other, or see it reflected in the other's eyes. Aside from some very intense sex, what are they actually doing together? Returning from adventures with stories to tell is not the same as sharing experiences. Because they are supposed to be concerned with how they treat each other, each must be careful not to hurt the other with accounts of "betrayals" or liaisons. So, as Mailer says, "the eye of one's own consciousness is forever looking at one's own action."[6] As long as Mona and the author have been living together but free to go out alone, this arrangement is supportable, but as the basis for a marriage it seems very unsteady. Nonetheless, Mona and the author decide to get married. Mona thinks the idea is a wonderful one:

> "'I'm so glad. I've been waiting to hear you say that. I want to start a new life with you. Let's get away from all these people! And I want you to quit that awful job. I'll find a place where you can write. You won't need to earn any money. I'll soon be making lots of money. You can have anything you want. I'll get you all the books you want to read. . . . Maybe you'll write a play—and I'll act in it! That would be wonderful, wouldn't it?'"

We have seen how the author feels about "establishing a new rhythm" to "bequeath new vitality." Now Mona echoes his belief in change, but one begins to realize at this point that all Mona and the author ever really have is an endless series of new starts. As the author says about Mona, "Inwardly she was like a column of smoke; the slightest pressure of her will altered the configuration of her personality instantly" (506). Perhaps marriage would provide both a new start and the basis for something permanent.

The author does not seem especially enthusiastic about another marriage, but he is "in love" with Mona and has vowed to do anything for that love, so he agrees. Various signs contribute to his suspicions he is making a mistake (at the divorce trial, the "judge looked like a scarecrow fitted with a pair of lunar binoculars"; there is a casual sexual incident with a girl in a bar after the trial; Mona deceives him at a theatrical performance; he meets *another* wife of an old friend; Mona vanishes for seven days and returns to promise *another* new beginning—

"Her whole body felt strangely different as I pressed her close. It was the body of a creature who had been reborn." [541].), but the author talks himself into believing, contrary to considerable evidence, that his *love* for her is so extraordinary that it will triumph over everything. He is now back at the beginning of *Sexus*, the conclusion of *Capricorn*, when he felt the first sharp pangs of romantic exultation. It is as if he has learned nothing during the first four volumes of *Sexus*. He is still the man who is ready to believe, in spite of all his experience, that some vague, idealized *love* will make everything wonderful. The ego of the narcissist is rampant. If he, the author does it, it must be right:

> The ground had opened up, the past had been swept away, drowned, drowned as deep as a lost continent. And miraculously —how miraculously I only realized as the moments prolonged themselves!—she had been saved, had been restored to me. It was my duty, my mission, my destiny in this life to cherish and protect her. As I thought of all that lay ahead I began to grow, from within, as if from a small seed. I grew inches in the space of a block. It was in my heart that I felt the seed bursting. (542)

But the "seed" of their marriage is still not quite ready to be planted. As volume five of *Sexus* begins, the author hesitates again, Mona threatens to leave again, they have another powerful sexual experience together (as Mailer says, "they tune each other superbly well,") and finally, they cross the Hudson to Hoboken to get married. The ceremony is a disaster ("O. K. Sign here. Bang, bang! Raise your right hand! *I solemnly swear*, etc. etc. Married. Five dollars, please. Kiss the bride. *Next, please. . . .*" (570)—all standard public rituals are mockeries in Miller's life) and the couple returns to a desultory celebration with a few old friends. The evening passes in a mixture of frenzy ("I'm whole again. All one piece. A man in love. A man who got married of his own free will. A man who was never really married before. A man who knew women, but not love. . . . Now I'll sing for you. Or recite, if you like. *What do you want?* [576]") and gloom ("Death is easy: it's like the booby-hatch, only you can't masturbate any more. You like your nookie, Ned says. Sure, so does every one. And what then? In ten years your ass will be crinkled and your boobs will be hanging down like empty douche bags [586]."") and winds down as the couple goes to a burlesque show. The marriage that follows is actually much worse than any of these unfortunate incidents would suggest.

The last twenty pages of *Sexus* is the crux of the triad, "The Artist as Actor," and unlike anything Miller wrote anywhere else. All of the sexual activity that comes before should be seen in terms of what happens here, and everything that the author has said about women and love ought to be reviewed in the light of this experience, because Miller uses it as a commentary on the author's previous limitations and blindness. One of the reasons that the author was reluctant to marry Mona was his instinctive awareness that his freewheeling sexual aggressiveness was a method for blotting out the emptiness of his life. Without a real sense of self, he had to depend on sexual passion as a means for expressing himself and even rationalizing his existence. He needed the fix of sex every day to dull the psychic pain. A non-starter as an artist, a relative failure as a provider, an outsider to the community, an invisible man to his parents and kin, the author had no basis for respecting himself as a human being. Because he sensed that marriage to Mona would not contribute anything vital to forming a viable concept for the self, he was hesitant about joining that union. As it turned out, the marriage not only put an end to his sexual adventures without providing anything in compensation, but led to a stunning reversal in sexual and social roles that threatened to drive the author literally out of his mind.

"Let us jump a few years," the author says, "into the pot of horror" (614). The details that have been skipped can easily be filled in by exaggerating the events of the first four volumes, with a particular emphasis on every moment that is an harbinger of disaster. We see the author now, uncharacteristically crushed in spirit, whining and complaining about what "they" have done: "It is night and I am sitting in a cellar. This is our home. I wait for her night after night, like a prisoner chained to the floor of his cell. There is a woman with her whom she calls her friend. They have conspired to betray me and defeat me. They leave me without food, without heat, without light. They tell me to amuse myself until they return" (614).

In a kind of terrible revenge for all the women the author has ignored, defamed, insulted and lied to, Mona and "her friend" are oblivious to the author's needs as a human being, using him as they will for their own amusement, giving him no respect of any kind. He cannot reach them, cannot make them acknowledge that he is a person who matters, even a factor they must make some adjustment to. In a devastating turnaround that sends the author practically careening into mental chaos, the two women talk about him as if he were not there or discuss him dispassionately the way one debates the merits of an acquisition, or the way in which men, throughout Miller's work, talk about some "feature" of a woman's body.

"When they return to torture me," the author says, "I behave like the animal which I have become," explaining that he must fake some passion "in order to stimulate my almost extinct emotions" (614–615). But the women are insensitive to his moods, and when he tries to reach them by wild gestures ("Stand up! I yell. Give me the other chair! Protests, howls, screams."), they remark coldly, "He'll never go away . . . he's just acting." The anger is genuine, but it is directed more at himself than at them or at the world. He has developed a self-hatred for accepting this treatment—the reverse of the narcissist's self-love, but a part of narcissistic behavior all the same. "One can detest oneself intimately and still be a narcissist," Mailer says.[7] The hatred is aimed at the author's vulnerability, and he knows that he has become defenseless because he has neglected his self (or his soul/spirit) throughout *Sexus* so that he might satisfy the narrow needs of the flesh each day.

The author flees temporarily, but goes nowhere, and a truck driver who picks him up describes his condition exactly: "You don't seem to care very much one way or another. You act like you were just riding around in the dark" (619). The author's defeat is measured in terms of his loss of spirit. It is not that the circumstances of his life have made him a "loser" because he has always *lost* by conventional standards of success and victory, but for the first time, he has lost the will to struggle, and this is a real defeat. His loss is a part of and goes back to his gradual but growing indifference to his qualities of humanity. Fittingly, he sees himself now as an animal with no human attributes: "He said roost, I said kennel—*under my breath,* to be sure. I liked kennel better. Roost was for roosters, pigeons, birds of feather that lay eggs. I wasn't going to lay no eggs. Bones and refuse, bones and refuse, bones and refuse. I repeated it over and over, to give myself the moral strength to crawl back like a beaten dog" (622).

How pathetic to try to hold onto a distinction between a dog and a rooster, but it is as a dog that the author sees himself now, and from the mind of a domestic pet, he expresses delight that his masters are home: "Near the bottom I heard muffled sounds of speech. They were home! I felt terrifically happy, exultant. I wanted to dash in wagging my little tail and throw myself at their feet. But that wasn't the program I had planned to adhere to" (623). He hears the two women talking—again a switch on the usual dialogue of men about women—and his "outsideness" is emphasized by their close joining:

> There were strange pauses, too, as if they were embracing. Now and then I could swear the big one gave a grunt, as though she were rubbing the skin off the other one. Then suddenly she let out a howl of delight, but a vengeful one. Suddenly she shrieked.
>
> "Then you do love him still? You were lying to me!"
>
> "No, no! I swear I don't. You *must* believe me, *please.* I never loved him."
>
> "That's a lie!"
>
> "I swear to you . . . I swear I never loved him. He was just a child to me."
>
> This was followed by a shrieking gale of laughter. Then a slight commotion, as if they were scuffling. Then a dead silence, as if their lips were glued together. (623–24)

Not only is his "beloved" denying him now, but he has been replaced, it seems, not only spiritually but physically by "the other one." The hint of lesbianism complicates the situation and further confuses the author, who expresses his distress and uncertainty by saying: "Then a curious physiological comedy took place. *I began to menstruate.* I menstruated from every hole in my body. When a man menstruates it's all over in a few minutes. He doesn't leave any mess behind either" (624–25). The strange image suggests a momentary identification with all those women who "bleed" whom he has mocked in the past, calling their "wound" a sign of weakness.

Like the dog he has become in his own eyes, the author "crept upstairs on all fours and left the house as silently as I had entered it." Alone on the street, he encounters one image after another of defeat and destruction. The "street" he is traversing begins to resemble a track or path through his subconscious mind, and he seems to be back on "the ovarian trolley" or living once again "in the night life." On the street, or in his mind "A drunk comes along and stands beside me. He pees all over himself and then suddenly he doubles up and begins to vomit. As I walk away I can hear it splashing over his shoes" (626). An old schoolteacher who "used to be sweet on me" gives him a nickel with a look that says, "You'll never be able to cope with the world." The author looks at the stars and sees "All my failures . . . a very embryo of unfulfillment." He is drawn back to his "kennel"—'an insane desire to repass the house I had been driven from took possession of me," and when he puts his ear to the window, he hears, in a parody of the love he misses: "They were singing a Russian song which the big one was fond of. Apparently all was his bliss in there" (627). He leaves the house and turns toward the river, usually a symbol of life in Miller's work, now (as once before in *Capricorn*) reversed as everything else is reversed for the author: "I retraced my steps to the river, to that grim, dismal street which ran like a shriveled urethra beneath the overhanging terraces of the rich" (627).

Abruptly, in this dark, blighted realm, part psychic place and part of the rotting city he lives in, he comes upon a shadowy figure. It is an avenger faceless and unrecognizable, perhaps some version of his conscience, now awakened from long hibernation and prowling in anger:

When he got within a few feet of me he flashed a gun. With that I instinctively put up my hands. He came up to me and frisked me. Then he put his gun back in his hip pocket. Never a word out of him. He went through my pockets, found nothing, cuffed me in the jaw with the back of his hand and then stepped back towards the gutter.

"Put your hands down," he said, low and tense.

I dropped them like two flails. I was petrified with fright.

He pulled the gun out again, levelled it, and said in the same even, low, tense voice: "I'm givin' it to you in the guts, you dirty dog!" (629)

The author curls up "like a foetus, crooking my elbow over my eyes to protect them," but is not hit by the fusillade. He staggers home, defeated and slinks into the house. He collapses into bed ("There were some cigarette butts at the foot of the bed—they felt like dead beetles.") and falls asleep, only to dream that he is some kind of animal again, tortured by a man with a whip, who attacks him repeatedly. The attack is like a reminder of all his sexual assaults on "willing" women, and he begins to bleed, "blood oozing from me as if I were a big sponge." Then he is shaken out of his dream and sees the two women bending over him. The "big one" implores him to stop screaming, and the other—Mona, but not named—says, "My God, Val, what's happened? Wake up, wake up!" (632). They argue and then leave. He falls asleep again. This time he dreams that he is in a dog show, "Two women whom I seemed to recognize were bickering about our respective merits and demerits."

This is the final degradation, the author reduced to a dog who is totally at the mercy of his master, completely ineffectual and impotent otherwise: " 'I knew you would win the prize for me,' she whispered. 'You're such a lovely, lovely creature,' and she began stroking my fur. 'Wait a moment, my darling, and I'll bring you something nice. Just a moment . . .' " (633). One sees here a kind of *love* in which the object of love (the pet) is adored, treasured, pampered, even worshiped. It has a familiar look to it. And the author, losing his final and his most cherished strength, his language, is only able to reply, "Woof woof! Woof woof!" The woman commands the pet to beg for a treat. " 'Woof woof! Woof woof!' " I was ready to jump out of my skin with joy" (633). And the final image of the author, as *Sexus* ends, is of a manipulated sexual implement, not man, not animal, just *thing*. The last paragraphs of the book describe the ultimate reduction of a man who has really just gotten everything that he asked for, although not quite in the form he had envisioned:

> Finally, to my astonishment, she stuck her tongue out and began to suck the marrow into her mouth. She turned it around and sucked from the other end. When she had made a clean hole through and through she caught hold of me and began to stroke me. She did it so masterfully that in a few seconds I stood out like a raw turnip. Then she took the bone (with the wedding ring still around it) and she slipped it over the raw turnip. "Now you little darling, I'm going to take you home and put you to bed." And with that she picked me up and walked off, everybody laughing and clapping hands. Just as we got to the door the bone slid off and fell to the ground. I tried to scramble out of her arms, but she held me tight to her bosom. I began to whimper.
>
> "Hush, hush!" she said, and sticking her tongue out, she licked my face. "You dear, lovely, little creature!"
>
> "Woof woof! Woof woof!" I barked. "Woof woof! Woof, woof, woof!" (634)

9 Nexus

The Retreat from Revelation

H ENRY Miller
is not a writer who depends on the development of an interesting situation for his effectiveness, but at the conclusion of *Sexus*
he has left the two primary characters of the book in a position
of uncertainty and tension that demands some kind of resolution. The suspense involving the survival of the author, both
psychically and physically, is sufficient to send any reader at all
interested in the central character of the triad eagerly to the
next book in the series. Miller intended to continue his narrative in *Plexus*, but during the seven years that passed before he
completed that book, he lost some of the animating fire that
inspired him to compose the desperate last pages of *Sexus*, and
Plexus, when it appeared, bore almost no relationship to its os-
tensible predecessor. There are two slightly familiar people
there called "Mona" and "Henry Miller," but they bear very
little resemblance to the tormented and vastly alive characters
of *Sexus*. Instead, they are a version of a relatively conventional
American couple, moderately happy, fairly poor, reticent about
their sexual interests (for Miller, they are practically celibate)
and living a generally homogenized existence. The book is like
a six-hundred-page sociology report, with some amusing anec-

dotes and some literary flashes (a nice parody or two) but not much to engage anyone who is attracted to any of the things that Henry Miller does well. The book might have been written by John Marquand and reviewed happily by J. Donald Adams, to mention respectable literary figures from the 1950s, but it has hardly any of the elements or ideas that have made Henry Miller's work so distinct and unusual. It is interesting, I think, that the only part of *Plexus* that Mailer includes is a "portrait" of a woman that might also have been included in a *Reader's Digest* excerpt with few complaints from the readers of that publication.

Miller must have realized that he had not successfully dealt with any of the implications of the frightening events at the conclusion of *Sexus*, because *Nexus* begins precisely as *Sexus* ended, owing nothing to any of the incidents related in *Plexus*. The last sentence of *Sexus* is literally the first sentence of *Nexus*: "Woof! Woof woof! *Woof! Woof!*"[1] Only the last two "barks" have been changed, italicized in this case to emphasize the desperation of the author, who describes himself "Barking in the night. Barking, barking. I shriek but no one answers. I scream but there's not even an echo" (7). Miller reaches back, in the beginning of *Nexus*, to recreate a condition of tension and desperation from which the author seems to have two possibilities of escape. Either he might slide further into madness and ineffectuality, or he might emerge triumphant with genuine new insights into his character that would permit him to begin the real work of his life. Of all the descents–ascents of Miller's writing, this is the most convincing, and for the first time, the stage has been set for an important discovery; even some significant revelation. By the end of *Sexus*, Miller has shown that he has some idea of what sexual exploitation, sexual aggression and male sexual politics is about. While he is too much a creature of his time and place to fully understand how women have been restricted in their lives, he has sufficient insight now to write with some real understanding about Mona and possibly the other female "characters" of his world.

Unfortunately, Miller was not really ready to resubmerge his mind and soul in the awesome chaos of what must have been one of the pivotal moments of his life. On the one hand, the reader (or the admirer of Miller) must be almost thankful that Miller is so far from this "time" that he finds it difficult to remember it. On the other hand, from a selfish artistic standpoint, one must almost regret Miller's inability to force himself back into the torment he must have felt. As Mailer says, in pointing out why Hemingway was shattered and Miller intact after a career of very introspective writing, it was necessary (for Miller) "to sacrifice a piece of one's talent in the act of becoming a man."[2] However Mailer means "man," Miller had put the terrors of 1927 in some safe part of his memory, walled in so that he could not be touched by those demons. Even more seriously, he did not have the imaginative power to regenerate the feeling of expectation, of new visions unfolding, that he most surely felt just before he left for Paris. The result is that *Nexus*, while not nearly as much a soporific as *Plexus*, stands as a disappointment, not only for what it fails to do but also as an example of so much that is not realized in Miller's writing.

Instead of moving through the fasces of his previous existence to some new level of revelation, Miller appears to step back from the edge of the abyss that beckoned hideously to the author in *Sexus*, look retrospectively over his entire life, and then give it all his blessings. To be sure, some adjustments will be made, but Henry Miller circa 1960 when *Nexus* was finished has grown rather fond of the author and the artist/hero and has decided to accept them as they are. The revelation that finally occurs in *Nexus* is, paradoxically, that there will never be any revelation; that it is all part of an ongoing process, and that it is the *process* itself which has been important. This is a valid position certainly, and it anticipates some very modern ideas about *art*, but after the way in which Miller has structured the triad, it is an unsatisfactory resolution to an important problem. The philosophy of "acceptance" which Miller has been so praised for by some critics is actually here an acceptance of defeat, an admission by implication that he cannot write effectively about his worst troubles with Mona and his decision to become a writer. As he tells J. Rives Childs in a letter written in 1951: "After that—*on verra*. Perhaps I will begin writing *Nexus*, a

long, long, volume—the hardest to do. It terrifies me, frank-
ly."³ Perhaps Miller suspected that he would not be able to
carry the narrative of *Nexus* to the point where one can see the
genesis of *Cancer* because the rage which gave him his tremendous energy was gone. Without that energy, *Cancer* would not
have been written, and without the rage, it is hard to imagine
the *energy* having its source in a man who accepts everything.
Indeed, the acceptance which *Nexus* projects undercuts much
of what made Miller so disturbing and compelling a writer in
the first place. As the "imminence of revelation" gradually
fades out of Miller's work forever in *Nexus,* one feels let down
rather than satisfied or fulfilled. The quality of serenity which is
offered in its place is not entirely convincing and can hardly be
called sublime or profound.

Nexus does begin with the author groping blindly amidst an
eternal night, his once-eloquent speech reduced to the futile
bark of a lost, frightened animal. The mood of *Sexus* is recapitu-
lated as exotic symbology assaults the author's senses, and he
must face a vast, uncharted universe without friends or even a
fixed sense of his own identity. But almost immediately, too
quickly, the author begins to move to firmer ground. Mona's
friend, the "other" woman, is named Stasia, a strange person
unlike anyone the author has met, but quite recognizable by
1960 as a young artist who has adopted a bohemian persona as
a means of handling her sexual ambivalence and insecurity.
Henry Miller is not particularly good at depicting the psychology of a woman with lesbian tendencies (Millett calls this
experience "lacerating" for him), and while he tries to appear
worldly and sophisticated, he is clearly on unsteady ground.
He does not understand her sexual inclinations, but he is willing to let that pass. What troubles him more is the "style" of
her life—her speech patterns, artistic preferences, the company
she chooses and her unusual relationship with Mona. The author's surprising conventionality is exposed by his difficulty in
dealing with someone who is *different,* rather disappointing in
one who has adopted for himself Rimbaud's proud designation
as "un autre." The candor in Miller's admissions of discomfort
is undermined by the narrowness of his knowledge concerning

the range of a woman's erotic interest. His problems with Mona can be seen now as a part of his too rigid sense of what a woman wants and needs. He is not really open to new experience, nor is he capable of learning by looking closely at phenomena he has not examined before. If, in *Nexus*, one could see the author attempting to regain his psychic balance by confronting what befuddles him and bringing his impressive intelligence to bear upon the varieties of new experience he encounters, the promise of *Sexus* (and all of Miller's previous work) might be realized. Instead, the pattern of the book is to accommodate everything that troubles him into an embrace that is genial if not passionate.

Consequently, he tries to be sympathetic to Stasia, and is repaid for his compassion by the reduction of a potentially fascinating woman to something like an overgrown, mixed-up adolescent. He decides that "love" is, indeed, as wondrous as he has always claimed, and that he just needs to start afresh with Mona. And so there are several "new beginnings" where he and Mona seem to have moved back to square one of their relationship, including a moment when they actually replay the first night they spent together (64). There is a rejection of a purely mental style of existence in the form of a one-shot mouthpiece character named Stymer who conveniently dies after expressing his nihilistic, bankrupt philosophy. Stymer is a balance for the totally sensual women of *Sexus* as the author seems to be striving for some safe middle ground, a consensus that includes a little of everything.

As the author tempers his excesses with understanding, he, Mona and Stasia grow closer together, less combative. The disappointing thing about this heart-warming development is that the author does not seem to understand himself, Mona or Stasia any better. He is just accepting everything. Again, while this is often an excellent idea for a troubled person, it is not much of an answer for a writer who has posed so many interesting questions. Without the hard scrutiny of the writer's probing consciousness, all phenomena reduce to unexamined surface. Because the entire structure of *Nexus* is directed toward an accommodation with the fact that the author will never make a quantum jump to a higher level of awareness, the small adjustments that he makes to ease the pain of conflict with the things he doesn't understand are like the lights of his artistic intelligence going out. Again, this would be easier to take if the subtheme of *Nexus* was not the gradual evolution of his will to become a writer.

The culmination of his quest for self-understanding, and the beginning of his resolve to be a writer come together as he visits his family on Christmas Day. After having condemned his family in rage in *Reunion in Brooklyn* in 1945, Miller retrospectively approves of his father circa 1927 from his perspective in 1960. His mother still appears as an impediment to his writing and quite possibly the source of his troubles with women, but he is able to forgive her, extending the understanding of a parent to *his parent*, something that he could do when he was nearly 70 but probably couldn't even think of in the 1920s. Mona and Stasia seem wise and tolerant as they join, temporarily, into a kind of enlarged family that is like the supporting community Miller often writes of with fondness. Miller is looking back with tolerance and is generally pleased with what he has done, and he has earned that pleasure, but the animating fire that should be driving him onward and inward in 1927 is doused by his good spirits. As the book progresses and he acknowledges all of his previous incarnations as direct spiritual descendants of the boy who grew up in the Fourteenth Ward, the intervening years fade into the recesses of his consciousness and all of the things he struggled with begin to matter less. When, in the midst of accepting things, the author rejects his old friend MacGregor (289–300), he is not just denying his kinship with those people (Van Norden, Fillmore, Ulric) who have not grown "spiritually" as he has, but is throwing out large chunks of his life as if they never happened. Miller is trying to show that the author will become "Henry Miller, the Writer" because he has a great capacity for self-perception and some capacity for self-disgust; because he can respond to the beauty and the burden of life; because he can grow spiritually and artistically. At the same time, his "acceptance" of everything that should be troubling him makes his claims hollow. As he reacts with a kind of benign amusement to the various incidents of *Nexus*, it becomes apparent that the rage which fed his energy, and the energy which demanded an outlet, cannot be replaced by a sort of spiritual grace, especially when the spirituality is never really demonstrated or even described, just asserted as a fact. There are too many passages in which the author says something like this, " 'It's funny, but in that state I was in everything seemed entirely as it should be. I didn't have to make the least effort to understand: everything was meaningful, justifiable and everlastingly real. Nor were you the devils I sometimes take you for' " (77).

When Dr. Kronski attempts to molest Stasia while he is "examining" her to see if she is "normal," Miller observes the sharer of his youthful sexual compulsions with a wry and distant eye. *Sexus* is too close in time and in the truth of its psychological depictions of the author for Miller to make this convincing. The author has abruptly and without explanation aged into the seer of Big Sur, the wise old man who writes erotic captions for Japanese woodcuts for *Playboy*. The change in the author's attitude toward sex can be explained by the intervention of twenty-five years in Miller's life, but *Nexus* is not supposed to be about the author as an old man. If Mona's husband has really changed that radically, then the book must explain why, and if he has, how can one reconcile this change with his origins as a writer, especially the man who is going to write *Tropic of Cancer* in a few years? Similarly, when the author and Mona talk at some length about their past and their hopes for the future (199–218), the urgency of their need for each other seems absent. Either this should be explored further as an intimation of their eventual separation, or it should be explained as a new manifestation of a man who still claims that he is in love, and has added the idea that love equals energy ("Like energy, which is still a complete enigma, love is always there, always on tap. Man has never created an ounce of energy, nor did he create love. Love and energy have always been, will always be. Perhaps in essence they are one and the same. Why not?" (40).) When the energy seems gone, it is hard to take the love seriously, and again, since *Cancer* is an explosion of energy, one

should see the author growing with power, not drifting into
spirituality. The confusion of the sensibility of 1960 with the
man living in 1927 leads to a fuzzing of the image that doesn't
really permit either figure to have a sharply defined personality. There are other versions of Miller at the age of 70 in print to
help delineate that aspect of his character, but the author who
is about to become the artist/hero is nowhere else discussed or
presented and he is the more interesting of the two as a literary
creation.

The defects in Miller's presentation are nowhere more apparent than in the treatment of the two women he presents as the
author's living companions. When the author seems incapable
of understanding anything about Stasia—and, what I think is
worse, is not particularly interested in trying to figure out how
Mona can be, somehow, in love with both of them—all of his
previous comments about the nature of woman begin to seem
suspect. Confronted with the very genuine article, he recoils in
dismay. One has to conclude that too much of his "information" is second hand—derived from literature and from suspect
male reports—and that he has not applied his own powers of
observation to the "species." Stasia, in particular, ought to
have some special interest for the author, because he is more
like her than he seems ready to acknowledge. She has some of
his freewheeling adventure-loving spirit, the same kind of hidden sensitivity beneath the tough surface, a surprisingly similar
artistic temperament. They both like artists who have an avant
garde ideology and when the author looks at Stasia's bookshelf,
he sees, in addition to a few titles which are supposed to suggest her lesbian inclinations (*Songs of Bilitis*), works by Baude-
laire, Mann, Bierce, Apuleius, Hardy, Twain, Sterne and James
Stephens—this could be Miller's own library. In addition, it
turns out that she is from the West, loves nature, and is driven
to rhapsodic moments of passion in its regions. What's more,
she can understand Mona better than the author. When the
author and Stasia finally begin to talk, they discover some tentative points of understanding and the author has an opportunity to show how tolerant he is of this strange, mutant creature,
but his spirituality here is not very impressive because his con-

tact with Stasia is also a demonstration of the thinness of the spirit's strength.

The problem with Mona is less specific and more complex. As Mailer points out, "we do not know by the end of *The Rosy Crucifixion* whether she breathed a greater life into his talent or exploited him. We do not know if Mona was a Great Ice Lady who chilled a part of him forever, or a beautiful much-abused piece of earth-mother."[4] One might deduce that the episode with Stasia marked the beginning of the author's changing attitude toward Mona, that he could not share her with any woman, although he was able to find ways to rationalize her visits to various men. But the sudden shift from total infatuation and great sexual desire at the end of *Sexus* to a kind of indifference in *Nexus* is never even explored. By 1960, Henry Miller probably was not very interested in the woman who had been Mona in the 1920s, but the author must not feel this way. Not only is the loss of interest hard to understand, the levels of mystery which made Mona so attractive seem to have been too easily ascended. The author visits her home and discovers that she has told him all sorts of lies about her origins. But he always knew that she embellished and created her own reality, as he does for himself, and to have the facts finally clear shouldn't make the woman less elusive since she never has paid much attention to the "facts" anyway. Actually, her "real" background, gypsy blood mixed with Rumanian Jewish ancestors, villages in the Carpathian mountains, interesting kin, strong streak of independence since childhood, hardly detracts from her appeal. And Mona hasn't changed at all. She is still the tempestuous, exotic, beautiful, headstrong woman that the author met at the end of *Capricorn*. While the author was kept in a state of frenzy thinking about her and trying to understand her in *Sexus*, now he seems more interested in his career as a writer and in his coming trip to Europe. Were Miller not writing about his "great love" from a distance of another two marriages, many affairs, and a long literary career, he might not be able to contain her so easily; and the author, it seems from all the evidence accumulated so far, should still be interested in, even fascinated by her mystery. What compounds the problem is that the author hardly seems attracted to women at all, and this is impossible to accept. The wild song of *Cancer* could not have been sung by this man. What really happened to his relationship with Mona is a question that demands an answer throughout *Nexus*. Is the ease with which they seem to accept each other a part of a genuine respect for the other's needs, or a matter of convenience since neither cares much any longer? Is the author's agreement to write a novel under Mona's name for a client of sorts called "Pop" just a matter of making money or a real partnership in which each person does what he can do best to support a mutual interest? Is the author's excitement about Europe a function of what Mona has told him and a reflection of his desire to share Europe with her, or the beginning of his life away from her? And beneath it all, what happened to the passion they felt for each other—the enormous lust that consumed them both and drove them to some wild high times that probably surpassed anything either of them had ever experienced with anyone else? If only Miller had done more, could have done more, with Mona and the author.

Finally, one is almost forced to adopt an attitude like the one Miller expresses in his later years and "accept" *Nexus*—and most of Miller's work—for what it is. Because it promises so much, one is bound to be disappointed at its final form, as Miller himself certainly was. But the questions that are raised, the ideas that are proposed, the vision that is revealed, the language that is created, the energy that is generated, these are aspects of an unusual writer and a very interesting man. One sees Miller's mark in many places as the twentieth century draws to a close: in bold considerations of sexual desires and attitudes; in Bob Dylan's own notes for *Highway 61 Revisited;* in Allen Ginsberg's *The Fall of America* (those lists!); in Norman Mailer's pantheon; and most important, on the shelves of bookstores everywhere. Is Miller a belated premodernist as Leslie Fiedler suggests, or is he a pioneer postmodernist, as an investigation of the criteria outlined by Ronald Sukenik, Roger Cardinal and David Lodge would imply?[5] It is these contradictions, quirks, intriguing arguments and ideas that remain vital which will continue to draw people to Miller's best work.

As *Nexus* draws to a close, one waits patiently for Miller to establish a realm of ecstasy to match the realm of despair at the beginning of the book. But the balancing ecstasy is in *Cancer;* the proof of the process which Miller has been trying to describe here is really that book's creation. The crucial connection between *Nexus* and *Cancer* is never made and for that reason, there is an open-ended quality to Miller's writing which will always remain. And Miller, knowing this, tried to bring it all together after *Nexus* was published, promising even in the early 1970s that there would be a second volume, and writing about his *Book of Friends* in 1976 saying, "What is herein given is just a handful. I hope to continue with the rest even if it takes the rest of my days."[6] But the real conclusion to Miller's writing is the end of *Nexus*. His output in the 1970s was full of casual tough talk that was like a parody of the early books, self-conscious and mannered in its attempt to sound like the legendary "Henry Miller." The last books were not helped by the removal of the modest restraints of respectability that Miller observed until his final years. These efforts don't matter much, though, since Miller had written forgettable things from the very beginning of his career and if anybody had earned the right to publish everything he wrote, it was surely Henry Miller. And many of the people who have enjoyed some part of Miller's work and wondered about the man will probably find his reminiscences diverting. But in the conclusion of *Nexus*, in a sudden plunge into his mind in 1960, the real place where the entire book unfolds, Miller bids good-bye to the terrain he has created, crossed and covered in his books. It is a brilliant farewell, ostensibly to America as he leaves for Paris, but actually to the realm of his writing, the most real "cosmos" he has inhabited. And it is also an extension of himself further into that *place*, not an ending so much as a merging:

> The boat will be pulling out soon. Time to say goodbye. Will I too miss this land that has made me suffer so? I answered that question before. Nevertheless, I do want to say goodbye to those who once meant something to me. What am I saying? *Who still mean something!* Step forward, won't you, and let me shake you by the hand. Come, comrades, a last handshake!

Up comes William F. Cody, the first in line. Dear Buffalo Bill, what an ignominious end we reserved for you! Goodbye, Mr. Cody, and Godspeed! And is this Jesse James? Goodbye, Jesse James, you were tops! Goodbye, you Tuscaroras, you Navajos and Apaches! Goodbye, you valiant, peace-loving Hopis! And this distinguished, olive-skinned gentleman with the goatee, can it be W. E. Burghardt Dubois, the very soul of black folk? Goodbye, dear, honored Sir, what a noble champion you have been! And you there, Al Jennings, once of the Ohio Penitentiary, greetings! and may you walk through the shadows with some greater soul than O. Henry! Goodbye, John Brown, and bless you for your rare, high courage! Goodbye, dear old Walt! There will never be another singer like you in all the land. Goodbye Martin Eden, goodbye, Uncas, goodbye, David Copperfield! Goodbye, John Barleycorn, and say hello to Jack! Goodbye, you six-day bike riders . . . I'll be pacing you in Hell! Goodbye, dear Jim Londos, you staunch little Hercules! Goodbye, Oscar Hammerstein, Goodbye, Gatti-Cassazza! And you too, Rudolf Friml! Goodbye now, you members of the Xerxes Society! *Fratres Semper!* Goodbye, Elsie Janis! Goodbye, John L. and Gentleman Jim! Goodbye, old Kentucky! Goodbye, old Shamrock! Goodbye, Montezuma, last great sovereign of the old New World! Goodbye, Sherlock Holmes! Goodbye, Houdini! Goodbye, you wobblies and all saboteurs of progress! Goodbye, Mr. Sacco, goodbye, Mr. Vanzetti! Forgive us our sins! Goodbye, Minnehaha, goodbye, Hiawatha! Goodbye, dear Pocahontas! Goodbye, you trail blazers, goodbye to Wells Fargo and all that! Goodbye, Walden Pond! Goodbye, you Cherokees and Seminoles! Goodbye, you Mississippi steamboats! Goodbye, Tomashevsky! Goodbye, P. T. Barnum! Goodbye, Herald Square! Goodbye, O Fountain of Youth! Goodbye, Daniel Boone! Goodbye, *Grosspapa!* Goodbye, Street of Early Sorrows, and may I never set eyes on you again! Goodbye, everybody . . . goodbye now! Keep the aspidistra flying! (315–16)

An impressive list from the modern Master of Lists! It is like a history in highlight of the cultural and personal features that made Miller's mind and heart so interesting, that made him an artist and a man of mighty opposites. Prizefighters, statesmen, revolutionaries, racehorses, legendary figures and places from early America, close friends, literary characters, composers, scenes from early childhood, what have you! And as a source of curiosity and a sly confession of his reluctance to give up his most important subject, Miller bids adieu to "Elsie Janis" and three Indian women, but not to any of the women he has known. Perhaps he wanted to keep them with him in memory and in person as long as he lived on this earth. And although he lived another twenty years after this passage was written, dying at the age of 88 just a month before *The World of Lawrence* was finally scheduled to be published, one might safely infer that thoughts of women and books filled his mind to the end of his days.

Notes

INTRODUCTION: "ACOLYTES AND ADVERSARIES"

1. Henry Miller, *Book of Friends: A Tribute to Friends of Long Ago* (Santa Barbara, Calif.: Capra Press, 1976); *My Bike and Other Friends*, Vol. II of *Book of Friends* (Santa Barbara, Calif.: Capra Press, 1978); *Joey*, Vol. III of *Book of Friends* (Santa Barbara, Calif.: Capra Press, 1979).

2. See George Wickes, *Henry Miller and the Critics* (Carbondale, Ill.: Southern Illinois University Press, 1963) for a comprehensive picture of critical responses to Miller's work during the early years of his writing career. For a more recent example of the same extremist tendencies, see Al Katz, "Free Discussion v. Final Decision: Moral and Artistic Controversy and the *Tropic of Cancer* Trials," *Yale Law Journal* 79 (December 1969): 209–252.

3. See Kate Millett, *Sexual Politics* (Garden City, N.Y.: Doubleday, 1970) 292–313. See also Anatole Broyard, "Tropic of Miller," *New York Times Book Review*, 20 Sept. 1981.

4. James Laughlin, letter to the author, February 25, 1981.

5. Gunther Stuhlmann, ed., *Henry Miller Letters to Anaïs Nin* (New York: Putnam, 1965), p. 30.

6. Miller, *Book of Friends*, Vol. III, p. 21.

7. The hilariously lurid cover which Kahane chose for the Obelisk Press edition of *Tropic of Cancer* is reproduced in Jay Martin's *Always Merry and Bright: The Life of Henry Miller—An Unauthorized Biography* (Santa Barbara, Calif.: Capra Press, 1978), p. 342.

8. See Karl Shapiro, *In Defense of Ignorance* (New York: Random House, 1960), p. 64. This essay originally appeared in *Two Cities* (Paris,

France, 1959) and serves as the introduction to the Grove Press edition of *Tropic of Cancer* (New York, 1961), pp. v–xxvii.

9. Alfred Perlès, *My Friend Henry Miller* (New York: Belmont, 1962), p. 86.

10. Robert Fink (untitled), *The International Henry Miller Letter* (Nijmegen, The Netherlands, 1961), p. 3.

11. Lawrence Durrell, "Studies in Genius," *Horizon* 20 (July 1949): 56.

12. Edward Mitchell, ed., *Henry Miller: Three Decades of Criticism* (New York: New York University Press, 1971), pp. 27–34.

13. Katz, "Free Discussion," p. 231.

14. But see Frederick Rafael et al., *The List of Books* (New York: Crown, 1981), where Miller is called "a whoremongering, narcissistic bore."

15. Kingsley Widmer, *Henry Miller* (New York: Twayne, 1963), p. i.

16. *Ibid.*, p. 1.

17. William Gordon, *The Mind and Art of Henry Miller* (Baton Rouge, La.: Louisiana State University Press, 1967), p. xxi.

18. *Ibid.*, p. ix.

19. *Ibid.*, p. 213.

20. *Ibid.*, pp. 214–215.

21. *Ibid.*, p. 216.

22. Leslie Fiedler, "Cross the Border, Close the Gap," *Playboy* 16 (December 1969): 241.

23. Ihab Hassan, *The Literature of Silence: Henry Miller and Samuel Beckett* (New York: Alfred Knopf, 1967).

24. Fiedler's remarks are directed toward an appreciation of Miller as a precursor of popular culture, while Hassan reserves Miller for inclusion in the pantheon of High Art.

25. Jane Nelson, *Form and Image in the Fiction of Henry Miller* (Detroit, Mich.: Wayne State University Press, 1970).

26. Henry Miller, *The Wisdom of the Heart* (Norfolk, Conn.: New Directions, 1941), pp. 22–23.

27. Laughlin, letter to the author.

28. For reproductions of Miller's plans and charts, see Martin, *Always Merry and Bright*. See also Thomas Moore, ed., *Henry Miller on Writing* (New York: New Directions, 1964), pp. 161–167.

29. Martin, *Always Merry*, p. 492.

30. Nelson, *Form and Image*, p. 30.

31. *Ibid.*, p. 55.

32. *Ibid.*, p. 107.

33. *Ibid.*, p. 114.

34. John Simon, *"A Spanking for Fellini Satyricon," The New York Times*, 10 May 1970.

35. Bertrand Mathieu, *Orpheus in Brooklyn: Orphism, Rimbaud and Henry Miller* (Paris: Mouton Press, 1976).

36. See *ibid.*, pp. 75–78, 146–149.

37. Norman Mailer, *Genius and Lust: A Journey through the Major Writing of Henry Miller* (New York: Grove Press, 1976), p. 395.

38. *Ibid.*, p. x.

39. *Ibid.*, pp. 185–190.

40. *Ibid.*, p. x.

41. *Ibid.*, p. xi.

42. As Miller told Martin, "I couldn't give you much help in your book, you know. Anyway, I've said the worst things that can be said about myself. You can say whatever the fuck you please about me." Thus, an "unauthorized biography."

43. Bern Porter, ed., *The Happy Rock: A Book about Henry Miller* (Berkeley, Calif.: Packard Press, 1945).

CHAPTER 1: LAND, SKIN, SPACE AND TIME

1. See Jane Jacobs, *The Death and Life of Great American Cities* (New York: Random House/Vintage, 1961) for an informative account of "life" in the streets of New York circa 1900.

2. Lawrence Ferlinghetti, "Rebirth of Wonder," *A Coney Island of the Mind* (New York: New Directions, 1958), p. 52.

3. As James Laughlin points out (Letter to author, February 25, 1981), during this time "Miller was trying to write for the pulps, although never with much success, he told me." Laughlin feels that Miller's activity in this area is interesting as demonstration of "from what kinds of acorns large oaks can grow."

4. Laughlin believes that Miller may have been influenced by William Carlos Williams in this quest, although he does not know which books of Williams Miller actually read. He says, "I am pretty certain that we sent him all the Williams books as they came from the press." (Letter to author.)

5. See Henry Miller, *The Books in My Life* (London: Icon Books, 1965), pp. 105–126.

6. Laurens Van Der Post, *The Dark Eye in Africa* (New York: Morrow, 1955), p. 36.

7. Henry Miller, *The Wisdom of the Heart* (Norfolk, Conn.: New Directions, 1941), p. 36.

8. Allen Ginsberg, epigram to Robert Creeley's *Pieces* (New York: Scribners, 1969), p. 1.

9. Miller, *Heart*, p. 3.

10. *Ibid.*, pp. 19–20.

11. Henry Miller, *Big Sur and the Oranges of Hieronymus Bosch* (New York: New Directions, 1957), pp. 316–317.

12. Miller, *Heart*, p. 6.

CHAPTER 2: THE REBEL HIS OWN CAUSE

1. George Orwell, "Inside the Whale," in *A Collection of Essays* (Garden City, N.Y.: Doubleday, 1954), p. 218.

2. Henry Miller, *Black Spring* (New York: Grove Press, 1963), p. 4.

3. Charles Olson, *Call Me Ishmael* (San Francisco: City Lights, 1947), p. 11.

4. Norman Mailer, *Genius and Lust: A Journey through the Major Writing of Henry Miller* (New York: Grove Press, 1976), p. 430. This is a quote from Henry Miller, *The Air-Conditioned Nightmare* (New York: New Directions, 1945).

5. Edward Mitchell, ed., *Henry Miller: Three Decades of Criticism* (New York: New York University Press, 1971), p. 40.

6. Jay Martin, *Always Merry and Bright: The Life of Henry Miller—An Unauthorized Biography* (Santa Barbara, Calif.: Capra Press, 1978), p. 188.

7. Thomas Moore, ed., *Henry Miller on Writing* (New York: New Directions, 1964), p. 193.

8. Kingsley Widmer, *Henry Miller* (New York: Twayne, 1963), p. 20.

9. Ihab Hassan, *The Literature of Silence: Henry Miller and Samuel Beckett* (New York: Alfred Knopf, 1967), pp. 38–39.

10. William Gordon, *The Mind and Art of Henry Miller* (Baton Rouge, La.: Louisiana State University Press, 1967), p. 164.

11. Mailer, *Genius*, p. xii.

12. Moore, *Henry Miller on Writing*, p. 213.

13. William Gordon, *Writer and Critic: A Correspondence with Henry Miller* (Kingsport, Tenn.: University of Tennessee Press, 1968), p. 31. See also, Martin, *Always Merry*, p. 492.

14. Gordon, *Writer and Critic*, p. 41.

15. *Ibid.*, p. 70.

16. *Ibid.*, p. 34.

17. *Ibid.*, p. 42.

18. George Wickes, ed., *Lawrence Durrell and Henry Miller: A Private Correspondence* (New York: E. P. Dutton, 1963), p. 42.

19. Mailer, *Genius*, p. 399.

20. Gordon, *Writer and Critic*, p. 60.

21. *Ibid.*, p. 5.

22. *Ibid.*, p. 39.

23. Emile Capouya, "Henry Miller," *Salmagundi* 1 (Fall 1965): 81.

24. Henry Miller, *Nexus* (New York: Grove Press, 1965), pp. 269–270.

25. Henry Miller, *The Wisdom of the Heart* (Norfolk, Conn.: New Directions, 1941), p. 23.

26. Capouya, "Henry Miller," p. 86.

27. See George Quasha and Jerome Rothenberg, eds., *America: A Prophecy* (New York: Random House/Vintage, 1974).

28. Charles Olson, "Projective Verse," in Donald Allen and Warren Tallman, *The Poetics of the New American Poetry* (New York: Grove Press, 1973), p. 149.

29. Mailer, *Genius*, p. 4.

30. Orwell, "Inside the Whale," p. 256.

31. John Barth, "The Literature of Exhaustion," *Atlantic Monthly* 220 (August 1967): 29–34.

32. Gunther Stuhlmann, ed., *Henry Miller Letters to Anaïs Nin* (New York: Putnam, 1965), p. 338. See also Martin, *Always Merry*, p. 430.

33. Mailer, *Genius*, p. 369.

34. Miller, *Black Spring*, pp. 25–26.

35. Albert Camus, *The Rebel*, tr. by Anthony Bower (New York: Random/Vintage, 1955), p. 10.

36. *Ibid.*, p. 13.

37. *Ibid.*

38. In addition to his efforts to write for the "pulps," Miller worked in New York City in the Parks Department, for Western Union, in a Greenwich Village restaurant, in various offices in entry level jobs for short periods of time, and at odd schemes which never amounted to much. Miller was also shaken by the collapse of his marriage to June Edith Smith, the Mara/Mona of his writing.

39. Camus, *The Rebel*, p. 16.

40. *Ibid.*, p. 17.

41. *Ibid.*

42. *Ibid.*

43. Alexsandr Solzhenitsyn, *The New York Times* (February 10, 1980), Sec. 5, p. 28.

44. James Laughlin (in a letter to the author, dated February 25, 1981) stresses the importance of Louis-Ferdinand Céline and Kenneth Patchen.

45. Mitchell, *Henry Miller*, p. 31.

46. William Gass, "The Essential Henry Miller, according to Norman Mailer," *The New York Times Book Review* (October 24, 1976), p. 3.

47. William Packard, ed., *The Craft of Poetry* (Garden City, N.Y.: Doubleday, 1974), p. 203.

48. *Ibid.*, p. 203.

CHAPTER 3: THE CARTOGRAPHY OF A COSMOS

1. Edward Mitchell, ed., *Henry Miller: Three Decades of Criticism* (New York: New York University Press, 1971), 82.

2. Karl Shapiro, in the Introduction to Henry Miller, *Tropic of Cancer* (New York: Grove Press, 1961), p. v.

3. Norman Mailer, *Genius and Lust: A Journey through the Major Writing of Henry Miller* (New York: Grove Press, 1976), p. 401. Miller's need for a good editor continues. In 1983 Grove Press published a book called *Opus Pistorum*, a six-part compilation of explicit pornography Miller wrote for Milton Lubovski in 1942 for a wage of a few dollars per page. In spite of praise from William Burroughs and Terry Southern, it is not surprising that Miller neither mentioned it nor attempted to get it published under his name during his lifetime. In 1985, Grove published the book in paperback, using as a title *Under the Roofs of Paris*, a translation of Miller's designation for the first part, *Sous les toits de Paris*. Considering the subject and style of the book, Miller's use of French here is probably designated as part of a somewhat obvious and vulgar pun.

4. Mailer, *Genius*, p. 6.

5. Jay Martin, *Always Merry and Bright: The Life of Henry Miller—An Unauthorized Biography* (Santa Barbara, Calif.: Capra Press, 1978), pp. 220–22.

6. Henry Miller, *My Life and Times* (New York: Gemini/Smith, 1971), pp. 58–77.

7. Considering Robert Coover's *The Public Burning* and E. L. Doctorow's *Ragtime*, just such a reconstruction may not be entirely unlikely in the future.

8. Guy Davenport, in the Introduction to *An Ear in Bartram's Tree: Selected Poems 1957–1967 by Jonathan Williams* (New York: New Directions, 1972).

9. Gunther Stuhlmann, ed., *The Diary of Anaïs Nin. Volume One, 1931–1934.* (New York: Harcourt Brace Jovanovich, 1966), p. 356.

10. Mailer, *Genius,* p. 402.

11. Henry Miller, *The Colossus of Maroussi* (New York: New Directions, 1941), p. 28.

12. *Ibid.,* pp. 240–241.

13. Martin, *Always Merry,* p. 444.

14. Mailer, *Genius,* p. 5; see also pp. 396–402.

15. Stuhlmann, *Diary of Anaïs Nin,* p. 356.

16. Martin, *Always Merry,* p. 324.

17. Gunther Stuhlmann, ed., *Henry Miller Letters to Anaïs Nin* (New York: Putnam, 1965), p. 320.

18. Martin, *Always Merry,* p. 254.

CHAPTER 4: *TROPIC OF CANCER*

1. Henry Miller, *Tropic of Cancer* (New York: Grove Press, 1961), p. 1. All references are to pages in this edition.

2. Kate Millett, *Sexual Politics* (Garden City, N.Y.: Doubleday, 1970), p. 295.

3. Jay Martin, *Always Merry and Bright: The Life of Henry Miller—An Unauthorized Biography* (Santa Barbara, Calif.: Capra Press, 1978), p. 262.

4. Edward Mitchell, ed., *Henry Miller: Three Decades of Criticism* (New York: New York University Press, 1971), pp. 134–135.

5. Millett, *Sexual Politics,* p. 302.

6. *Ibid.,* p. 296.

7. Norman Mailer, *Genius and Lust: A Journey through the Major Writing of Henry Miller* (New York: Grove Press, 1976), pp. 92–93.

8. Mailer, *Genius,* p. 94.

9. Millett, *Sexual Politics,* p. 313.

10. *Ibid.*

11. *Tropic of Cancer,* pp. 119–120.

12. Millett, *Sexual Politics,* p. 313.

13. *Ibid.,* p. 308; see also Mailer, *Genius,* pp. 92–94.

CHAPTER 5: *BLACK SPRING*

1. See Jay Martin, *Always Merry and Bright: The Life of Henry Miller—An Unauthorized Biography* (Santa Barbara, Calif.: Capra Press, 1978), pp. 292–294.

2. William Gordon, *The Mind and Art of Henry Miller* (Baton Rouge, La.: Louisiana State University Press, 1967), p. 215.

3. Henry Miller, *Tropic of Cancer* (New York: Grove Press, 1961), p. 287.

4. Henry Miller, *Black Spring* (New York: Grove Press, 1963), pp. 6–7. All references are to pages in this edition.

5. Peter Conrad, *Imagining America* (New York: Oxford, 1980), p. 234.

6. Hugh Kenner, *A Homemade World: The American Modernist Writers* (New York: Morrow, 1975), p. 20.

7. Gunther Stuhlmann, ed., *Henry Miller Letters to Anaïs Nin* (New York: Putnam, 1965), pp. 188–193.

8. Kenneth Dick, *Colossus of One* (Nijemegen, The Netherlands: Alberts-Sittard, 1967), p. 186.

9. Norman Mailer, *Genius and Lust: A Journey through the Major Writing of Henry Miller* (New York: Grove Press, 1976), p. 501.

10. Mailer, *Genius*, p. 6.

11. Dick, *Colossus of One*, p. 42.

12. Martin, *Always Merry*, p. 294.

13. Henry Miller, *The Cosmological Eye* (Norfolk, Conn.: New Directions, 1939), pp. 63–75.

14. Miller, *The Cosmological Eye*, pp. 75–107.

15. Jane Nelson, *Form and Image in the Fiction of Henry Miller* (Detroit, Mich.: Wayne State University Press, 1970), pp. 51–52.

CHAPTER 6: *THE COLOSSUS OF MAROUSSI* AND *BIG SUR*

1. Bertrand Mathieu, *Orpheus in Brooklyn: Orphism, Rimbaud and Henry Miller* (Paris: Mouton Press, 1976), p. 149.

2. Norman Mailer, *Genius and Lust: A Journey through the Major Writing of Henry Miller* (New York: Grove Press, 1976), p. 398.

3. Charles Olson, *Mayan Letters* (New York: New Directions, 1966), p. 88.

4. Sherman Paul, *Olson's Push: Origin, Black Mountain and Recent American Poetry* (Baton Rouge, La.: Louisiana State University Press, 1978), p. 73.

5. *Ibid.*, p. 73.

6. *Ibid.*, p. 250.

7. George Wickes, ed., *Lawrence Durrell and Henry Miller: A Private Correspondence* (New York: E. P. Dutton, 1963), p. 138.

8. *Ibid.*, p. 173.

9. *Ibid.*, p. 183.

10. Mathieu, *Orpheus in Brooklyn*, p. 4.

11. Henry Miller, *The Colossus of Maroussi* (New York: New Directions, 1941), p. 28. All references are to this edition.

12. Guy Davenport, in the Introduction to *An Ear in Bartram's Tree: Selected Poems 1957–1967* by *Jonathan Williams* (New York: New Directions, 1972).

13. Mathieu, *Orpheus in Brooklyn*, p. 209.

14. *Ibid.*, p. 213.

15. *Ibid.*, p. 212; see also p. 6.

16. Gunther Stuhlmann, ed., *Henry Miller Letters to Anaïs Nin* (New York: Putnam, 1965), p. 194.

17. Stuhlmann, *Henry Miller Letters to Anaïs Nin*, pp. 193–194.

18. Mailer, *Genius*, p. 428.

19. *Ibid.*, p. 459.

20. Henry Miller, *Big Sur and the Oranges of Hieronymus Bosch* (New York: New Directions, 1957), frontispiece. All references are to pages in this edition.

CHAPTER 7: *TROPIC OF CAPRICORN*

1. Jay Martin, *Always Merry and Bright: The Life of Henry Miller—An Unauthorized Biography* (Santa Barbara, Calif.: Capra Press, 1978), p. 385.

2. Kate Millett, *Sexual Politics* (Garden City, N.Y.: Doubleday, 1970), p. 295.

3. *Ibid.*, p. 297.

4. Laurie Stone, "The Big P," *The Village Voice* (February 25, 1980), p. 35.

5. *Ibid.*, p. 35.

6. *Ibid.*, p. 36.

7. *Ibid.*

8. *Ibid.*, p. 35.

9. Ann Douglas, "Soft-Porn Culture," *The New Republic* (August 30, 1980), pp. 26–29.

10. Henry Miller, *The Books in My Life* (London: Icon Books, 1963), p. 97.

11. Millett, *Sexual Politics*, p. 309.

12. Martin, *Always Merry*, p. 325.

13. Henry Miller, *Tropic of Capricorn* (New York: Grove Press, 1961), p. 9. All references are to pages in this edition.

14. Norman Mailer, *Genius and Lust: A Journey through the Major Writing of Henry Miller* (New York: Grove Press, 1976), p. 91.

15. Ihab Hassan, *The Literature of Silence: Henry Miller and Samuel Beckett* (New York: Alfred Knopf, 1967), p. 42.

16. Jane Nelson, *Form and Image in the Fiction of Henry Miller* (Detroit, Mich.: Wayne State University Press, 1970), p. 17.

CHAPTER 8: *SEXUS*

1. Henry Miller, *Sexus* (New York: Grove Press, 1965), p. 9. All references are to pages in this edition.

2. Gunther Stuhlmann, the editor of *Henry Miller Letters to Anaïs Nin* (New York: Putnam, 1965), says that Nin's letters to Miller "would have added little to this story. They are a part of her own autobiography which has found its most eloquent crystallization in her Diary" (p. xxvi).

3. Norman Mailer, *Genius and Lust: A Journey through the Major Writing of Henry Miller* (New York: Grove Press, 1976), p. 186.

4. *Ibid.*, p. 185.

5. *Ibid.*

6. *Ibid.*, p. 188.

7. *Ibid.*, p. 185.

CHAPTER 9: *NEXUS*

1. Henry Miller, *Nexus* (New York: Grove Press, 1965), p. 7. All references are to pages in this edition.

2. Norman Mailer, *Genius and Lust: A Journey through the Major Writing of Henry Miller* (New York: Grove Press, 1976), p. 504.

3. Richard Wood, ed., *Collector's Quest: The Correspondence of Henry Miller and J. Rives Childs, 1947–1965* (Charlottesville, Va.: University Press of Virginia, 1968), p. 61.

4. Mailer, *Genius*, p. 191.

5. William Spanos, ed., *Boundary 2*, vol. 6, no. 3; vol. 7, no. 1 (Spring/Fall 1978): 503–507.

6. Henry Miller, *Book of Friends: A Tribute to Friends of Long Ago* (Santa Barbara, Calif.: Capra Press, 1976), p. i.

Bibliography

WORKS BY HENRY MILLER

Tropic of Cancer. Paris: Obelisk, 1934; New York: Grove Press, 1961.
What Are You Going to Do about Alf? Paris: Lecram-Servant, 1935.
Aller Retour, New York. Paris: Obelisk, 1935.
Black Spring. Paris: Obelisk, 1938; New York: Grove Press, 1963.
Max and the White Phagocytes. Paris: Obelisk, 1938; Norfolk, Conn.:
    New Directions, 1939.
The Cosmological Eye (including *Max and the White Phagocytes*). Norfolk,
    Conn.: New Directions, 1939.
Tropic of Capricorn. Paris: Obelisk, 1939; New York: Grove Press, 1961.
The World of Sex. New York: JHN Press, 1940. Revised edition, Paris:
    Olympia, 1959; New York: Grove Press, 1965.
The Wisdom of the Heart. Norfolk, Conn.: New Directions, 1941; New
    York: New Directions, 1960.
The Colossus of Maroussi. San Francisco, Calif.: Colt, 1941; Norfolk,
    Conn.: New Directions, 1941.
Hamlet. 2 vols. Santurce, P.R.: Carrefour, 1939–1941. *Correspondence
    Called Hamlet.* 2 vols. London: Carrefour, 1962.
Murder the Murderer: An Excursus on War. Big Sur, Calif.: 1944; Norfolk,
    Conn.: New Directions, 1947.
Sunday after the War. Norfolk, Conn.: New Directions, 1945.
The Air-Conditioned Nightmare. New York: New Directions, 1945.
Henry Miller Miscellanea. Berkeley, Calif.: Packard/Bern Porter, 1945.
Maurizius Forever. San Francisco, Calif.: Colt, 1946.
Remember to Remember. Vol. 2, *The Air-Conditioned Nightmare.* Norfolk,
    Conn.: New Directions, 1947.

The Smile at the Foot of the Ladder. New York: Duell, Sloan and Pearce, 1948.

Sexus. 2 vols. *(The Rosy Crucifixion. Book One).* Paris: Obelisk, 1949; Paris: Olympia Press, 1962; New York: Grove Press, 1965.

Books in My Life. Norfolk, Conn.: New Directions, 1952. *The Books in My Life.* London: Peter Owen, 1952; London: Icon, 1963.

Plexus (The Rosy Crucifixion. Book Two). Paris: Olympia Press, 1953; New York: Grove Press, 1965.

Quiet Days in Clichy. Paris: Olympia Press, 1956; New York: Grove Press, 1965.

A Devil in Paradise. New York: New American Library, 1956; New York: New Directions, 1957.

The Time of the Assassins: A Study of Rimbaud. New York: New Directions, 1956.

Big Sur and the Oranges of Hieronymus Bosch (including *A Devil in Paradise).* New York: New Directions, 1957.

Reunion in Barcelona: A Letter to Alfred Perlès. Northwood, England: Scorpion Press, 1959.

The Red Notebook. Highlands, N.C.: Jargon/Jonathan Williams, 1959.

Nexus (The Rosy Crucifixion. Book Three). Paris: Olympia Press, 1960. New York: Grove Press, 1965.

To Paint Is to Love Again. Alhambra, Calif.: Cambria Books, 1960.

Stand Still like the Hummingbird. New York: New Directions, 1962.

Just Wild about Harry: A Melo-melo in Seven Scenes. New York: New Directions, 1963.

Lawrence Durrell and Henry Miller: A Private Correspondence. Edited by George Wickes. New York: E. P. Dutton, 1963.

Henry Miller Letters to Anaïs Nin. Edited by Gunther Stuhlmann. New York: Putnam, 1965.

Order and Chaos Chez Hans Reichel. Tucson, Ariz.: Loujon Press, 1966.

Collector's Quest: The Correspondence of Henry Miller and J. Rives Childs, 1947–1965. Edited by Richard Wood, Charlottesville, Va.: University Press of Virginia, 1968.

Insomnia: Or the Devil at Large. Euclid, Ohio: Loujon Press, 1971; Garden City, N.Y.: Doubleday (Gemini/Smith), 1974.

My Life and Times. New York: Gemini/Smith–Playboy, 1971.

On Turning Eighty. Santa Barbara, Calif.: Capra Press, 1972.

Reflections on the Death of Mishima. Santa Barbara, Calif.: Capra Press, 1972.

First Impressions of Greece. Santa Barbara, Calif.: Capra Press, 1973.

The Waters Reglitterized: The Subject of Water Color in Some of Its More Liquid Phases. Santa Barbara, Calif.: Capra Press, 1973.

Reflections on the Maurizius Case (A Humble Appraisal of a Great Book). Santa Barbara, Calif.: Capra Press, 1973.

Letters of Henry Miller and Wallace Fowlie (1943–1972). New York: Grove Press, 1975.

Book of Friends: A Tribute to Friends of Long Ago. Santa Barbara, Calif.: Capra Press, 1976.

Mother, China and the World Beyond. Santa Barbara, Calif.: Capra Press, 1977.

Gliding into the Everglades. Lake Oswego, Oregon: Lost Pleiade Press, 1977.

My Bike and Other Friends. Vol. 2, *Book of Friends.* Santa Barbara, Calif.: Capra Press, 1978.

Henry Miller: Years of Trial and Triumph, 1962–1964: The Correspondence of Henry Miller and Elmer Gertz. Edited by Elmer Gertz and Felice Flanery Lewis. Carbondale, Ill.: Southern Illinois University Press, 1978.

Joey. Vol. 3, *Book of Friends.* Santa Barbara, Calif.: Capra Press, 1979.

The World of Lawrence: A Passionate Appreciation. Edited by Evelyn Hinz and John Teunissen. Santa Barbara, Calif.: Capra Press, 1980.

Opus Pistorum. New York: Grove Press, 1983; *Under the Roofs of Paris.* New York: Grove Press, 1985.

Dear, Dear Brenda: The Love Letters of Henry Miller to Brenda Venus. New York: William Morrow & Co., 1986.

GENERAL

Barrett, William. "His Exuberant Reflections. Henry Miller: Man in Quest of Life." *Saturday Review* 40 (August 30, 1957): 9–10.

Barth, John. "The Literature of Exhaustion." *Atlantic Monthly* 220 (August 1967): 29–34.

Bataille, Georges. "La Morale de Miller." *Critique* 1 (June 1946): 3–17.

Baxter, Annette Kar. *Henry Miller, Expatriate.* Pittsburgh, Pa.: University of Pittsburgh Press, 1961.

Bennett, John, ed. *Black Messiah: A Tribute to Henry Miller.* Ellensburg, Wash.: Vagabond Press, 1981.

Bess, Donovan. "Miller's *Tropics* on Trial." *Evergreen Review* 6 (March–April 1962): 12–37.

Brady, Mildred. "The New Cult of Sex and Anarchy." *Harpers* 73 (April 1947): 312–332.

Camus, Albert. *The Rebel.* Translated by Anthony Bower. New York: Random/Vintage, 1955.

Capouya, Emile. "Henry Miller." *Salmagundi* 1 (Fall 1965): 81–87.

Cott, Jonathan. "Henry Miller: 1891–1980," *Rolling Stone* (July 24, 1980): 25.

Creeley, Robert. *Pieces.* New York: Scribners, 1969.

Crouser, G. Thomas. *American Autobiography: The Prophetic Mode.* Amherst, Mass.: University of Massachusetts Press, 1979.

Davenport, Guy. *An Ear in Bartram's Tree: Selected Poems 1957–1967 by Jonathan Williams.* New York: New Directions, 1972.

D'Azevedo, Warren. "Henry Miller and the Fifth Freedom—A Communication." *The New Republic* 110 (February 14, 1944): 124–131.

Dick, Kenneth. *Colossus of One.* Nijemegen, The Netherlands: Alberts-Sittard, 1967.

Douglas, Ann. "Soft-Porn Culture," *The New Republic* (August 30, 1980): 26–29.

Durrell, Lawrence. "Studies in Genius: VIII—Henry Miller." *Horizon* 20 (July 1949): 45–61.

———, ed. *The Henry Miller Reader.* New York: New Directions, 1959.

Eliot, George P. "A Brown Fountain Pen." *Kenyon Review* 24 (Winter 1962): 62–79.

Fiedler, Leslie. "Cross the Border, Close the Gap." *Playboy* 16 (December 1969): 149–151, 228–230, 258–260.

Fink, Robert. (Untitled). *The International Henry Miller Letter* 1 (June 1961): 3–7.

Fowlie, Wallace. "Shadow of Doom: An Essay on Henry Miller." *Accent Quarterly* 1 (Autumn 1944): 34–42.

Gass, William. "The Essential Henry Miller, according to Norman Mailer," *The New York Times Book Review* (October 24, 1976): 1–3.

Gilman, Richard. "Norman Mailer Searches the Tropics—'Mr. Miller, I Presume?' " *Village Voice* (October 4, 1976): 43–44.

Glicksbrug, Charles. "Henry Miller: Individualism in Extremis." *Southwest Review* 33 (Summer 1948): 311–314.

Gordon, William. *The Mind and Art of Henry Miller.* Baton Rouge, La.: Louisiana State University Press, 1967.

———. *Writer and Critic: A Correspondence with Henry Miller.* Kingsport, Tenn.: University of Tennessee Press, 1968.

Grenier, Roger. "Henri Miller ou l'obsession du panthéisme." *Les Temps Moderne,* I Anée, no. 8 (mai 1946): 1527–1533.

Hassan, Ihab. *The Literature of Silence: Henry Miller and Samuel Beckett.* New York: Alfred Knopf, 1967.

Haggard, H. Rider. *She.* River City, Mo.: 1976.

Jacobs, Jane. *The Death and Life of Great American Cities.* New York: Random House/Vintage, 1961.

Jung, Carl Gustav. *Aion: Research into the Phenomenology of the Self.* Princeton, N.J.: Princeton University Press, 1968.

Katz, Al. "Free Discussion v. Final Decision: Moral and Artistic Controversy and the *Tropic of Cancer* Trials." *Yale Law Journal* 79 (December 1969): 209–252.

Kazin, Alfred. "An Ordinary Bloke." *The New Republic* (October 12, 1978): 44–46.

Kees, Weldon. "To Be or Not: Four Opinions on Henry Miller's *Smile at the Foot of the Ladder.*" *The Tiger's Eye* 1 (October 20, 1948): 68–72.

Kellman, Steven. *The Self-Begetting Novel.* New York: Columbia University Press, 1980.

Kempton, Sally. "Cutting Loose." *Esquire* 66 (July 1970): 54–58, 156–162.

Kenner, Hugh. *A Homemade World: The American Modernist Writers.* New York: Morrow, 1975.

Klein, Don. "Innocence Forbidden: Henry Miller in the Tropics." *Prairie Schooner* 33 (Summer 1959): 125–130.

Kreigel, Leonard. *Of Men and Manhood.* New York: Dutton, 1979.

Krim, Seymour. "The Netherworld of Henry Miller." *Commonweal* 57 (October 24, 1952): 68–71.

———. "Sitting Shiva for Henry," *The Village Voice* (June 23, 1980): 38.

Laughlin, James. Letter to the author, February 25, 1981.

Lelchuk, Allan. "Miller's Lawrence." *The New York Times* (July 14, 1980): 34–37.

Leonardini, Jean-Pierre. "Libertaire à tout crin." *L'Humanité* (9 Juin 1980): 9.

Littlejohn, David. "The Tropics of Miller." *The New Republic* 132 (March 5, 1962): 478–480.

Mailer, Norman. *Genius and Lust: A Journey through the Major Writing of Henry Miller.* New York: Grove Press, 1976.

Martin, Jay. *Always Merry and Bright: The Life of Henry Miller—An Unauthorized Biography.* Santa Barbara, Calif.: Capra Press, 1978.

Mathieu, Bertrand. *Orpheus in Brooklyn: Orphism, Rimbaud and Henry Miller.* Paris: Mouton Press, 1976.

McDowell, Edwin. "1942 Miller Work Being Published," *The New York Times* (June 7, 1983): C11.

Millett, Kate. *Sexual Politics.* Garden City, N.Y.: Doubleday, 1970.

Mitchell, Edward, ed. *Henry Miller: Three Decades of Criticism.* New York: New York University Press, 1971.

Moore, Thomas, ed. *Bibliography of Henry Miller.* Minneapolis, Minn.: Henry Miller Literary Society, 1961.

————. *Henry Miller on Writing*. New York: New Directions, 1964.

Muller, Herbert. "The World of Henry Miller." *Kenyon Review* 2 (Summer 1940): 312–318.

Nelson, Jane. *Form and Image in the Fiction of Henry Miller*. Detroit, Mich.: Wayne State University Press, 1970.

Norris, Hoke. "*Cancer* in Chicago." *Evergreen Review* 6 (July–August, 1962): 40–66.

Olney, James. *Autobiography: Essays Theoretical and Critical*. Princeton, N.J.: Princeton University Press, 1980.

Omarr, Sydney. *Henry Miller: His World of Urania*. London: Villiers, 1960.

Orwell, George. *A Collection of Essays*. New York: Signet, 1954.

Packard, William, ed. *The Craft of Poetry*. Garden City, N.Y.: Doubleday, 1974.

Paul, Sherman. *Olson's Push: Origin, Black Mountain and Recent American Poetry*. Baton Rouge, La.: Louisiana State University Press, 1978.

Perlès, Alfred. *Art and Outrage: A Correspondence about Henry Miller between Alfred Perlès and Lawrence Durrell*. New York: Dutton, 1961.

————. *My Friend Henry Miller: An Intimate Biography*. New York: J. Day and Company, 1956; New York: Belmont, 1962.

Porter, Bern. *Henry Miller: A Chronology and Bibliography*. Baltimore, Md.: The Waverly Press, 1945.

————, ed. *The Happy Rock: A Book about Henry Miller*. Berkeley, Calif.: Packard Press, 1945.

Putnam, Samuel. *Paris Was Our Mistress*. New York: Viking, 1947.

Quasha, George. "Impure Americana, Fixtures of Place." *Stony Brook* 1/2 (Fall 1968): 223–232.

————, and Jerome Rothenberg, eds. *America: A Prophecy*. New York: Random House/Vintage, 1974.

Rahv, Philip. "Spellbinder in Greece." *The New Republic* 106 (January 12, 1942): 59–60.

————. "The Artist as Desperado," *The New Republic* 104 (April 21, 1941): 557–559.

————. *Image and Idea*. New York: New Directions, 1949.

Read, Herbert. *The Tenth Muse*. New York: Arno, 1957.

Rexroth, Kenneth. "Neglected Henry Miller." *The Nation* 179 (November 5, 1955): 386.

Shapiro, Karl. "The Greatest Living Author," *Two Cities* 3 (December 15, 1959): 24–44.

Shattuck, Roger. "A Loner's Lark through Brooklyn," *The New York Times* (September 2, 1962): 6.

Spanos, William, ed. *Boundary 2*, vol. 6, no. 3; vol. 7, no. 1 (Spring/Fall 1978): 503–507.

Simon, John. *"A Spanking for Fellini Satyricon,"* *The New York Times* (May 10, 1970): 11.

Solotaroff, Theodore. "All That Deep-Cellar Jazz: Henry Miller and Seymour Krim." *Commentary* 33 (October 1961): 319.

Stuhlmann, Gunther, ed. *The Diary of Anaïs Nin. Volume One, 1931–1934.* New York: Harcourt Brace Jovanovich/Harvest, 1966; *Volume Two, 1934–1939.* New York: Harcourt Brace Jovanovich/Harvest, 1967; *Volume Four, 1944–1947.* New York: Harcourt Brace Jovanovich/Harvest, 1971.

Trilling, Lionel. "Angels and Ministers of Grace." *The Mid-Century* 31 (October 1961): 79–85.

Van Der Post, Laurens. *The Dark Eye in Africa.* New York: Morrow, 1955.

West, Herbert. *The Mind on the Wing.* New York: Arno, 1957.

White, Emile, ed. *Henry Miller: Between Heaven and Hell.* Big Sur, Calif.: Emile White, 1961.

Wickes, George. "The Art of Fiction, XXVIII: Henry Miller." *Paris Review* 7 (Summer–Fall 1962): 128–139.

———. *Henry Miller and the Critics.* Carbondale, Ill.: Southern Illinois University Press, 1963.

———. *Henry Miller.* Minneapolis, Minn.: University of Minnesota Press, 1966.

Widmer, Kingsley. *Henry Miller.* New York: Twayne, 1963.

Wilson, Edmund. "A Review of *Sunday after the War.*" *New Yorker* 20 (October 21, 1944): 83–84.

Index

245

DATE DUE